T0280085

Enslaved, Indentured, Free

Enslaved, Indentured, Free

Five Black Women on the Upper Mississippi,
1800–1850

Mary Elise Antoine

WISCONSIN HISTORICAL SOCIETY PRESS

Published by the Wisconsin Historical Society Press
Publishers since 1855

The Wisconsin Historical Society helps people connect to the past by collecting, preserving, and sharing stories. Founded in 1846, the Society is one of the nation's finest historical institutions.
Join the Wisconsin Historical Society: wisconsinhistory.org/membership

© 2022 by the State Historical Society of Wisconsin

For permission to reuse material from *Enslaved, Indentured, Free: Five Black Women on the Upper Mississippi, 1800–1850* (ISBN 978-0-87020-989-5; e-book ISBN 978-0-87020-990-1), please access www.copyright.com or contact the Copyright Clearance Center, Inc. (CCC), 222 Rosewood Drive, Danvers, MA 01923, 978-750-8400. CCC is a not-for-profit organization that provides licenses and registration for a variety of users.

Front cover images, top: detail of Courtney's petition, Circuit Court Records, University Libraries, Washington University in St. Louis; bottom: print of Prairie du Chien, Wisconsin in 1830, WHI IMAGE ID 22616.

Printed in the United States of America
Cover designed by TG Design
Typesetting by Integrated Composition Systems
26 25 24 23 22   1 2 3 4 5

Library of Congress Cataloging-in-Publication Data
Names: Antoine, Mary Elise, author.
Title: Enslaved, indentured, free : five Black women on the Upper Mississippi, 1800–
    1850 / Mary Elise Antoine.
Description: [Madison, Wisconsin] : Wisconsin Historical Society Press, [2022] | Includes bibliographical references and index.
Identifiers: LCCN 2022000342 (print) | LCCN 2022000343 (e-book) | ISBN
    9780870209895 (paperback) | ISBN 9780870209901 (epub)
Subjects: LCSH: African American women—Wisconsin—Prairie du Chien—
    Biography. | African American women—Wisconsin—Prairie du Chien—
    Social conditions. | Women slaves—Wisconsin—Prairie du Chien—Biography. |
    Women slaves—Wisconsin—Prairie du Chien—Social conditions. | Prairie du
    Chien (Wis.)—Biography. | Prairie du Chien (Wis.)—Social conditions.
Classification: LCC E185.93.W58 A58 2022 (print) | LCC E185.93.W58 (e-book) |
    DDC 306.3/62082077574—dc23/eng/20220518
LC record available at https://lccn.loc.gov/2022000342
LC ebook record available at https://lccn.loc.gov/2022000343

♾ The paper used in this publication meets the minimum requirements of the American National Standard for Information Sciences—Permanence of Paper for Printed Library Materials, ANSI Z39.48-1992.

Dedicated to "The Ladies," who guided me throughout this journey.

The Ladies sent suggestions for research, helped me to make connections, and inspired me to keep on looking. They often faced what seemed to be insurmountable barriers. Yet, they led gracious and meaningful lives, and they passed to their children the importance of family.
They are an inspiration to all.

CONTENTS

ACKNOWLEDGMENTS

The writing of this story has been a long journey that began with many beginnings.

In the very white community of Prairie du Chien, Wisconsin, the story of Marianne Labuche has always fascinated residents. The few details of her life recorded by James Lockwood, an early white settler of Prairie du Chien, were told and retold. I, too, heard and retold those few lines from Lockwood's *Recollections*. But I, like others, felt that Marianne, a free Black woman at Prairie du Chien, must have been an anomaly.

Then, in the 1990s, I had the opportunity to work with legal history scholar Lea VanderVelde. She had begun her research on Dred Scott and introduced me to the US Army paymaster papers on which officers stationed at Fort Crawford had claimed reimbursement for the enslaved men and women whose lives were controlled by the officers' demands. The funding for an exhibit Lea had hoped to develop on Dred and Harriet Scott and other enslaved men and women in the upper Mississippi River Valley never was approved, and I put all I had learned aside.

About ten years later, in 2016, Chris Lese, a social studies teacher at Marquette University High School, asked to bring his students to Fort Crawford. For a number of years, Chris had taken students on trips to study slavery in the United States. On each trip, the students slept in buildings where enslaved people had worked and lived. In April 2017, Chris brought his students to Fort Crawford. They had spent the previous night in Henry Dodge's cabin, where Toby, Tom, Lear, Jim, and Joe, who were enslaved by Dodge to work his smelting furnace, had once lived. The students would now sleep in the Fort Crawford Hospital. Accompanying Chris and his students was Joseph McGill Jr., a history consultant for Magnolia Plantation in Charleston, South Carolina. He is also the founder and director of the Slave Dwelling Project. Building on what I had learned with Lea, I did more research on the presence of slavery at Fort Crawford. This I shared with Chris, Joseph, and the others. I was moved as I watched the emotion on Joseph's face as he absorbed the information and studied what the officers had written on the paymaster vouchers. He looked up at me and murmured, "These are my people." I decided then that their story needed to be told.

But there were so many people listed on the paymaster forms, and most of them had just first names. So, I began with what I knew: the few details about Marianne. Then, census records told me that other Black people had lived at Prairie du Chien at the same time as Marianne and her family. Mariah Faschnacht was listed as Black. Mariah acquired land from François and Helene Galarneau, Marianne's daughter and son-in-law. Then Mariah sold land to Courtney, who was listed as Black as well. I was learning that Marianne was not an anomaly.

I knew about Patsey from my research on Joseph Street and the Winnebago School on the Yellow River. I had discovered connections among three Black women—Marianne, Mariah, and Courtney—who lived at Prairie du Chien in the 1830s. Patsey lived on the prairie at the same time. Did she know them? I continued my research and learned much more about Patsey and her sons.

Rachel v. Walker is a well-known freedom suit because of Dred Scott's infamous suit, *Scott v. Sanford*, heard before the US Supreme Court in 1857. Rachel's suit for freedom, which occurred more than twenty years earlier, was cited in the court arguments and many publications about Dred and Harriet's fight for freedom, and included in these citations was always the note that Rachel had based her suit for freedom on the years she had spent at Prairie du Chien. But in all of those writings, little attention had been paid to Rachel as a person. She was just a name on legal documents, much like the Black men and women listed on the paymaster documents. So, I learned more about Rachel, and she brought me back to Courtney.

Of all the many Black men and women who had lived at Prairie du Chien in the first half of the nineteenth century, I found enough details about these five women and their families that I believed I could tell their life stories. And so, more and more research led to more connections and finally to a manuscript.

Along this journey, I was fortunate to meet descendants of Marianne, Patsey, and Courtney. Grace Meyer, a descendant of Marianne through her son Regis Gagnier, gave me a treasured memento. Estelene Bell, a descendant of Patsey through her son Henry H. Triplett, shared with me family research, pointed me in the direction of Joseph Street's correspondence, and made sure I had my facts correct. Debbie Furman, a descendant of Courtney through her son James Barr, shared family research and photographs. Tobe Melora Correal, a descendant of Courtney through her son James Barr, sent spiritual encouragement.

As I was conducting my research, Walt Bachman was focusing his research on the many Black men and women enslaved by officers in the United States Army in the first half of the nineteenth century. Walt generously shared with me information he compiled to form the Bachman Army Slave Database.

Many thanks are due to Lea, Chris, Joseph, Grace, Estelene, Debbie, Tobe, and Walt. You all helped me immensely. And I learned so much from each of you. Thank you also to the Wisconsin Historical Society for funding a research trip to the National Archives to see the paymaster records.

Last, but not least, thank you to Elizabeth Wyckoff for being a wonderful, understanding editor, and Sara Phillips, who brought this all together. And thank you to the Wisconsin Historical Society Press for publishing the story of these five strong women, their families, and their compatriots.

Introduction

A round 1800, two girls were born into slavery. Mariah took her first breath in a cabin in Maryland. Farther west, Patsey opened her eyes in the new state of Kentucky. No records of their births have been found, nor have the names of their mothers. Sixteen years later, when Mariah and Patsey were told to sign letters of indenture binding themselves to the white men who were their enslavers, the men described both women as "coloured," with Mariah further described as "mulatto."[1] Their fathers may have been white men, perhaps the men who had enslaved Mariah's and Patsey's mothers.

Twelve to fourteen years after the births of Mariah and Patsey, two other girls were born into slavery. They were named Courtney and Rachel. With her birth, Courtney became the property of the Garland family of Albemarle County, Virginia. Rachel became one of a vast number of enslaved people whose birthplaces were never recorded. Later, men who enslaved Courtney and Rachel identified each as "Black."[2]

As they grew into girlhood and young womanhood, Mariah, Patsey, Courtney, and Rachel were removed from the care of their mothers, given or sold to strangers, and gradually transported westward and then northward by their enslavers. Through various circumstances, each came to reside in the small community of Prairie du Chien, spread along the east bank of the Mississippi River. Here, at different times and in different combinations, they came to know one another.

Mariah, Patsey, Courtney, and Rachel had been born into slavery. Through no choice of their own, they had been taken from their mothers and families, and they had been transported by their enslavers to various places, which ultimately included Prairie du Chien. At the prairie, perhaps for the first time in their lives, each woman had the ability to explore beyond the confines of the house in which she labored. And when each woman walked the prairie, she saw women and men of color who were free. By some means, perhaps of their own making, each woman met Marianne, the matriarch of a large Black family in the settlement. Marianne had been born free, and all of her children and grandchildren were free. They owned and lived in their own homes, and they farmed their land. Marianne likely made an impression on Mariah, Patsey, Courtney, and Rachel. Each of them would go on to fight for and obtain freedom before the end of her life.

—||—

When the four women were brought to Prairie du Chien, the federal government considered that land to be part of Michigan Territory, created by the US Congress in 1805 and then expanded in 1818. Michigan Territory, which in 1818 stretched from Lake Huron to Lake Superior to the mouth of the Mississippi River, had been formed out of what was previously the vast Northwest Territory, established in 1787. According to Article VI of the Northwest Ordinance, slavery and involuntary servitude were not allowed in the Northwest Territory. However, the ordinance did permit slavery as punishment for the conviction of a crime, and it allowed fugitives who had escaped the bonds of slavery from other states to be returned to their enslavers.[3] So, though the ordinance made the institution of slavery illegal in the Northwest Territory, Congress did allow slavery to be perpetuated in the United States.

Additionally, the United States had no way to enforce Article VI, leaving its interpretation up to territorial governors, judges, and legislatures for the next twenty-five years, until Congress had partitioned the land into territories and then state constitutions had been approved. As a result, many Black people remained unfairly enslaved and indentured in the so-called free territory. This was not legal slavery (also known as *de jure* slavery), but slavery in practice (*de facto* slavery).

In the first half of the nineteenth century, an enslaved person in the United States and in the country's territory east of the Mississippi River was considered to be the property of their enslaver. An enslaved person was not paid for their work. Each state and territory enacted its own slave code, but all were similar in that they restricted enslaved people's movements, limited or prevented their ability to marry, prohibited them from gathering, and regulated the ways in which enslavers could punish them, usually going so far as to apply no penalty to an enslaver who accidently killed an enslaved person while punishing them. Enslaved people could obtain their freedom through illegal means, like escaping or overthrowing their enslavers. They could also obtain their freedom through nonviolent acts if their enslavers allowed them to purchase their freedom or granted them freedom, often as a stipulation in their will. Or, in certain states and territories where slavery was practiced, enslaved people could file freedom suits. If an enslaved person could provide satisfactory evidence proving he or she should be free, the court would grant the person freedom. But even a legally free Black person was at risk of being kidnapped and forced into slavery in the United States at this time.

Unlike an enslaved person, an indentured servant was a person who had signed a legal contract or document obligating them to work for their employer for a specific period of time without pay. According to the law, only a free person could enter into an indenture, but the indenture then placed them into a third category: neither enslaved nor free, but indentured. An indenture signed voluntarily was usually an obligation for the indentured person to repay a loan, learn a skill, or fulfill an agreement with their employer. At the end of the set time, the indentured person was meant to gain a recompense for their labor—both the length of the indenture and the recompense were detailed in the document. Yet, in practice, many people came to be indentured involuntarily, either through coercion, deception, or other means.

Some enslavers bringing enslaved people into the Northwest Territory used indentures as a means of complying with the law, while others, knowing that the law was rarely enforced, continued to illegally enslave Black people within the territory. Some Black people were held enslaved under the pretense of indenture, as some indentures were written to bind the indentured person into servitude for life. According to most state and territorial laws of the time, children born to indentured servants were not considered legally free until they reached adulthood, and employers often treated such children as their property in practice.

Lithograph of Prairie du Chien in 1830, printed in *Das Illustrite Mississippithal* by Henry Lewis and based upon a sketch by Seth Eastman. Prairie du Chien is depicted with the first Fort Crawford and a few of the houses that stood in the Main Village. In the background are houses that stood in the southern part of the Village of St. Friole. WHI IMAGE ID 22616

Mariah, Patsey, Courtney, and Rachel had been brought into the North-west Territory as enslaved women. Yet, although they became residents of the Northwest Territory, they did not become free at that time; their enslavers continued to hold them in bondage or indentured servitude.

Although the four women were not free, the isolation of Prairie du Chien meant that their enslavers did not restrict their ability to move around as much as they might have in more settled or less remote areas. Prairie du Chien was a community surrounded by vast tracts of open prairie that melded into virgin forests, and rivers offered the only means of travel. The closest settlements were Green Bay at the end of the Wisconsin–Fox waterway 240 miles to the east, Fort Snelling several days' journey up the Mississippi River, and the lead-mining district of Galena along the Fever River sixty miles to the south. People traveled between these communities by river, and for that, one needed a boat. It would have been nearly impossible for any of the women to attempt an escape to freedom. During any instance when the women had time without demands, or in the course of completing an errand, they could have trudged along the well-worn trail that stretched the length of the prairie, noting the crops planted by the residents and recording the passing of seasons. Or they might have proceeded to Water Street, catching a glimpse of the neatly hewn log houses built to face the street and the river. While they and other enslaved people living on the prairie were able to move about relatively freely, their isolation and inability to obtain transportation bound them to the prairie.

In Prairie du Chien, the four women met other enslaved and indentured Black people. But they also encountered Black people who were free. During their time on the prairie, either while performing duties or enjoying a moment between tasks, each woman met Marianne Labuche, the matriarch of a large family whom the census taker in 1820 noted as "free-coloured."[4] Mariah, Patsey, Courtney, and Rachel soon learned that Marianne was married and that she had maintained her last name through three marriages. She owned property and raised crops both to nourish her family and as a source of income. She provided healing skills to the community. The isolation of Prairie du Chien gave Marianne the security to raise her children without the fear of them being taken away. She was able to gather her children, their French Canadian spouses, and her grandchildren in a home that she owned.

Although Mariah, Patsey, Courtney, and Rachel surely understood that freedom from slavery was not the same as equality and acceptance among white people, Marianne must have stood as an ideal to them. She lived a life that none of the four women had experienced. And she may have inspired them as they fought for ways out of their enslavement or indentured servitude. Each of the four women eventually obtained freedom, albeit through different means and under different circumstances. This book follows these four remarkable women on their various paths to freedom.

—||—

It would seem that Marianne, Mariah, Patsey, Courtney, and Rachel could not read or write. They left no written evidence of thoughts or recollections of their lives. No one recorded their histories for posterity beyond a few sentences by James Lockwood about Marianne and a conversation recorded by Ida Street in which she has Patsey speaking in dialect.[5] There is one letter written by Henry Triplett, Patsey's son, in which he remembers details of his life when he was enslaved by George Wilson.[6] But no letters, diaries, photographs, or mementos have been found that were created or kept by the five women. Attempting to understand them and their lives requires piecing together bits of information from the records of the white men and women who enslaved them; legal and religious documents that recorded their births, baptisms, and marriages; requests for pay by the US Army officers who held them in bondage; and documents and transcripts of court cases maintained by the US legal system. It also requires a fair amount of speculation—residents' and visitors' descriptions of Prairie du Chien and the events that took place there when the women lived in the community have been used to fill in the gaps. Finally, envisioning the world in which these women lived necessitates a study of the complex legal history of slavery that shaped American life leading up to the early 1800s.

Slavery was an issue that the delegates to the Continental Congresses, the Constitutional Convention, and the early Congresses of the United States debated from the time of the drafting of the Declaration of Independence in 1776. It continued to be a contentious issue among members of Congress and their constituents for the next seventy-five years. As the United States increased in size, acquiring territory through numerous treaties and the forced removal of Native nations, debates over slavery and the position of Black people in American society grew more heated. The legal enactments arising from these debates restricted enslaved people even more as the years passed, eventually resulting in the Fugitive Slave Act of 1850, which required that freedom seekers be returned to their former enslavers, even if they had escaped into a free state. Interpretation of the federal and state laws by justices and courts would determine whether or not Mariah, Patsey, Courtney, and Rachel could obtain their freedom.

Thomas Jefferson claimed people as property in his personal life and simultaneously attempted to control the spread of slavery in his role as an early American statesman. In 1784, Jefferson wrote a Plan for Government of the Western Territory, which included a provision stating that after 1800 there would be neither slavery nor involuntary servitude in all the western territories. His plan failed to pass the Congress of the Confederation, but this plan and the Ordinance of 1785 influenced provisions that came to be included in the Northwest Ordinance of 1787.

Article VI of the Northwest Ordinance states, "There shall be neither slavery nor involuntary servitude in the said territory, otherwise than in the punishment of crimes, whereof the party shall be duly convicted: provided always, that any person escaping into the same, from whom labour or service is lawfully claimed in any one of the original states, such fugitive may be lawfully reclaimed and conveyed to the person claiming his or her labour or service aforesaid."[7] Although the article begins with a phrase that seems to condemn slavery, it ends in a statement that supports the institution, declaring that enslaved people escaping into the Northwest Territory may be returned to their enslavers.

Slavery had existed in what became known as the Northwest Territory long before the land became part of the United States in 1783 as agreed to by the United States and Great Britain in the Treaty of Paris. The French began to settle in the western Great Lakes in the early 1700s, and within a few years, enslaved Black men and women had been transported into Detroit and Michilimackinac by their enslavers. Around the same time, France established the colony of Louisiana. For a few years, ships brought captured Africans to the colony, but most enslaved people arriving in the colony were either captured from the British or smuggled from the Caribbean. Slavery continued after most of North America came under the rule of Great Britain in 1763. By this date, enslaved people lived and worked within the communities of Kaskaskia, Vincennes, and Cahokia in the Illinois Country. After the Illinois Country was captured by an American force in 1778, enslavers from Virginia, Kentucky, and other Southern states migrated into the territory, bringing enslaved men and women with them.[8]

The federal government had no ability to enforce Article VI of the Northwest Ordinance, so for the next seventy-five years, territorial governors, judges, and legislatures would interpret the article in court cases. Enslaved people living in the territory continued to live in bondage and were treated as property to be sold, given to enslavers' friends and family members, and bequeathed in wills.[9]

However, a territorial acquisition made sixteen years after the purchase of the Northwest Territory resulted in a new set of laws regarding slavery. On October 20, 1803, the US Senate ratified the purchase from France of 827,000 square miles of land located west of the Mississippi River. With completion of the Louisiana Purchase, the form of slavery that had existed in the lands west of the Mississippi River under French and Spanish rule became part of the institution within the United States.

Slavery had already existed in Louisiana, as it had in the Northwest Territory, for close to one hundred years. But in 1724, the French had introduced the *Code Noir* (or Black Code) in Louisiana, which set rules for those who claimed people as property and for the enslaved.

While the movement of and rights of enslaved people were restricted under the *Code Noir*, the *Code* offered some protections for enslaved people. Four articles described in detail how enslaved people were to be clothed, fed, and housed. Article XX stated, "Slaves who shall not be properly fed, clad, and provided for by their masters, may give information thereof" to the legal authorities. The article also stated that "the attorney-general shall prosecute said masters without charging any costs to the complainants. It is our will that this regulation be observed in all accusations for crimes or barbarous and inhuman treatment brought by slaves against their masters."[10]

When Spain took control of the Louisiana Territory in 1763, the Black Code was modified to provide enslaved people with more rights. Enslaved men and women were now allowed to own property, and they could also purchase their freedom. And in 1769, the Spanish governor, citing a law of 1542, banned the further importation, buying, and selling of enslaved American Indians.

In 1764, the French began to settle St. Louis as a trading post to trade with the Osage who lived along the Missouri River and westward. People from the Illinois Country moved to the settlement, and the community grew. By the time of the Louisiana Purchase in 1803, St. Louis was populated by a mix of French, Spanish, American Indian, and free and enslaved Black people. The new territorial legislature passed a set of laws regulating slavery in 1804, which defined slaves as "personal estate" (movable property) and placed restrictions on the mobility of enslaved individuals.[11] In 1806, the Laws of the Territory of Louisiana were enacted, including a Black Code that detailed "the rules and conduct to be observed with respect to negroes and other slaves of the territory." The following year, Chapter 35, "An Act to enable persons held in slavery, to sue for their freedom," was added. The act stated: "It shall be lawful for any person held in slavery to petition the general court or any court of common pleas, praying that such person may be permitted to sue as a poor person, and stating the grounds on which the claim to freedom is founded."[12]

With this law, petitioners could claim that they were free people illegally being held in slavery. A petitioner did not need manumission papers or other documents from enslavers that made their freedom official. If such documents did not exist, oral testimony or written depositions could be used to prove to the jury that the individual had been granted freedom in a will or deed, had been born free, or had resided on free soil. Petitioners were allowed to sue as paupers, and the court assigned counsel to represent them. Until a decision had been made regarding the petitioner's freedom, the petitioner was protected from being "subjected to any severity because of his or her application for freedom." The defendant (usually the person who claimed ownership of the enslaved person) had to post a bond guaranteeing the petitioner's appearance and good treatment. Under law, Black people were forbidden to testify in cases involving white people, but in so-called freedom suits, petitioners were allowed to call Black men or women to testify on their behalf.[13]

Chapter 35 was the act that would allow Courtney and Rachel to sue for their freedom in St. Louis in the mid-1830s. After being added to the Laws of the Territory of Louisiana in 1807, Chapter 35 remained a part of the law when Missouri Territory was formed from Louisiana Territory in 1812. The chapter was reaffirmed after Missouri was admitted to the Union in 1821 as a slave state as a result of the Missouri Compromise. And the 1820 Compromise prohibited slavery everywhere in the Louisiana Territory north of the 36°30' latitude line, with the exception of Missouri. The Compromise reinforced the Northwest Ordinance and made slavery illegal in the part of the territory that would become Iowa and Minnesota.

The administration of the new state of Missouri took very seriously its role in the national compromise on slavery. After much debate, Congress had admitted Missouri as a slave state and Maine as a free state in order to preserve a delicate balance between pro- and antislavery forces in the nation. The Missouri legislature chose to maintain that balance within the state of Missouri, though it prioritized the economic interests of enslavers over the rights of Black people.[14] The state's laws regulating slavery reflected slave codes of the older United States, but they also set limits on the overseers and owners of enslaved people and allowed owners to manumit

an enslaved person. The Missouri statutes also offered recourse if manumission agreements were violated or if a person who was free was captured
by enslavers. Then, in 1824, the Missouri Legislature passed a law re-
affirming the old territorial statute allowing enslaved people to sue for
their freedom.[15]

So, by 1820, two acts of the United States Congress—the Northwest
Ordinance of 1787 and the Missouri Compromise—had defined the
portion of the country in which slavery was ostensibly not permitted. Yet,
these laws were not adequately enforced, and enslavers continued to keep
Black people enslaved and indentured in these areas, including in the
settlement of Prairie du Chien. After the passage of the Northwest Ordinance in 1787, Prairie du Chien was a part of several different territories
before it finally became part of the state of Wisconsin in 1848. And each
territory had its own constitution and laws regarding slavery.

Ohio was the first state to be created from the Northwest Territory,
and it took a relatively bold stance against slavery. Article VIII, Section 2,
of the Ohio Constitution of 1803 stated,

> There shall be neither slavery nor involuntary servitude in this State,
> otherwise than for the punishment of crimes, whereof the party shall
> have been duly convicted; nor shall any male person, arrived at the
> age of twenty-one years, or female person arrived at the age of eigh-
> teen years, be held to serve any person as a servant, under the pre-
> tense of indenture or otherwise. . . . Nor shall any indenture of any
> negro or mulatto, hereafter made and executed out of the State, or if
> made in the State, where the term of service exceeds one year, be of
> the least validity, except those given in the case of apprenticeships.[16]

The law could be enforced far more easily than Article VI of the Northwest
Ordinance because court systems with justices existed in populated areas
of the new state. Of course, these laws would be enforced only if the authorities in Ohio wished to do so.

The remainder of the territory, including Prairie du Chien, came under
the jurisdiction of Indiana Territory. Although slavery continued to be
illegal according to the Northwest Ordinance, territorial governor William Henry Harrison asked Congress for a ten-year suspension of the

This map from the *American Pocket Atlas* depicts the Northwest Territory according to its boundaries between 1809 and 1818. COURTESY OF MARY ELISE ANTOINE

slavery ban. Congress finally agreed to the petition, so in 1805, the Indiana Territory House of Representatives passed the "Act Concerning the Introduction of Negroes and Mulattoes into this Territory." The act stated that "within thirty days of bringing slaves into the territory, the owner or master should take them before the Clerk of Court, and have an indenture between the slave and his owner entered upon record, specifying the time which the slave was compelled to serve the master."[17] In other words, human bondage was allowed to continue under a different name: voluntary indenture.

In 1809, when Illinois became a separate territory (in which Prairie du Chien was included), the territorial legislature passed a law similar to that of Indiana Territory, which also placated enslavers. The law provided that

> any person, being the owner of any negroes or mulattoes of and . . . above the age of fifteen years, and owing service and labor as slaves in any of the states and territories of the United States, or any person purchasing negroes or mulattoes, might bring the same into the territory[,] provided . . . the owner or master within thirty days should take them before the clerk of the court and have an indenture between the slave and his owner entered upon record specifying the time which the slave was compelled to serve his master. If, however, the negro or mulatto was under fifteen years, the owner was given power to hold the males until they were thirty-five years of age and the females until they were thirty-two. Children born of a parent who owed service of labor, by indenture, were required to serve, the males until the age of thirty, and the females until the age of twenty-eight.

The law further provided that when an enslaved person was brought into the territory and refused to be indentured, the enslaver had sixty days in which to move the enslaved person from Illinois Territory into a state where they could be legally held as property. The period of indenture into which most enslaved people were coerced was typically ninety-nine years.[18]

Illinois Territory included what is now Illinois, Wisconsin, eastern Minnesota, and the upper peninsula of Michigan. The southern portion of the territory was admitted to the Union as the state of Illinois in 1818.

But unlike the legislatures of Ohio and Indiana, the Illinois legislature did not prohibit slavery in the new state. Rather, it ruled that each person who had been bound to service by a contract or indenture under the laws of Illinois Territory was still bound to fulfill all obligations detailed in the contracts and "shall serve out the time appointed by said laws." However, the children of enslaved or indentured people could become free—"males at the age of twenty-one years, females at the age of eighteen years."[19]

When Illinois was granted statehood in 1818, the land that would become Wisconsin and eastern Minnesota came under the jurisdiction of the territory of Michigan. Michigan Territory had had to deal with the legality of slavery soon after it became a territory in 1805. In the 1807 *Denison v. Tucker* case, Justice Augustus Woodward ruled that "under the Jay Treaty settlers continued to enjoy their property of every kind." And because enslaved people were recognized as property, "Slaves [born before May 31, 1793] in the possession of the settlers on July 11, 1796 continued such for life." But children born after July 11, 1796, the date the Jay Treaty was approved, were "free from birth." By 1810, only a handful of enslaved Black people lived in Michigan Territory, and most lived in Detroit. Others who had been born before July 11, 1796, had either died or escaped across the Detroit River to Canada.[20]

When Mariah arrived at Prairie du Chien in 1816 as an indentured servant, many white men and women kept Black men, women, and children enslaved and indentured in portions of the United States that were considered free. Black people living in these free states and territories could be enslaved until they died or until their indenture terminated. The states, territories, and future states formed from the Northwest Territory, where slavery was technically prohibited, offered no means by which a person illegally held in servitude could gain his or her freedom. Conversely, Missouri, a state in which slavery was legal, did offer a means by which an enslaved person could gain his or her freedom.

This ostensibly free territory of Michigan was the world into which Mariah, Courtney, Patsey, and Rachel were transported by their enslavers. But, whether enslaved or indentured, the women had no freedom in this so-called free land.

CHAPTER 1

MARIANNE, 1769–1816

Marianne Labuche had lived at Prairie du Chien for almost twenty years when Mariah arrived at the prairie in 1816. Like Mariah, Patsey, Courtney, and Rachel, Marianne had been born in a section of the United States where slavery was legal. But unlike the others, Marianne had been born, and continued to be, free.

As far as we know, Marianne never recorded anything about herself. Therefore, her origins and family history prior to her arrival at Prairie du Chien must be pieced together from census reports, church records, personal reminiscences, correspondence, land records, and an interview with her granddaughter. But all who wrote about her agreed that she was Black.

At the time of her 1817 marriage to her third husband, Marianne told the officiating Catholic priest about her parentage. Father Marie Joseph Dunand recorded that she was the daughter of Pierre Labuche and Marianne (no last name recorded), of New Orleans.[1] However, his documentation makes it unclear who was born in New Orleans: Marianne, her mother Marianne, or both women.

The younger Marianne was described as having "mixed African and white blood," suggesting that one parent was Black and the other parent white or that one or both of her parents were of mixed descent.[2] At least one, if not both, of Marianne's parents was probably born into slavery, for in 1769, a few years before the time Marianne was born, only 99 free Black people lived in the city of New Orleans, whereas 1,227 Black people in the city were enslaved.[3]

From the time France constituted the colony of Louisiana in 1682 until control passed to Spain in 1763, freedom was not easily granted to enslaved people there.[4] It became easier for an enslaved person to gain freedom when Spain gained control of Louisiana. The Spanish modified the *Code Noir* that had been instituted by the French, easing the requirements for manumission and ability to purchase one's freedom. Under Spanish rule, enslavers in Louisiana could free their captives. Enslaved people in the territory could also purchase their freedom or petition the court to grant them freedom. More women than men gained their freedom by self-purchase. This trend occurred, in part, because enslaved women were considered less valuable than enslaved men, and the price of a woman's freedom was often lower. Women could more easily acquire the necessary funds to purchase their freedom by selling produce in the markets, sewing and mending, taking in laundry, and acting as nurses. And in New Orleans, where self-purchase was more common than in other parts of the country, free and enslaved Black women outnumbered free and enslaved Black men.[5]

Free Black people in the lower Mississippi Valley in the 1700s recognized their individuality. They constantly sought to protect their identities, and as a result, family ties were very important. Free people of color almost always married other free people of color, including people of mixed race or American Indian ancestry. Additionally, marriages occurred between free people of color and white people. Free Black people took pride in their heritage and saw themselves as separate, in some ways, from the enslaved Black population.[6] Marianne was one of these free Black people who recognized her individuality. Throughout her life and her unions with three successive husbands, Marianne never relinquished her birth name and was always known as Marianne (or sometimes Mary Ann) Labuche.

According to Article XLV of the *Code Noir*, *gens de couleur libres* or, in Spanish, *gente de color libre* (free people of color) and manumitted slaves in French and Spanish Louisiana possessed all the "same rights, privileges, and immunities which are enjoyed by free-born persons." So, Marianne and other free people of color in Louisiana were able to move within Spanish Louisiana and maintain their freedom. North of New Orleans, up the Mississippi River, Ste. Genevieve became part of Spanish Louisiana in 1763. The following year, St. Louis was established as a fur trading post. Free Black people and formerly enslaved people who had gained their freedom in Louisiana could travel up the river, but they did so with caution. Local ordinances sometimes imposed restrictions that were not part of the *Code Noir*. Free Black people living in Ste. Genevieve were required to have passports to cross the Mississippi River and were not permitted to congregate after dark.[7]

Marianne's last name, Labuche (in various spellings), appears in documents and accounts in both Ste. Genevieve and St. Louis dating from the 1770s. In each instance, the person with the name Labuche was a *gens de couleur* (person of color), and many were free. Though none are named Marianne, they may have had a connection to Marianne or her parents.

For instance, a French Canadian named Jean François LeBuche lived outside the old town of Ste. Genevieve during the middle to late 1700s. According to baptism records from 1778, he and a Black woman named Elizabeth had two girls and two boys, one named Pierre. Apparently, Jean François was attacked and scalped by the Osage later that same year.[8]

Genevieve Labuche, another potential extended family member, was born in about 1765. She and her husband, Joseph Labadie dit St. Pierre, lived in St. Louis. They were both free Black people. In 1835, the General Assembly of the State of Missouri passed an act stating that all free Black people living in the state who sought work were required to have a Freedom License.[9] That year, seventy-year-old Genevieve applied for a license as a seamstress, and her sons—twenty-three-year-old Pierre and thirty-one-year-old Antoine—applied for licenses as butchers. All three are described as "light mulatto." Also in that year, two women with the last name Labuche—Genevieve, a thirty-seven-year-old "mulatto woman," and Adelaide, a twenty-four-year-old "light mulatto woman with a freckled face"—applied for licenses as seamstresses in St. Louis.[10]

Though no direct connection can be determined between Marianne and the LeBuches of Ste. Genevieve or the Labadie/Labuches of St. Louis, these individuals have more than just a name in common—they were all free and of mixed descent.

Marianne's first marital union was with a member of the Duchouquette family. No marriage record has been found, but Marianne's eldest son's name was recorded on census records and legal documents as Duchouquette. Duchouquette (sometimes spelled Du Chouqette) was an established name in St. Louis and the Illinois Country across the Mississippi River from St. Louis. Perhaps Marianne married one of the sons of

François Lafleur Duchouquette, a trader at New Chartres. He had four sons—Henri, Jean Baptiste, Pierre, and François—who lived in the area of Kaskaskia.[11] Though no records confirm the first name of Marianne's first husband, James Lockwood, a resident of Prairie du Chien who knew Marianne, stated that she married and had two sons with a "man by the name of Du Chouquette."[12] One son was François, who resided with Marianne at Prairie du Chien. The other son was very likely named Pierre. On May 8, 1787, Pierre Labuche, "Nat.[ural] son of Marianne Labuche," was baptized at Holy Family Church in Cahokia.[13]

Sometime after the birth of her son François, Marianne met the man who would become her second husband, Claude Gagnier. Claude was a white man of French Canadian ancestry. By 1778, he owned land and farmed at Cahokia, a French settlement founded by missionaries from Quebec and located across the Mississippi River from St. Louis. He had also worked a number of trading seasons for Michel Brisbois, who lived at Prairie du Chien. Michel traded with the Ho-Chunk, and Claude transported pelts to Chicago that Michel had acquired in those trades. Claude, in traveling between the three communities, would have been familiar with Prairie du Chien.[14]

By 1790, the population of the Illinois Country was greatly increasing with the influx of Americans from the eastern United States. The fur trade had almost ceased, and the French society in the Illinois Country was marginalized and being displaced. Several Illinois Frenchmen including Pierre and Michel Antaya dit Pelletier and Joseph Crelie had already moved their families to Prairie du Chien, and Claude decided to follow their example and relocate to the prairie.

The Meskwaki had lived on and used the prairie since the early 1700s. For a time, they had a village on the prairie, but by the 1770s, they had relocated and formed villages along the Wisconsin River, allowing non-Native people to use the prairie to trade. In 1780, as it became obvious that the newly formed United States would succeed in its revolt against Great Britain, the non-Native men living at Prairie du Chien became concerned that they held no titles to the land on which they resided.[15]

In May of 1781, Lieutenant Governor Patrick Sinclair met with chiefs of the Ojibwe Nation (referred to as the Chippewa by white people at the time), who were joined by chiefs from other nations, and signed a treaty purchasing Prairie du Chien from the Ojibwe.

Michel Brisbois, who lived at Michilimackinac at the time and was present at the treaty signing, stated that when the Native people learned of the white residents' concerns that Britain, in fact, owned Prairie du Chien, a Meskwaki chief named Nanponis ratified "an ancient sale" of the prairie to the French.[16] In 1792, Claude Gagnier paddled up the Mississippi River to Prairie du Chien, seeking a lot on which to make a home for his family. Like the French Canadians who had settled on the prairie before him, Claude selected a tract of land. It was located at the far north end of the prairie. When the United States sent a surveyor to Prairie du Chien in 1820, the tract came to be known as Farm Lot No. 2. In 1794, Claude selected a very large strip of the prairie a half mile south of Farm Lot No. 2. Claude partitioned that property and sold the northern portion to Pierre LeFleur.[17]

Claude cultivated and then occupied the southern portion of the tract, and it came to be called Farm Lot No. 13. Much larger than Farm Lot No. 2, Farm Lot No. 13 was six arpent wide (1,150 feet) and stretched from the Mississippi River to the bluffs. West of the dirt road that traversed the prairie, Claude built a sizeable house on this lot for Marianne and what would become their large family. By 1794, Marianne and her son from her first union, François Duchouquette, joined him at Prairie du Chien.

Like all the houses and barns constructed at Prairie du Chien in the late-1700s and first thirty years of the 1800s, Claude's house was built of logs carefully hewn in the method used by other French settlers from the Illinois Country. The home was a story-and-a-half high with a door facing the Mississippi. A door in the opposite wall faced the road and Claude's cultivated fields, which stretched to the bluffs. With both doors open, cooling breezes flowed through the two large first-floor rooms. It was a comfortable and finished structure, intended to be a permanent home. A veranda shaded the east and west sides of the house, the interior was plastered and white-washed, and a large fireplace heated the home in the colder months, reminiscent of the homes built in the Illinois Country. Claude enclosed the west yard with a fence to keep animals out of the garden created and tended by Marianne.[18]

Farm Lots No. 2 and No. 13, from *Plat of the Private Land Claims at Prairie du Chien, 1828* by Lucius Lyon, surveyor, were initially claimed by Claude Gagnier. He gave Farm Lot No. 2 to his wife, Marianne Labuche, who married Charles Menard after Claude's death in 1803. WHI IMAGE ID 113245 (DETAIL)

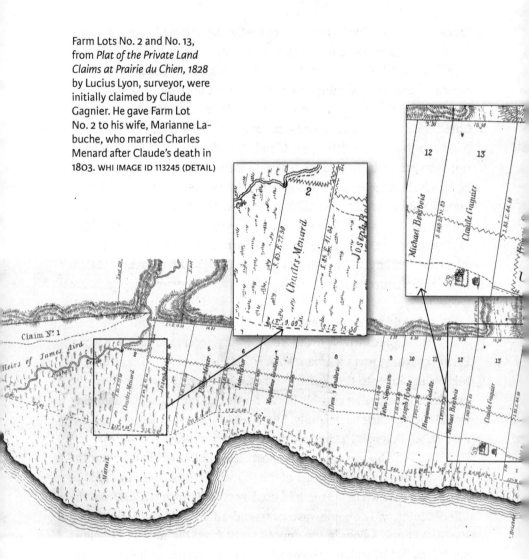

The arrival of Marianne and François brought a new culture to an already diverse community. For untold years, the Native nations of the upper Mississippi had congregated at the prairie to trade among themselves. Hostilities were left behind during these seasonal gatherings, and the Dakota did not disturb the Meskwaki who made a home on the prairie up until the 1760s. By the mid-1700s, a vast variety of traders—Native, European, and of mixed heritage—gathered on the prairie before dispersing to their winter trading sites. Then they would meet again in the spring to celebrate the trade with kegs of spirits that had been stored on the prairie for the rendezvous. The prairie saw traders from the Province of Lower Canada, Michilimackinac, the Illinois Country, New Orleans, and even as far away as New York and Connecticut. Though some groups were competitors in other contexts, all toasted the end of the trading season with brandy and in friendship.

The often-conflicting politics of the European countries that benefitted from North American trade were not discussed among the French Americans from the Illinois Country and those who traded under license from the Spanish governors, nor among the British Canadians and their French compatriots. Politics, religion, and racial differences were not as important as discussions of the trading season and how it compared to previous years. During these gatherings, many French-speaking and British men formed consensual marital relationships with women of the Dakota and Ho-Chunk nations. Consequently, when permanent settlement began at Prairie du Chien in the early 1770s, cultural diversity could be found in the main village on the island west of the prairie and in the two smaller villages that soon took root on the mainland, all of which, with forty-three farm lots, constituted Prairie du Chien.

In addition to expanding the cultural diversity of the community, Marianne provided a benefit to the community that was greatly needed. With knowledge learned from her mother, Marianne walked the prairie and riverbank selecting roots and plants that she knew had healing benefits. Once she had distilled or dried the plants into tinctures and powders, she used her skills and medicines to ease pains and cure ailments.

No record of a marriage between Claude and Marianne has been found, but in the few years they were together before Claude's death, they had six children, born between 1795 and 1802. They named their sons François Regis, Claude, and Bazil. Their daughters were Helene, Adelaide, and Melanie. Adelaide and Melanie may have been twins, as they were both fifteen when they were baptized in 1817.[19]

At some point, Claude gave Farm Lot No. 2 to Marianne. It was a small, narrow lot, bounded on the west by the backwaters of the Mississippi River and on the north where the bluffs bordered Fisher's Creek. Very little of this land could be cultivated, but Fisher's Creek flowed with clear, cool spring water and kept the land verdant. A host of plants rooted themselves along the creek bank, crisp watercress waved in the eddies, and seasonal grasses

and flowers blossomed up the coulee slope. This land provided the vege-
tation Marianne required for the distillations and medicines she made.

By 1803, Marianne had established herself as vital to the Prairie du
Chien community and was welcome in every household. She was a skilled
midwife and knew how to mix herbs and plants to prepare tonics for illnesses. She would have very ill people brought to her home, where she
nursed them back to health. Even after the arrival in 1816 of a surgeon at
the military post on the prairie, Marianne was credited with providing
better cures than the medical professional. James Lockwood, who arrived
at Prairie du Chien in 1817, later recalled that the residents of the prairie
called her "Aunt Mary Ann." James described her as "an excellent nurse"
and remembered that he and others "frequently joked the physician about
Mary Ann's superior skill in the healing art."[20]

An exchange or trade economy existed at Prairie du Chien into the
1840s. Most of the men living at the prairie were employed in the fur trade
as traders or voyageurs. Those who farmed produced food for themselves
and exchanged the surplus for manufactured goods that were part of the
fur trade. The farmers took their ground grain to Michel Brisbois, the
village baker. In return, he baked their flour into bread, keeping some of
the flour as pay for his services. The corn and pease grown on the prairie
provided sustenance not only for the families but for the men who would
spend the winters at their trading sites up the Mississippi River. When the
farmers exchanged grain with the traders, they received a credit with
which they could acquire blankets, tools, tea, and a variety of other goods.
So, when Marianne charged for her services and took her pay "in the produce of the country," she was participating in Prairie du Chien's exchange
economy as other free residents did.[21]

Claude and Marianne's family resided on Farm Lot No. 13 until Claude's
death in 1803. The lot then passed to Claude's children, and Marianne
continued to live on the property and, with help from her neighbors,
raised cattle and horses and tended the crops of pease, rye, and barley.[22]

Within a year of Claude's death, Marianne formed a union with a man
who would become her third husband, the French Canadian Charles
Menard, who had only recently arrived at the prairie. He had been born
in Chambly, Lower Canada, and was the son of Joseph Menard and Marie
Sabourin. With Charles, Marianne gave birth to twin girls (possibly her

second set of twins) Julie and Marguerite in 1805 and three sons: Charles in 1807, Louis in 1809, and Pascal in 1814. By her three marriages, Marianne gave birth to thirteen children, at least twelve of whom lived to adulthood.

In April 1817, Father Marie Joseph Dunand, a Trappist priest, made a treacherous journey up the Mississippi River from St. Louis to minister to the Catholics living at Prairie du Chien. Not only did he solemnize Charles and Marianne's union, he baptized the six children born to Claude Gagnier and Marianne and the eldest children born to Charles and Marianne. The youngest, Louis and Pascal, had already been baptized in August 1814 in St. Louis.

By 1817, Marianne's eldest daughter, Helene, had been married to François Galarneau for several years. Father Dunand also blessed this union in the spring of 1817. In 1818, Adelaide married Jean Baptiste L'Emerie, and then François Regis married Therese Chalifoux. The house was too crowded for this extended family, so Marianne had a hewn log house constructed above the south bank of Fisher's Creek on her farm lot. By 1820, this house became Charles and Marianne's home. As her sons grew older and brought their wives to the farm, a second house was constructed just south of the original family home on Farm Lot No. 13.[23]

By this time, the eldest of Marianne's children, François Duchouquette, had ventured forth on his own. He had gone looking for employment in the fur trade, an industry in which one's skill and ability were more important than skin color or cultural heritage. After finding passage from Prairie du Chien to Michilimackinac around 1810, François joined an expedition establishing fledgling trade posts in the west for the Southwest Company. Following the route of the Lewis and Clark expedition, François and his compatriots experienced a harrowing journey to the Oregon Country. They arrived at Fort Astoria in 1812, and François found employment as a blacksmith. He and his compatriots spent the winter of 1812–1813 at Astoria, but competition from the North West Company was too great for the venture to continue, and the North West Company bought out John Jacob Astor's venture. François was a lead *milieu*, or voyageur, in one of the canoes that returned the Astorians to the Great Lakes. By fall of 1815, François had traveled to Detroit, where he served as an interpreter during treaty negotiations between William Henry Harrison and the Delaware, Seneca,

Shawnee, Miami, Chippewa, Ottawa, and Potawatomi Nations. Then, François headed back to the Oregon region, where he began a relationship with Mary Margueritte Lapetite, the sister of an Okanogan chief. About 1819, a son was born to them and named François Duchouquette.[24]

According to the 1820 census, six of Marianne's eleven children who had been born at Prairie du Chien had not yet married. Marianne and these six children were listed as "free colored." Marianne's eldest daughter, Helene Galarneau, also was enumerated as "free coloured." But Adelaide, who had married L'Emerie, was recorded as "white."[25] By 1830, Charles Menard Jr. and Melanie had both married. When counted in the 1830 census, neither Marianne nor any of her children were listed as "Black." In 1834, a census was taken to determine the population of Michigan Territory as the portion of the territory east of Lake Michigan and south of Lake Superior completed the process to gain statehood. In this census, Marianne was described as "Black," but her children were not. And so it continued until 1860. In that year, Pascal Menard and Helene's son David Galarneau were deemed to be "Mulatto."[26]

By 1839, all of Marianne's children had married. Each had chosen as a spouse a young man or woman who was either French Canadian or of mixed French Canadian and Native ancestry and who lived on the prairie. The family home and the new house on Farm Lot No. 13 were filled with young couples and Marianne's grandchildren. Though Marianne and Charles had moved to the log house along Fisher's Creek, Marianne never ceased to be a part of her children's lives.

To her children and grandchildren, Marianne was known as Maman or Grand-Mère. To other residents of the prairie, Marianne was Madame Gagnier, Mrs. Menard, or as James Lockwood noted, Aunt Mary Ann. No brother or sister had joined Marianne or Claude at Prairie du Chien, so Marianne was no one's aunt by relation. Yet she was referred to as an aunt by many residents of the prairie—a fact that had different implications depending on the race of the person using the term.

Most African men, women, and children who were enslaved in North and South America had once lived in West Africa. There they had lived in societies that valued family and kinship and in which significant roles were assigned to uncles and aunts. The slave trade threatened to destroy these traditional kinship and family patterns. Upon arrival in North America, enslavers disbursed the kidnapped Africans, often separating families and disrupting connections forged during the Middle Passage. Yet, Black people managed to perpetuate some aspects of their African culture in the face of these violent separations, and many enslaved parents continued to instill in their children a deep respect for family and kinship. Children were sometimes taught to refer to Black women and men as *aunt* and *uncle*. And in some cases, if an enslaver separated a child from a parent, the child could turn to these fictive aunts or uncles for emotional or physical support. In this way, among others, enslaved Black people created networks of care that extended beyond blood and marriage. Often, this network remained intact even if a member became free.[27]

While Marianne shared her skills to help many on the prairie, the appellation of *aunt* may have been used only by Lockwood and other white people who had migrated to the prairie from New York and New England. Lockwood wrote his reminiscences in 1856, at a time when the issue of slavery was dividing the United States. Lockwood may have used *aunt* to suggest that he had regard for Black people and disassociate himself from slavery, though a young Black enslaved man had been part of his household in the 1830s.[28]

Just after Marianne's youngest child, Pascal, was born in April 1814, the prairie was the scene of a battle. In the summer of 1814, a contingent of US infantry and Missouri volunteers led by William Clark arrived at Prairie du Chien and constructed a fort in the main village.

In June 1812, the United States had declared war on Great Britain. The resulting conflict, which we now refer to as the War of 1812, ranged throughout the American Northeast and Southeast, and into Canada, the Northwest Territory, and even the Atlantic Ocean. Among the many reasons the United States declared war was Great Britain's control of the fur trade in the Northwest. William Clark, who was the principal Indian agent for the Louisiana Territory and became governor of Missouri Territory in 1813, wished to gain control of Prairie du Chien and thereby the upper Mississippi, the Fox-Wisconsin waterway, and Green Bay. In May of 1814, Clark led a force composed of US Infantry and Missouri volunteers to Prairie du Chien, where they built a fort within the Main Village. In response, the residents of the prairie and the Native nations who lived in the region saw the American force as a threat to their way of life. In July of 1814, a small

British force of volunteers formed at Michilimackinac to capture the prairie. The force included residents of Green Bay and Prairie du Chien as well as men from the Menominee, Ho-Chunk, Ojibwe, and Dakota Nations. The men laid siege to the American fort, and after three days, the US force surrendered. The upper Mississippi and western Great Lakes region remained under British control until the summer of 1815.

With the end of the war in 1815, the United States revitalized the government's three-part policy to establish an Indian agency, a fur factory, and a military installation at strategic locations along bodies of water. With these three elements placed in proximity to one another, the United States believed it could keep British–Canadian trade and influence from the upper Mississippi and western Great Lakes regions and, in time, gain the loyalty of the Native nations and assimilate their people into American culture. The War Department had already established an Indian agency at Prairie du Chien in 1807, and Nicolas Boilvin, the agent, returned to the prairie as soon as the news of the British abandonment of the prairie reached St. Louis.

In the spring of 1816, representatives of the other two components of the tripartite plan were ordered to Prairie du Chien. And life for Marianne and her neighbors greatly changed.

As of 1816, Marianne and her children seem to have been the only people of African heritage living on the prairie. In time, each of Marianne's children would marry a spouse of French Canadian or mixed French Canadian and Native heritage. These unions were blessed by Catholic priests, the children were baptized, and the families continued to own, reside on, and farm the land the United States had patented to Claude Gagnier and Marianne Labuche. Upon their deaths, they were buried in the community cemetery and blessed by an attending priest.

Every member of Marianne's family would have known about slavery. When people from Prairie du Chien traveled to St. Louis, the Illinois Country, Detroit, or Montreal, they would have encountered enslaved individuals. Most enslaved people in the United States were of African descent, but in the lower Mississippi, some enslaved people were of First Nations descent, sometimes called *Panis slaves*. One formerly enslaved American Indian man named Nicolas Colas lived at Prairie du Chien. He had been brought to the prairie in the 1790s by Jean Marie Cardinal and had possibly gained his freedom with the death of Jean Marie. Nicolas then married Jean Marie's widow, Marie Souligne. Nicolas and Marie lived two farm lots south of the Gagnier farm.[29] In the early nineteenth century, race did not automatically exclude people of color from various institutions on the prairie. However, when white American men brought people of African heritage with them to the prairie, they also brought racial inequality.

CHAPTER 2

MARIAH, 1800–1829

In the spring of 1816, Mariah arrived at Prairie du Chien. Although the prairie would become her new home, just as it had for Marianne, Mariah set foot on the river's shore through no choice of her own. No husband awaited her arrival. No newly built house stood in the midst of a field lush and green with spring wheat, and no welcoming greetings reached her ears. Rather, when she arrived at Prairie du Chien, her enslaver, John W. Johnson, likely ordered Mariah to collect her parcel and get off the boat.

Mariah was the first of almost two hundred Black people brought to the prairie between 1816 and 1845 as captives. Each of these men and women, in some manner, was enslaved by a man who was an employee of the US government or an officer in the US Army.[1]

—⊣|⊢—

Mariah was born around 1800. Her mother, about whom no records have been found, was an enslaved woman. At the time of Mariah's birth, her mother lived and worked on a tobacco plantation in Aquasco, Prince George's County, Maryland, that was owned by Rinaldo Johnson. In 1789, Rinaldo married Ann Eilback Mason of Fairfax County, Virginia. Ann was the daughter of George Mason, a Virginia enslaver and plantation owner and a delegate to the US Constitutional Convention. Ann brought seventeen enslaved individuals to the marriage. These included Sissy, Nan, Bess, Aracajah, and Bess's and Aracajah's children. Mariah's mother could have been one of these women or a woman already enslaved by Rinaldo.[2]

John W. Johnson was Rinaldo's younger brother. When their father, Thomas, died severely in debt, John had to find a means to produce an income, and he used his sister-in-law's family connections to do so. In 1807, President Thomas Jefferson had appointed Ann's brother, John Mason, as the US superintendent of Indian trade. Using this connection, John W. Johnson secured the appointment of factor for the US trading house that was to be instituted for the Sauk and Meskwaki. The factory, as the US–owned fur trading post was called, would be located about a mile from the mouth of the Des Moines River. John traveled from Maryland to St. Louis, then journeyed with a military squadron up the Mississippi River to the proposed site. Under Lieutenant Alpha Kingsley and John's directions, the soldiers began construction of the new post and the factory building in September 1808. John remained as the fur factor for Fort Madison until September 1812, when the post commander ordered the factory buildings burned to prevent the Sauk and Ho-Chunk from firing on the factory and fort.

After the conflict between the United States and Great Britain officially ended with a treaty signed by both countries in December 1814, John sought another government posting. President Madison and the secretary of war still believed all that was needed to gain the trust of the Native nations was a fur factory offering fair trade prices and no liquor. Instead of rebuilding the factory on the Des Moines River, they decided to open a US factory at Prairie du Chien, where Fort Crawford was being constructed. Like the Indian agency, the factory needed to be located close to the new post. John Mason still held his position in the Indian Office located in Georgetown, and he recommended John W. Johnson for the appointment as the US factor at Prairie du Chien. The appointment was approved.[3]

John traveled to the nation's capital at Washington City to be confirmed in his new position, and while there he ordered the goods he needed for trade at the Prairie du Chien factory. Before leaving for his new posting, John returned to Maryland. There he acquired two enslaved people, likely from his brother Rinaldo—Mariah and a young man named Henry. Then, as ordered by John Mason, John W. Johnson left for Prairie du Chien, accompanied by Mariah, Henry, and Robert B. Belt. Robert, a white man, had been John's assistant at Fort Madison and was now the assistant factor for Prairie du Chien, with the duties of clerk and bookkeeper.[4]

John may have already known that slavery was illegal on the northeast side of the Mississippi River. But in Illinois Territory, which included Prairie du Chien at that time, an enslaver could quite easily circumvent the Northwest Ordinance and bring human property into the territory.

To be in compliance with Illinois Territorial law, which prohibited slavery but allowed for indentured servitude, John conveyed Henry and Mariah to Josiah Randle, the circuit court clerk for Madison County. In all likelihood, John set the terms of Mariah's and Henry's indentures, which were then written down. In the presence of Josiah, Henry and Mariah each affixed an X to a legal document. Though this changed their legal status to indentured, they remained bound to John.

On April 10, 1816, John filed the first indenture, which placed Henry, age eleven, into service for John. No date was recorded for the length of Henry's indenture. He was described as "a Certain Negro boy ... of a yellow complexion."[5]

In the indenture of April 11, 1816, Mariah became indentured to John. Mariah was described as having been "lately Brought to said territory by the Said John W. Johnson" and "agreeing to and with her said Master, to serve him faithfully During the Term of Seventeen years from the first day of January in the year of Our Lord one thousand Eight hundred and Sixteen."[6] At the signing of her indenture, Mariah was about sixteen years old.[7]

Mariah and Henry arrived at the prairie with John and Robert and a stock of trade goods in May 1816. John Mason had suggested that once John W. Johnson arrived at the prairie, he should occupy "some of the houses that are public property, or to rent of individuals on easy terms." If the structures needed repairs, John was to apply to the officer commanding the new military post being constructed at Prairie du Chien. That officer had been told to supply soldiers to repair and improve the structures John would use for the US factory. The soldiers were to be paid "Ten cents and a gill of whiskey per day."[8]

Along with all the goods and documents required to operate the factory, John had brought copies of the indentures with him to the prairie. These he kept safe in case anyone was to question him about Mariah and Henry. In 1816, according to the laws of the Territory of Illinois, Henry's and Mariah's indentured servitude was legal, but John probably knew that

Indenture dated April 11, 1816, between Mariah and John W. Johnson. With this document, Johnson altered Mariah's status from enslaved to indentured for a "Term of Seventeen years." It was recorded at Prairie du Chien on August 8, 1829. COURTESY OF CRAWFORD COUNTY REGISTER OF DEEDS

human bondage in any form was technically illegal in the Northwest Territory.[9]

When Mariah and Henry stepped from the flat-bottomed barge that had transported them to Prairie du Chien, a panorama of color and activity moved before them. Officers barked orders to sweating men who were engaged in hewing, notching, and assembling logs to form barracks for the military post. Mariah's gaze may have moved from the construction site to the other buildings ranging along the waterfront and to the south on the island. She may have wondered if all buildings were made of logs in this strange place. And she may have been curious about some people gathered around one of the hewn log houses. Their skin was brown, but not as dark as hers. They wore soft leather on their feet; the men stood straight and tall. Some wore strands of colorful beads and silver discs

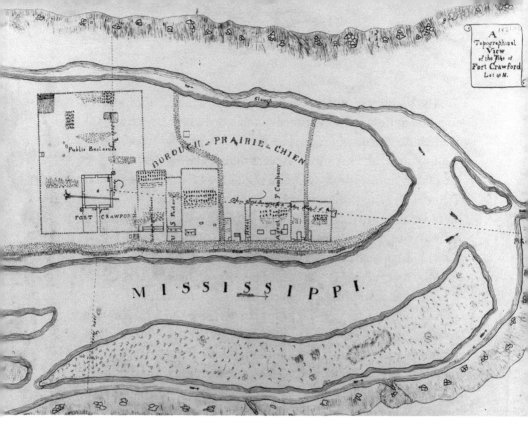

Abbreviated drawing of the Main Village of Prairie du Chien, 1821. It places the locations, from left to right, of the first Fort Crawford, the US Indian Agency, the US Factory where Mariah worked, the home of Michel Brisbois, two private homes, the "Hotel" of Jean Brunet, and the property of Joseph Rolette, who is noted as "Agent A F Company."
WHI IMAGE ID 42267

around their necks. If Mariah or Henry had never come in contact with American Indians in Maryland or southern Illinois, they would soon learn that members of the Ho-Chunk and Sauk-Meskwaki Nations often visited the prairie. As they walked on the dirt road, following John and Robert to the buildings that would become their new home and house the factory, they discovered that their new residence lay just south of the US Indian Agency.

Finding that François Bouthellier had previously rented the village lot he owned to various British traders, John examined the two structures on the lot and determined the property fit his needs as the location of the US factory. He entered into an agreement with François to rent the buildings for twenty-seven dollars a month and had his goods unpacked and displayed for trade by the time General Thomas A. Smith and a contingent of the Rifle Regiment disembarked at Prairie du Chien on June 20.[10]

The buildings John had rented were constructed of carefully hewn logs and quite sturdy. Every room had wood plank floors, and the logs were chinked so no wind blew into the rooms. The logs and chinking were whitewashed, and the windows were tightly glazed. Heat radiated from a rectangular cast iron stove. John would need much of the space for the factory store and storage of trade goods, as well as the pelts and lead he would soon be exchanging for the goods. Exactly where Mariah and Henry were given space to sleep and keep their few belongings is not known, but it would have been in one of the two log structures.

John had purchased Mariah not to work as a field hand but to provide domestic labor within the setting of the factory for which he was responsible. While he had been the factor at Fort Madison, John had formed a relationship with Tapassa, a woman of the Sauk Nation, and had fathered three daughters with her. But John had left them behind when the factory buildings had been destroyed in 1812. As a single man, John desired someone who would assume the domestic responsibilities of a household when he arrived in Prairie du Chien. John chose Mariah for this work.

Mariah likely learned to perform the tasks expected of a house servant during her childhood in the Johnson plantation house. She was likely trained by her mother or other enslaved women to work in the yard, help in the kitchen, and wait on table. Other duties for house servants could include washing clothes, making soap and candles, and spinning and weaving.[11]

Not all of these skills would have been needed for the work Mariah did for John. Commodities stocked at US factories included soap, candles, and piece goods, which ranged from satinette to coarse linen. But it can be assumed that Mariah cooked the meals for the Johnson household, toted water, maintained an orderly living space, cleaned and washed the clothes for John and Robert, and tended a kitchen garden similar to those behind other homes in the settlement. Henry probably helped in the factory, moving trade goods from boats to the store and carrying packs of pelts and lead from the store to boats waiting to lift anchor for St. Louis.

Mariah, Henry, John, and Robert had been in Prairie du Chien for about a month when General Smith and Major Richard Grant entered the factory building on June 20. According to John, Smith and Grant "commenced regulating the village" the day after their arrival at the prairie. General Smith was filled with scorn for the residents of the community, whom he considered traitors for having assisted the British in the war. Every Prairie du Chien resident was required to present to Grant their licenses allowing them to trade; if they had no license, their goods were seized. The soldiers had been living in tents since they had disembarked at the prairie in April. Smith found this unacceptable and therefore took possession of some houses, declaring them housing for the soldiers until barracks were constructed. Michel Brisbois, a resident whose home was next to the factory buildings, was arrested and sent to St. Louis for trial. His wife and children were forced out of their home. Smith also seized the buildings John W. Johnson had rented, declaring them public property and forbidding John to pay rent. Soon thereafter, John shared these events in a letter to François Bouthellier, who was now at Galena, and advised him not to write in return. "Thus you find how things are changed," he wrote.[12]

Two buildings existed on François's property when Smith commandeered them for the use of the US factory, but even though they were good-sized buildings, they could not accommodate the stock of trade goods available at the factory and the subsequent storage of pelts. Using funds allocated to the Office of Indian Trade, John retained soldiers to repair the sizable log structures and construct several outbuildings.[13] More buildings were needed not only because of the business of trade but also to provide quarters for John, Robert, and five other individuals who worked to make the factory function. Mariah and Henry were likely relegated from one of the large structures to one of the outbuildings. These, too, would have been constructed of tightly chinked hewn logs.

Another man, John P. Gates, soon arrived at the factory. Neither John W. Johnson nor Robert Belt could converse with the American Indians with whom they were to conduct trade. Therefore, the War Department had retained Gates as an interpreter for Johnson and Belt. Mariah now had another person for whom to prepare meals and do laundry.[14]

As Mariah and Henry assessed their new home, to the north soldiers continued to busily construct the log barracks of the new fort, named Crawford for Secretary of War William Harris Crawford. Once General Smith had established his authority, life may have settled into a routine. Then Smith transferred, and soon a newly appointed commanding officer arrived at the prairie, assessed his new post, and began instituting laws for the community that surrounded it.

Lieutenant Colonel Talbot Chambers had been previously posted at Fort Howard in Green Bay. To the residents of that community, he behaved in a professional manner. But at Prairie du Chien, Chambers forced certain residents to move their homes to the end of the village because they stood on land Chambers wanted for the military tract. He demanded to see trading licenses and arrested those who could not produce the document. He also banished Joseph Rolette, the main trader at Prairie du Chien, to an island seven miles up the Mississippi River for some infraction. John Shaw, who had built a sawmill on the north end of the prairie, found Chambers's "petty tyrannies" so offensive that he sold the mill to Chambers at a loss and moved to Illinois.[15]

One of Chambers's rants against a resident of the prairie was so odious that not only Shaw but James Lockwood remembered the incident when he wrote his reminiscences forty years later. Once, after imbibing too much, Chambers chased a young girl across the prairie and into the home of Charles Menard and Marianne Labuche. Menard challenged him. In response, Chambers had Menard arrested. Brought before a court martial, Chambers accused Menard of selling liquor to some soldiers. Menard protested that he had not sold whiskey to any soldiers, for he did not keep liquor to sell. No matter his protest, the court found Menard guilty and sentenced him to receive twenty-five lashes with a cat-o'-nine-tails. The punishment was public spectacle, and many residents were present, including Nicolas Boilvin's ten-year-old son. Moved by what was about to happen, the boy ran to Chambers and, crying, pled that Menard not be publicly humiliated. The drumroll began, but after two or three lashes, Chambers ordered the drummer to stop, and the whipping ceased. Chambers then ordered that a bottle be hung around Menard's neck. Under guard, Menard was marched through the village. The post musicians followed Menard, playing "The Rogue's March."[16]

Mariah and Henry may have watched this spectacle. If so, this event may have been the first time that Mariah saw Marianne and her children. They would have been present to witness Menard's punishment, with Marianne prepared to treat her husband's slashed back. Mariah and

Henry may have been familiar with whipping as a form of punishment for enslaved Black people, but they had likely never seen a white man being whipped.

John W. Johnson, in his short term of service as US factor at Prairie du Chien, demonstrated the abilities and knowledge he had gained as a private trader before he had become a US factor. He engaged in trade with the Sauk, Meskwaki, Ho-Chunk, Menominee, Ioway, Kickapoo, Potawatomi, and Dakota. With the southern tribes, John preferred to trade government goods for lead rather than furs. He used A. P. Vanmeter and Jesse Shull as middlemen to acquire lead from the Ho-Chunk and the Sauk and Meskwaki. According to government reports, John and George Davenport, agent for the American Fur Company, acquired a good deal of the lead mined on Sauk and Ho-Chunk land for trade until the US factory system was abolished in 1822.[17]

Not only did Native people mine lead in the region, but also many white men sought wealth in the mines. The early American miners came from Missouri and Kentucky, where slavery was legal. Many brought their Black captives with them to do the hard work of mining. John used this connection to add to his household. John did not have a wife, and although Mariah maintained the living quarters, cooked, and did laundry for him, Belt, and Gates, John felt that he needed more help. He retained the services of two more "coloured people."[18]

John may have sent to Missouri for the young man and young woman, as they were part of his household by 1820, though no indentures for these two people were filed in Illinois or at Prairie du Chien. The only record of the existence of the young people are the tally marks in the column *Free Coloured* in the 1820 federal census forms for Prairie du Chien. Their names were not recorded, nor were they noted as enslaved or indentured, but it is reasonable to assume that they were bound to John in some manner. The woman was about twenty, the same age as Mariah, and the boy was under the age of fourteen, so possibly about the same age as Henry.[19]

Beyond Mariah, Henry, the boy, and the young woman who worked alongside them, and the members of Marianne Labuche's family, only four other "free coloured" people were recorded as living at Prairie du Chien at that time. A young man described in the 1820 federal census as a "coloured male" lived in the household of Michel Brisbois, and another young man listed as a "coloured male" in the census worked in the household of François Bouthellier. Both were described as being between the ages of fifteen and twenty-six. Two "free coloured" women lived with Joseph and Jane Fisher Rolette and their children in the Rolette house located several lots to the south of the factory. When Jane had married at the age of fourteen, she had become a stepmother to Joseph's three daughters by his first marriage to Marguerite DuBois, so the two Black women probably maintained the house and helped care for the three girls and Jane and Joseph's children. One of the Black women in the Rolette household was about the same age as Mariah, and the other was older. One of the two women was named Polly.

John W. Johnson, as US factor, was to trade only with the American Indians who came to Prairie du Chien. Nevertheless, he found profit in providing goods to the non-Native residents of the prairie as well, including the Rolette household. Jane Rolette often sent Polly to the factory for tea or silk. On one occasion, Polly received "1 pair coarse shoes," shoes with leather soles and uppers for working outdoors, for herself.[20]

It is possible that Polly and the other Black woman in the Rolette household were paid servants and not indentured. Joseph Rolette, who was one of the justices for Crawford County, certainly knew that slavery was not legal in Prairie du Chien. In 1831, Pierre Chouteau, who lived in St. Louis and worked for the Western Outfit of the American Fur Company, wrote to Joseph, offering to send him a "servant maid." Joseph replied, "The law prohibits slavery, therefore I must decline purchasing."[21]

John's accounts indicate that Polly came to the factory regularly, and therefore, Mariah may have found friendship with Polly or the other Black woman who lived with Joseph. It can be proved with more certainty that Mariah became a friend of Helene Gagnier Galarneau, the mixed-race eldest daughter of Marianne Labuche and Claude Gagnier.[22]

Helene was about six years older than Mariah. When Mariah arrived at Prairie du Chien in 1816, Helene was already married to François Galarneau and had two children. Her husband had been born in the parish Berthier-en-Haut, Quebec, and had entered the fur trade to transport trade goods bound for Michilimackinac. At the end of his engagement, he remained in the country and learned the blacksmith trade. At Green Bay, the merchant and fur trader Jacob Franks hired François to manage his blacksmith shop, which he did for a few years until François resettled and established his own smithy at Prairie du Chien in the Main Village.[23]

The Main Village contained fewer than twenty homes, and the families who lived in these houses were connected by the economy of the fur trade. Some of the men, such as Michel Brisbois and Joseph Rolette, traded for the American Fur Company. Other men, including François, engaged in some other occupation that was vital to the trade. François may have received work from John, as the American Indians often brought broken guns and tools to John and Nicolas Boilvin, the Indian agent, for repair. This work would be done by a blacksmith. In such a small community, bound by the commonality of the trade, Mariah would have soon met Helene. And a friendship began.

Mariah served John for the length of his stay in Prairie du Chien, which ended in 1829. But John's position as US factor at Prairie du Chien lasted only until 1822, when the entire system of government trading houses was abolished. The factory system had operated on the belief that as the factor offered goods to the American Indians at face value, they would see that they received more goods for their furs from the factors than they did from the private traders. According to this line of thinking, Native people would choose to trade furs at the US factory rather than with private traders. But the factory system failed to understand the protocol of the established trading system, which had been in operation for generations.

Both French and British officials had frequently given presents to the American Indians prior to the negotiations over furs, and private trading companies continued the tradition of gift giving. In addition, the Native people maintained no reserve of necessities. They had become accustomed to using manufactured goods that were part of the trade, and they often needed to replace items between trading seasons. Consequently, a system had developed in which the British and American private traders provided American Indians with needed supplies on credit. The United States, however, would not engage in the tradition of gift giving, and factors could not extend credit. Factors also did not travel beyond the factory and live among the tribes during the winter so as to secure the best pelts in the spring. Furthermore, many of the Canadian and American agents of the large private fur companies were married to women who were members of the tribes with which the men traded, thereby ensuring that trade continued within the families. John W. Johnson established a relationship with Tapassa when he was at Fort Madison, but it may have been a relationship of convenience, for John never reconnected with her upon his return to the Mississippi Valley in 1816.[24] In contrast, Joseph Rolette, Augustin Roc, and other traders at the prairie entered into unions with women from the Dakota Nation that were sanctified by marriage, and these unions lasted until the death of one partner.

By 1816, the year John arrived at Prairie du Chien, St. Louis merchants had begun to lobby for the dissolution of the factory system. Within a few years, Ninian Edwards, governor of Illinois, and Lewis Cass, governor of Michigan Territory, supported their argument. Finally, early in 1822, Senator Thomas Hart Benton, chairman of the Senate Committee on Indian Affairs, introduced a bill that would end the factory system. As part of the investigation by the committee, Benton demonstrated that the factories at Chicago and Green Bay served no purpose, as most of the factories' sales were to white civilians. In five of the six years of its operation, John's agency at Prairie du Chien had lost the government $12,300 and had incurred debts of $14,404, which could not be recovered. Evidence presented to the Indian Affairs committee documented the goods John had sold to Joseph Rolette and several members of the Brisbois family.[25] In March 1822, the US Congress abolished the system of government trading houses.

Even though he had lost his position with the federal government, John remained in Prairie du Chien, as did Mariah. John had garnered judicial appointments and become a force within the community. In the spring of 1819, the first court for Crawford County was organized by Michigan Territory. The territorial legislature appointed three men to be justices of the peace for Crawford County: Nicolas Boilvin, John W. Johnson, and James H. Lockwood. The justices elected John the chief justice. Two years later, on September 17, 1821, the governor and justices of Michigan Territory approved the incorporation of the Borough of Prairie du Chien. The borough was to be administered by a warden and two burgesses, assisted by a clerk and treasurer. In the first election, held in 1822, John was elected warden.

When the factory system was dissolved, John moved out of the structures that had once housed the US factory and acquired a large tract of land at the south end of the Main Village on which he planned to live. John brought Mariah with him, and she continued to serve him at his new residence. Several lots to the north of John's land was the lot to which François and Helene Galarneau had relocated in 1817.

—ı⊢—

In addition to being influenced by the people Mariah likely met through the US factory in Prairie du Chien, such as Helene Galarneau and the Black women living in the Rolette household, Mariah's life was significantly altered by a Fort Crawford soldier named Jacob Faschnacht. The construction of Fort Crawford was completed, and in 1819, the War Department transferred responsibility for the command and operation of the garrison to the Fifth Regiment of Infantry. All regiments within the US Army appointed officers to travel throughout the country to recruit men to enlist so that the many new garrisons established on the vast American frontier would be fully manned. Periodically, a young lieutenant or a captain serving at a frontier post was ordered to temporary recruiting duty. These men would return to the East, visiting communities and giving talks about the benefits of enlisting in the army. One young man who heard a talk encouraging him to enlist and venture to the frontier was Jacob Faschnacht.

When he enlisted in December 1817, Jacob was twenty years old. Born in York, Pennsylvania, he was of German heritage, five-foot-six with dark hair and dark eyes. He mustered into the service the following March, soon regretted his decision, and deserted. But he was returned to duty in September, and the military quickly transported Jacob and other recruits west for a posting at Detroit. In April 1818, he was transferred into another company that was assigned to Fort Crawford, and so Jacob arrived at Prairie du Chien. He did not desert again but remained at Fort Crawford for the duration of his enlistment until he received his discharge on December 9, 1822.[26]

Jacob served at Prairie du Chien during the same years that Mariah resided in John's household at the US factory, and by some means, they came in contact with each other. Fort Crawford stood only a few hundred feet north of the government factory buildings, and Jacob may have been one of the soldiers assigned to improve the structures of the fur factory. However they met, they talked and learned about each other's lives prior to coming to Prairie du Chien. Mariah may have been the reason that Jacob remained in Prairie du Chien after his return to civilian status. Even after Mariah and John no longer resided at what had been the US factory, Jacob and Mariah continued to maintain their relationship, and at some point, Jacob proposed to marry Mariah.

Mariah was still indentured to John and, therefore, not free. She needed his permission to marry. As the employer in the indenture, John could forbid Mariah from marrying, and he could loan, rent, or sell her at any point during the duration of her indenture. But she must have received his permission, because on October 25, 1824, Crawford County Justice of the Peace James H. Lockwood married Jacob and Mariah. Lockwood recorded the couple as "Jacob Forsnot of PdC and Maria, a mulatto woman."[27]

Once married, Jacob may have lived and worked in the Johnson household. But Jacob intended to provide for Mariah. Many of the officers stationed at Fort Crawford employed servants to cook and wait upon them when they were not engaged in military duties. About two months after Mariah and Jacob married, Jacob found employment as servant to Second Lieutenant P. Andrews stationed at Fort Crawford. Jacob worked for the officer from January through April in 1825. With his wages, plus other money, Jacob purchased a plot of land from François and Helene Galarneau.[28]

When François arrived at Prairie du Chien, he had established his smithy north of the Indian agency. In 1817, Lieutenant Colonel Chambers arrived at Fort Crawford and ordered residents in close proximity to the fort to take down their houses. They were relocated to the south end of the Main Village. In that area, more lots existed, and the dislocated residents reestablished their homes. François and Helene had been forced to move and were granted Main Village Lot No. 24. On this narrow tract, they built a house, and François reestablished his smithy so that it faced the street that lay along the waterfront.[29] As of 1820, they did not have a title to the land, but they lived on the lot with their children, and François produced an income as one of several blacksmiths working at the prairie.[30]

In 1824, Congress granted François and Helene a patent to their lot in the Main Village. In that same year, the couple sold Jacob a portion of their village lot that lay behind their home. Jacob constructed a house on his newly purchased lot, which was 50 feet by 366 feet—less than half an acre.

Though still indentured to John, Mariah obtained permission from John to live with her new husband. Mariah was now Helene's neighbor, and their friendship deepened.[31]

Though married and living in her own house at Prairie du Chien, Mariah remained indentured to John. In the mid-1820s, John may have rented Mariah to officers who had been temporarily transferred from Fort Snelling to Fort Crawford. Captain Robert A. McCabe was posted at Fort Crawford from the spring of 1823 to the end of 1825. In July 1825, just before the Great Council and Treaty of Prairie du Chien, Robert assumed command of the post. He officiated at the treaty, signed the document, and continued to hold the position of commanding officer until he was transferred to Fort Snelling. Second Lieutenant Henry Clark arrived at Fort Crawford at the end of October 1825 and was posted at Prairie du Chien for only two months until he, too, was removed to Fort Snelling. Mariah must have accompanied one, possibly both, of the officers when they returned to duty at the fort along the Minnesota River. First Robert McCabe and then Henry Clark claimed Mariah on their Fort Snelling pay returns.[32] According to the document Mariah had signed in 1816, her term of indenture would not end until January 1, 1833, so John could rent her to other individuals and keep the income.

Unlike most indentured men and women, Mariah was married and lived in a house that she could call hers by her marriage to Jacob. But by selling her services to Robert and Henry, John wrenched Mariah back to the reality of her situation. After finding herself once again on a boat, being transported northward to an unknown future, Mariah may have found some comfort when she arrived at Fort Snelling. There were other Black people living here. All were enslaved, and like Mariah, all had been born and raised on a Southern plantation. These were her companions for the winter months while she lived at isolated Fort Snelling.

Once the river opened in the spring of 1826, Mariah would return to Prairie du Chien and her home with Jacob. As she watched the first boat arrive at Fort Snelling that spring, carrying supplies and passengers, she would have seen an officer disembark with his wife and infant children. Mariah may have glimpsed a slight young Black woman trailing behind them, perhaps pausing to crane her neck at the stone walls of her new home. As Courtney arrived at Fort Snelling, Mariah departed, but in that short space of time, they may have made the initial connection that would later grow into an important friendship.

By the summer of 1826, though still indentured, Mariah had a home to return to after completing her service for Robert McCabe and Henry Clark. Jacob had begun raising crops on their small piece of land. Mariah had neighbors who had become her friends. Because of their cultural bond, Mariah may have been included in the gatherings of Marianne Labuche's large family. If so, Mariah would have been present to celebrate the birth of Helene's fourth child, Marguerite Galarneau, the day before Christmas of 1826.

As spring awakened on the prairie in 1827, the hush of the wind was the only background to the sounds of men calling to their oxen pulling plows across the fields. Gone were the shouts of sergeants, the drumming of marching feet, and the clink of swords against belt harnesses. The War Department had ordered the abandonment of Fort Crawford the previous fall, and most residents were glad to watch the leave-taking as the soldiers loaded food and equipment on keelboats that would transport the goods and men to Fort Snelling. But there was a disquiet about the community. Tensions existed between the Ho-Chunk and the men of the lead-mining district, who consistently encroached on Ho-Chunk land to dig into the rich mineral deposits. In March 1826, a confrontation had occurred along the Yellow River, across the Mississippi River from Prairie du Chien. François Methodè and his wife had been killed, along with their three children and the family dog. After collecting evidence, Major Willoughby Morgan, who commanded Fort Crawford, came to the conclusion the Ho-Chunk had killed the Methodè family. He demanded the Ho-Chunk surrender the four men that Willoughby suspected had attacked the family. Though they protested their innocence, the Ho-Chunk men were imprisoned. When the military abandoned Prairie du Chien, two of the men were released and two were taken to Fort Snelling and imprisoned.

But in the spring of 1827, a shout announcing the arrival of a visitor to the prairie and the gladness that most residents felt upon his appearance caused any uneasiness about the arrests to dissipate. Father François Vincent Badin had come to minister to the spiritual needs of the community. Father Badin had been sent by the Diocese of Detroit as a missionary to the Catholic residents of Prairie du Chien and Galena. He was the first Catholic priest to visit the community since Father Dunand's five-week stay in 1817. Many local couples wished to have their marriages blessed, and many children and adults awaited the sacrament of baptism.

As had Father Dunand, Father Badin arrived in May. He immediately began to offer Mass, using a part of the Fort Crawford barracks with a solid floor and a roof that did not leak as his residence and chapel. At once, he began a busy schedule, administering at least four baptisms a day. As a friend of Helene, Mariah may have been invited to witness the occasions. Marianne, the family matriarch, surely watched as her grandchildren François and Marie Louise, the son and daughter of François Regis Gagnier and Therese Chalifoux, were baptized. Two of Marianne's other children, François Duchouquette and Adelaide Gagnier, stood as godparents for François. Neighbors Denis and Theodiste Courtois stood as Marie Louise's godparents. Marianne's family celebrated again on June 25 when Father Badin blessed the marriage of Joseph Gardipie and Julie Menard.[33]

Unknown to Marianne, her family and friends, and all of the community, including Mariah, events were transpiring that would destroy this short-lived happiness. A rumor had been circulating that the two Ho-Chunk men who had been imprisoned at Fort Crawford and then transported to Fort Snelling had been murdered at the fort. Although they were, in fact, alive and would later be released, this rumor was believed by the Native people in the Dakota and Ho-Chunk villages where the story spread.

Trusting that the two Ho-Chunk men had been killed at the fort, the Ho-Chunk felt obligated to seek restitution and restore peace by killing the murderer or someone close to him. The Ho-Chunk considered Fort Snelling too well defended for them to approach, but Prairie du Chien was the next closest settlement in which Americans resided.

The Prairie Lacrosse band of Ho-Chunk lived the closest to Prairie du Chien. They planned to make restitution for the two deaths. Red Bird, a Ho-Chunk chief, was ordered by the elders of the band to go to Prairie du Chien and kill two Americans. This was not a responsibility he wanted, as he knew many residents at the prairie and was liked by all who knew him. But he was forced to accept the directive.[34]

On June 28, Red Bird and three companions completed their journey to Prairie du Chien. When they did not immediately find any Americans as they walked down the prairie, they continued toward the home of Thomas

Marie Louise Gagnier, born in 1823, was the daughter of François Regis Gagnier and Therese Chalifoux and the granddaughter of Marianne Labuche. She was wounded during the Winnebago War of 1827. In 1843, she married Amable Moreau. After his death, she married Combe Cherrier. Marie Louise lived to age sixty-seven and was the mother of thirteen children. PRAIRIE DU CHIEN HISTORICAL SOCIETY

McNair. But before arriving at the McNair home, they encountered the small log house in which Regis Gagnier, Therese, and their two children lived, along with a retired soldier named Solomon Leipcap. Visiting at the time was Pascal Menard, Regis's half-brother.

The family of Marianne Labuche suffered in the Ho-Chunk's need for retribution. Her son Regis was killed, and her granddaughter Marie Louise was wounded. When the residents of the prairie heard of the attack, all took refuge in the tavern owned by Jean Brunet, and word was sent upriver to Fort Snelling. While all crowded into the tavern, Marianne may have helped prepare her son for burial. In his church records, Father Badin recorded: "François Regis Gagne, 30 years of age, killed by the Indians yesterday about noon, was buried in the cemetery of this parish by the undersigned priest, June 29, 1827, in the presence of John Simson and Augustin Hebert."[35]

When news reached the prairie that another band of Ho-Chunk had attacked two keelboats coming from Fort Snelling, all the residents temporarily relocated to the old Fort Crawford. The local militia re-formed under the command of Thomas McNair and proceeded to fortify the block-house as best they could. Three of Marianne's sons—François Duchouquette, Bazil Gagnier, and Charles Menard—were privates in the militia, which was quickly designated a military company by General Henry Atkinson. They were joined by two of Marianne's sons-in-law, Joseph Gardipie and Jean Baptiste L'Emerie. Joseph had had his marriage to Julie Menard blessed by Father Badin only four days previously.[36]

Four companies of the Fifth Regiment, under the command of Colonel Snelling, finally arrived at Prairie du Chien in mid-July. Feeling secure, the residents returned to their homes and fields, and life returned to some normality.

Soon after the arrival of the troops from Fort Snelling, Father Badin continued to administer the sacrament of baptism to children and adults and to bless the union of many couples. On August 5, Marianne attended the baptism of two of her grandchildren, Marie and Rosalie Loyer, with Charles Menard standing as godfather to both grandchildren. Four days later, Helene Galarneau's two daughters, ten-year-old Sophie and seven-month-old Marguerite, were baptized. Three days later, Helene's son David and daughter Tharsile were baptized. Then, to culminate his stay before traveling to Galena, Father Badin blessed the marriage of Adelaide Gagnier and Jean Baptiste L'Emerie on August 17. This marriage warranted a family celebration, as Father Badin recorded that relatives and friends, which may have included Mariah, were present when he blessed the marriage.[37] Perhaps some joy offset the sadness Marianne held in her heart for her son Regis.

After the events of the summer of 1827, the War Department decided a garrison was still needed at the prairie, but a better site was vital. The events also forced a change in US Indian policy and provided justification for the United States "to enable the President to extinguish the title to certain mineral Lands claimed by the Winnebagoes [Ho-Chunk], Potawatamis, Ottawas [Odawa], and Chippewa [Ojibwe] Indians East of the Mississippi and south of the Ouisconsin River."[38] President John Quincy Adams appointed John McNeil, Pierre Menard, and Caleb Atwater commissioners to conduct a council with these nations and demand the cession of Ho-Chunk lands to the United States. Representatives of the nations and the United States government convened in formal council in July 1829 at Prairie du Chien. A show of force by US troops and a talk by Sauk leader Keokuk convinced the Ho-Chunk to surrender their land to the United States. While John W. Johnson held no position pertaining to the treaty negotiations, he was present. On July 29, he signed as a witness to the treaty with the Council of Three Fires (Ojibwe, Odawa, and Potawatomi). On August 1, he signed as a witness to the treaty with the Ho-Chunk.[39]

While discussing the final terms of the treaty with the Ho-Chunk in July 1829, the commissioners ordered an announcement to be made that anyone who had a claim against the nation was to submit it to the commissioners. If one's claim was determined valid, the individual would receive reimbursement for the loss. Mariah submitted a claim, stating that a horse and a colt she owned had been stolen by the Ho-Chunk. The value of the animals was assessed at sixty dollars.[40] Though still indentured to John, Mariah owned personal property and clearly had a life beyond her indentured servitude.

After the signing of the treaties in the summer of 1829, John decided to leave Prairie du Chien for St. Louis. This provided an opportunity for Mariah to gain her freedom, and she probably approached John to request it.

This view of the Mississippi River, Fort Crawford, and Prairie du Chien was sketched by Lieutenant Seth Eastman in October 1829. Eastman had been posted to Fort Snelling and stopped at Prairie du Chien. The sketch is the earliest known and most detailed record of the villages and structures and their location on the prairie. The second structure to right of the fort is the building used by the US Factory. PEABODY MUSEUM, HARVARD UNIVERSITY, OBJECT 41-72-10/80

Because Mariah was married, it would have proven difficult and might have led to litigation for John to force Mariah to come with him to St. Louis to complete her indenture. Also, Mariah had now lived for more than ten years in Michigan Territory, where slavery was not allowed. Based on the questionable legality of the indenture John had made Mariah sign, he may not have wished to force her to complete her term of indenture. His decision to change Mariah's status from enslaved to indentured had been a tacit acknowledgment that Mariah was a free woman under Illinois law. He probably believed he would be on shaky legal ground if he pressed Mariah to complete the term of her indenture. John was likely also swayed by the fact that he would have the opportunity to purchase other enslaved people in St. Louis.

Instead of freeing Mariah from the obligation to work for him for the entire seventeen years, John required her to pay for her freedom. He must have calculated the value of her labor for the remaining four years of her indenture and told her that was the price of her freedom. On August 8,

1829, John created a document stating that he "released her [Mariah] from her said Indenture and do hereby cancel said Indenture and release her from all and every claim which I have or ever had on her." With her indenture cleared, Mariah purchased her freedom from John for the price of $210.[41] At this time, farm laborers in Maryland, where Mariah had been born, earned $8.62 per month plus board.[42] Perhaps Mariah took in washing, did paid work for others, and sold any surplus from what she raised on her small tract of land to accumulate the amount needed to purchase her freedom.

By whatever means, Mariah accomplished her goal. At the age of thirty, Mariah Faschnacht was a free woman. She owned a home in Prairie du Chien and land on which to grow enough to support herself with a surplus to sell. Mariah had not obtained her freedom by escaping her enslaver, and she did not have the option to file a freedom suit—she had worked hard to earn the money that allowed her to purchase her freedom when the opportunity arose. But two other factors may have influenced John's decision: for thirteen years, Mariah had lived in a part of the United States where slavery was illegal, and Johnson had made her sign an indenture, as required by Illinois territorial law. But Prairie du Chien was now a part of Michigan Territory. In 1827, the Michigan territorial legislature had passed a law that set an age limit of twenty-one years for childhood indenture. As Mariah was older than twenty-one and governed by Michigan law, it was possible that the indenture John had had Mariah sign might no longer be considered legal if tested in the courts.[43]

Mariah continued to live with François and Helene Gagnier Galarneau and their children as her neighbors. François and Helene had demonstrated their regard for Mariah by selling her part of their land. And through them, she had formed attachments with Helene's older brothers and sisters.

CHAPTER 3

PATSEY, 1800–1880

The year before Mariah purchased her freedom in 1829, another indentured Black woman arrived at Prairie du Chien. Patsey, in her late twenties, was forced to accompany the wife and children of the settlement's newly appointed US Indian agent, Joseph Montfort Street. With Patsey were her two young sons, Charles and James; at least two other Black people indentured to the Streets; and Eliza Street and her ten children. Joseph Street had come to Prairie du Chien ahead of the rest of the household and had rented a house on land adjacent to the farm lot owned by Marianne Labuche. As soon as Patsey entered the community of Prairie du Chien, she became one of Marianne's neighbors.

By the time Patsey arrived in Prairie du Chien, she had already been working for the Streets for twenty years, since the age of seven or eight. Though little is known about the early years of her life, there is a record of her birth in Kentucky in 1800. Somehow, she came to be enslaved by General Thomas Posey. Thomas had been born on a farm in Virginia adjacent to Mount Vernon and knew George Washington. Thomas served as a general in the Continental Army and accepted land near Henderson, Kentucky, in reward for his military service. He was appointed lieutenant governor of Kentucky in 1805, and when he was appointed governor of Indiana Territory in 1813, he espoused the legalization of slavery in the territory.

Thomas was the father of several sons and a daughter, Eliza Maria. When Eliza came of marriageable age in 1807, Thomas "gave" Patsey to his eldest daughter to be trained as Eliza's maid. About this time, Eliza met the man who would become her husband, Joseph Montfort Street. Joseph had been born in Lunenburg County, Virginia, in 1782, the youngest of eight children. His father, Anthony, owned a plantation and enslaved a number of people who worked the land. By 1805, Anthony Street was in debt, which may have been the impetus for Joseph to leave the family home for Richmond. There he met John Wood, who convinced Joseph to join him on a tour "through the country west of the Mississippi and south of the Missouri." They journeyed as far as Frankfort, Kentucky, where in 1806 they began publication of the *Western World*. After publishing unfounded attacks on Aaron Burr, the newspaper lost its credibility, and Joseph, who had become its sole owner, sold the paper. In debt, Joseph left Frankfort for Henderson, Kentucky.[1]

From Henderson, Joseph wrote his father that he had decided to make Kentucky his "perpetual residence" and that he planned to purchase land to begin a plantation. In response, Anthony offered to "distribute" to Joseph "2 or 3 Negroes who would be willing to go out with you." Anthony was contemplating selling the people he kept enslaved on his property but stated, "I rather let you have Little & Big Negroes and settle with you that way. . . . I have mentioned it to several of my Negroes and they seem perfectly willing to go to Kentucky: and if they keep that mind They shall go."[2]

When Joseph Street married Eliza Maria Posey in October 1809, Eliza brought nine-year-old Patsey with her to work in the Street household, which by 1810 included eight enslaved individuals.[3] Joseph and Eliza's first son, Thomas Posey, was born while the home Joseph planned for his family was under construction. Joseph later recalled to his son that "with Patsey not quite as large as Ann Eliza [Joseph's granddaughter, who was eight years old] [, Patsey] kept house with your mother, myself and your Uncle Alexander, who lived for us a time. . . . We had one cow which your mother milked—Patsey had not learned to milk then—I nor your mother believed we could cook for ourselves. Your mother was but just from Mrs. Beck's School in Lexington and at her Father's had been waited on by several servants, and never been in the Kitchen but out of curiosity. This is the error of Slave countries." So, perhaps Patsey's duties, at the age of nine, included preparing the meals and teaching Eliza how to cook, in addition to "keeping house," which likely consisted of caring for young Thomas, tending the kitchen garden, and cleaning. She may also have been responsible for washing the family's clothing.[4]

Joseph Montfort Street (1782–1840) was appointed the US Indian agent for the Prairie du Chien Indian Agency in 1827. He and his wife, Eliza Posey Street, held Patsey and her children as indentured servants until Eliza's death in 1847. WHI IMAGE ID 26632

In July 1812, Patsey accompanied the Streets in a move from Kentucky to Illinois that allowed Joseph to avoid certain financial obligations. He acquired land forty miles west in the frontier community of Shawneetown, Illinois. There he had a log house constructed for his family and called the property Westwoodplace.[5]

At Shawneetown, Joseph continued to be active in politics. He was elected clerk of court for Gallatin County and became a brigadier general in the local militia, resulting in his being known afterward as "General" Joseph Street. Either while in Kentucky or after his move to Illinois, Joseph acquired London, an enslaved Black man. London had been born in Virginia and may have been one of the "2 or 3 Negroes" Anthony Street had said he would send to Joseph. According to the Street family, London was of mixed African American and American Indian descent.[6]

In 1818, Illinois achieved statehood, and its constitution stated: "Neither slavery nor involuntary servitude shall hereafter be introduced into this State, otherwise than for the punishment of crimes, whereof the party shall have been duly convicted."[7] The constitution went on to qualify the legal parameters of indentured servitude: "Nor shall any male person, arrived at the age of twenty-one years, nor female person, arrived at the age of eighteen years, be held to serve any person as a servant under any indenture hereafter made, unless such person shall enter into such indenture while in a state of perfect freedom, and on condition of a bona fide consideration received or to be received for their service."[8]

To conform to Illinois law while still keeping Patsey and London in servitude within his household, Joseph circumvented the law by declaring Patsey and London free and then having them sign an indenture.

As John W. Johnson had done with Mariah and Henry, Joseph executed indentures with Patsey and London so that he would be in compliance with Illinois law. In August 1818, Joseph drew up the two indentures. London, described by Joseph as a "free man of colour," placed his mark on one document, which stated:

> For divers good causes and consideration him thereunto moving and for in consideration of his board cloathing maintenance and good treatment . . . and, for in consideration of one dollar current money by the said Joseph M. Street to the said free man of colour London . . . hath put placed and bound himself unto the said Joseph M. Street his heirs executors administrators or assigns as an indentured servant for and during the term of sixty years . . . until the eighteenth day of August in the year of our Lord one thousand eight hundred and seventy eight.[9]

The indenture continued with details as to how London was to conduct himself and obey Joseph during the length of his indenture, which would almost certainly last his lifetime.[10]

Joseph also recorded an indenture with Patsey, whom he described as "a free negro Girl of colour about seventeen years of age." Like London, Patsey was made to "place and bind herself unto the said Joseph M. Street . . . for and during the term of fifty years." Joseph then ordered Patsey to place an X on the indenture. In so doing, Patsey bound herself to

> well and truly serve and all his commands obey and perform every where and chearfully [sic] and that she the said Patsey will not waste or embezzle or knowingly permit to be wasted or embezzled or uselessly destroyed any of the goods chattels & property of the said Street put or placed under her management or controul or care, . . . nor will she drink or dissipate or absent herself from the service of the said Street during the term of service set out in this indenture [and] like a good and diligent and faithfull servant shall and will always demean herself towards her said master Joseph M. Street his heirs and assigns after the manner of a bound or indentured

Document written by Joseph Montfort Street in which Patsey, described as "a free negro
Girl of colour about seventeen years of age," was indentured to Street for a term of fifty
years. Dated August 18, 1818. YALE UNIVERSITY LIBRARY MANUSCRIPTS AND ARCHIVES, STREET
FAMILY PAPERS, BOX 3, FOLDER 48

servant. . . . As the object of the said Patsey is to sell to said Street her personal services.[11]

For each "breach or failure," Joseph could add one year to her service.[12]

Though Joseph described Patsey and London as free on the indentures, no freedom papers were ever filed for the two. The indentures were in compliance with Illinois law. In Gallatin County, where Joseph lived, other enslavers also employed the use of indentures to maintain the people they enslaved while still abiding by the law.

As the clerk of court for Gallatin County, Joseph witnessed the signing of many other documents of indenture involving "free coloured" people and would continue to do so until 1825. Each indenture witnessed by Joseph was signed by Black men and women described as "free of colour" or "free Negro," and was also signed by the people who would receive the benefits of their indentured servitude. As clerk, Joseph also witnessed the manumission of several Black enslaved individuals by residents of Gallatin County. No records indicate that Joseph ever considered freeing London or Patsey.[13]

This practice, of enslavers forcing the Black people they enslaved to sign indentures that documented them as free, was not restricted to Gallatin County where Joseph was clerk of court. Indentures involving Black people designated as free were signed in Edwards, Madison, Pope, Randolph, and St. Clair Counties in Illinois.[14]

On the same day that Patsey and London signed their indentures, Dick, who was described as "a free man of color about twenty years of age," signed an indenture with John Forrester. By signing the document, Dick became bound to John for sixty years. Joseph witnessed the signing of Dick's indenture just as John had witnessed the signing of Patsey's and London's indentures.[15]

In 1819, less than a year after Patsey signed her indenture, she gave birth to a daughter whom she named Betsey. In July 1821, she had another daughter, Judy. And then, in November of 1822, she gave birth to a son, Charles. Judy lived less than two years, dying in May 1823. Joseph Street recorded all of these births and Judy's death in the family Bible. For Charles, Joseph listed the father's name: "Charles a boy born of Patsey and Dick on the _____ of November 1822."[16] Charles would be known as

Charles Forrester. Dick, who was indentured to John Forrester, may have been the father of all three of Patsey's children born between 1819 and 1822.

According to Section VI of the Illinois Constitution, children of indentured servants were also indentured. They were to become free, "the males at the age of twenty-one years, the females at the age of eighteen years."[17] Therefore, Patsey and her children were all under Joseph's control.

John rented Dick out to work in lead mines in Missouri, an action that went against Illinois law, which stated that indentured servants could not be taken out of the state. In early 1820, Dick escaped, and John placed an ad in the Shawneetown newspaper.

> **$100 REWARD**
>
> Runaway from the U.S. Saline, Illinois on the 14th inst. A Negro man named Dick, 5 feet 8 or 9 inches high, stoutly made, twenty-two or twenty-three years old, and very black and ugly. He has a small scar on his forehead, cut with a knife, and one on his left breast. His feet singularly shaped, being very narrow at the heel and broad at the toes—his eyes generally red. From some circumstances I am disposed to think he will go down the river, but whether he will endeavor to get into Texas, or stop in any of the states or territories bordering the Mississippi is doubtful. Any person taking up said Negro within this state shall receive a reward of $50.00, and if taken any where out of the state, and notice given me thereof so that I obtain possession of him again, a reward of $100.00, and all reasonable charges for bringing him to me.
>
> JOHN FORRESTER
> Shawneetown, Ill. — February 20, 1820[18]

What became of Dick is not known, but as he was likely the father of Charles, who was born in 1822, Dick must have been returned to John in Shawneetown before that date. Patsey and her two living children, Betsey and Charles, continued to live in the Street household, all indentured and thus bound to Joseph.[19]

By the spring of 1827, Joseph Street wished to move from Gallatin County. According to his letters written to friends, he wanted to live among people in the northern counties where he would be in "the midst of people who love and respect me, [and] all my neighbors will be warm and unchanging friends." There, he believed, he and his wife could one day "live happily in our retirement."[20]

Street had met Ninian Edwards, the governor of Illinois, and in 1827, he began a correspondence with Edwards expressing his wish to receive a government appointment as Indian agent, preferably the position located in Prairie du Chien, which he knew was vacant. Street had purchased a small farm in Sangamon, Illinois, but he still needed employment and the ability to pay for the property he had purchased. Street therefore requested that Edwards write to Henry Clay and John Taliaferro of King George, Virginia, to recommend Street for the position. Street knew both men and believed they could promote his interest to Secretary of War James Barbour.[21]

Taliaferro responded to Street's letter "with warm protestations of friendship and a desire to serve." Edwards told Street that he had seen Clay, who had "parted with [Barbour] under the belief that you would be appointed."[22]

Nicolas Boilvin had been the Indian agent at Prairie du Chien in early 1827. Boilvin had raised his son, also named Nicolas, to assist him in his responsibilities as Indian agent, and the son had often sat with his father in council with tribal leaders. In the summer of 1827, the elder Boilvin died unexpectedly while traveling down the Mississippi River to St. Louis. His son may have assumed he would be appointed to take his father's place as Indian agent, but this was not to be. Instead, Edwards and Clay had importuned Barbour to appoint Street for the position. Street received notice of his appointment and left in mid-September of 1827, making his way to the prairie slowly because of an injury from a fall and arriving on the first of November.[23]

Street arrived at the prairie just as residents were beginning to settle after the Ho-Chunk attacks. Red Bird and his companions had surrendered to Major William Whistler and were now imprisoned at Fort Crawford. Discussions within the War Department had begun in earnest as to when a treaty conference would be held to restrict the movements of the Ho-Chunk and remove them from their traditional lands. Street was now at the center of events, and his presence was needed at Prairie du Chien. In his role as Indian agent, he was expected to treat with nations in the vicinity of Fort Crawford, which included convening councils, conducting treaty negotiations, listening to and attempting to solve grievances presented by the Indian nations, and communicating official policy to them. Governor William Clark, who was superintendent of Indian affairs, made it known to Street that Clark expected him to relocate to Prairie du Chien. Street had planned to make his home in Sangamon and travel to Prairie du Chien as needed. But Street realized that if he did not make his home at the prairie, Clark would "endeavor to have me removed." Street told Edwards, "I shall certainly move, for I cannot do without it." He then speculated, "If commissioners are appointed to treat with the Indian for these lands or other purposes, and I could be one of them, the addition[al] sum would enable me to move without any great sacrifice. And I believe I could write a much better treaty than 2/3ds of those I see."[24]

Street soon had temporary quarters made for him in the council house located on the Indian agency property. Major John Fowle sent workmen from Fort Crawford to build a partition across the council chamber to create a private space in which Street lived. With this done, Street found the accommodations "very respectful and friendly." Either London or Charles may have accompanied Street to Prairie du Chien in 1827. If so, one of them may have slept in the council chamber. Patsey, who had just given birth to her second son, James, on June 6, 1827, remained with Eliza Street and the children in Shawneetown. Realizing the need to live permanently at Prairie du Chien, Joseph Street now needed to find suitable accommodations for his household of "12 white persons" and five "free coloured" people.[25]

Patsey had been with Eliza Street for almost twenty years, caring for her and the many children she had borne since her marriage in 1809 while also caring for her own children. But Joseph had never been able to manage his finances. Sometime after Joseph left Shawneetown for Prairie du Chien, the sheriff of Gallatin County seized his property to sell at auction to pay Joseph's debts. The seizure included Patsey. She was sold at a sheriff's sale and was purchased by Dr. Alexander Posey, Eliza Street's brother. Eliza wanted Patsey's assistance, for she had just given birth to Eliza and Joseph's tenth child. In May of 1828, Alexander took Patsey to Shawneetown's county clerk of court. There, Patsey was told to place an X on another indenture. The indenture read:

> I do hereby covenant and agree with said Posey to remain with Mrs.
> Street as her servant, during the full period for which the aforesaid

Patsey's second indenture, dated May 24, 1828, was signed by Patsey at the behest of
Alexander Posey. By placing her mark on this indenture, Patsey bound herself to Eliza
Posey Street and agreed to travel with Mrs. Street to Prairie du Chien. COURTESY OF
CRAWFORD COUNTY REGISTER OF DEEDS

indentures were taken, and furthermore I do hereby voluntarily and
of my own accord agree to go with the said Mrs. Street to Prairie du
Chien or where else she may reside, and to serve her in the capacity
of a servant as above stated; and I do hereby again aver that my going
with Mrs. Street as aforesaid is of my own free will and accord, and
not through the compulsion of exertion of said Posey or any other
person.[26]

When Eliza, Patsey, and the rest of the Street household arrived at Prairie du Chien, the indenture was recorded with the register of deeds at Prairie du Chien.

While the indenture Patsey signed technically conformed to Illinois law because Joseph had stated that Patsey was free, the sale and the purchase of Patsey were illegal not only by the terms of the Northwest Ordinance but by the laws of the State of Illinois, as selling and purchasing a human being constitutes slavery. The Street family was flouting federal, state, and territorial laws, and they would continue to do so for more than twenty-five years.

Though the Indian agency council house stood south of Fort Crawford on Main Village Lot No. 13, the home in which the previous agents had lived did not belong to the United States. Boilvin and his family had lived on his personal property, which was the western portion of Main Village Lot No. 13, while he was the Indian agent at Prairie du Chien, and the Boilvin family did not offer the house to Street. He was therefore in need of a home, but he was unable to locate a house close to the Indian agency council house or in the Main Village. Street needed a home with many rooms for his large family and servants. After learning of Street's needs, Joseph Rolette offered to rent him property beside the creek that flowed through Rolette's Coulee. A vacant house, built several years earlier, lay along the creek bank. The location was not ideal, for the coulee was about three miles north of the Main Village. The US Indian agent was expected to live adjacent to the military post, for he could be needed any time of the day to resolve an issue. Only the Indian agent, not the military, could treat with the Indians. But, with no other option, Street rented the house from Rolette for two hundred dollars a year.[27]

Once Joseph Street had secured a home, Eliza, Patsey, and the household's many children traveled up the Mississippi to Prairie du Chien. As the indenture had stated, Patsey stayed with Eliza to serve her, and Patsey's sons Charles and James moved with her. What became of Patsey's daughter Betsey is not known. She may have died, or, since she was now eight years old, she may have been illegally sold to another person—even at the same sheriff's sale where Patsey had been sold to Alexander. The house that Joseph had rented stood on land adjacent to the farm lot owned by Marianne Labuche. Patsey was now a neighbor of Marianne. As Patsey worked in the

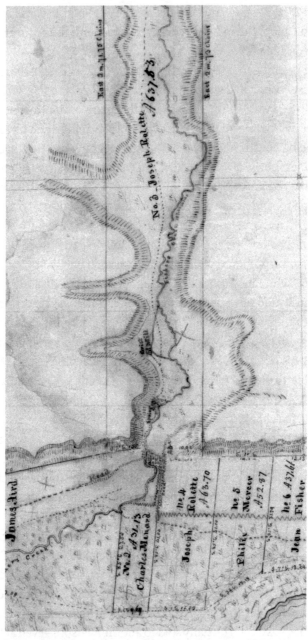

Farm Lot No. 3 from *Plat of the Private Land Claims at Prairie du Chien, 1828* by Lucius Lyon, surveyor. Patsey and the Street family lived on the extensive Lot No. 3, located to the east of the platted plots, when they arrived at Prairie du Chien in 1828. WHI IMAGE ID 113245 (DETAIL)

kitchen garden, or perhaps as she nursed the Street children, she would have seen Marianne gathering plants along the stream and witnessed Marianne's freedom to move about the community. Marianne may have been called upon to prescribe remedies for Eliza, whose continual child-bearing had led to ill health.

From the time of his arrival at Prairie du Chien as Indian agent, Joseph Street had been visited by Ho-Chunk who were, as he recorded, "greatly discontented with our people and dissatisfied with the conduct of our Government in relation to the lead mines." Street characterized the miners as "low, gross, and like blackguards."[28] On two separate occasions, Street asked Major Fowle to send troops from Fort Crawford to evict lead miner Henry Dodge from Ho-Chunk lands, where he was mining illegally. Fowle refused, and when Street complained to Governor Clark, a new survey was conducted that deemed that Dodge was not on Ho-Chunk lands. One year after his appointment as Indian agent, Street, along with Major Stephen Watts Kearney, confiscated timber that had been illegally cut on Ho-Chunk land by Jean Brunet and others. Brunet sued Street and Kearney and won. With no support from the US military or the Indian Department, Street resigned himself to his task, writing, "[Ho-Chunk] removal is certain beyond all human control as the ultimate fact of their removal west, the time is under the influence of measures in the power of the [War] Department." He therefore did what he thought was best to help the tribe and lessen the influence of the fur traders as the Ho-Chunk lost their land to the United States in treaties signed in 1829 and 1830 at Prairie du Chien.[29]

Beginning in 1829, Street wished to employ a blacksmith at the Indian agency for the benefit of the Ho-Chunk. As he began looking for a man to fill the position, Street was told that Marianne Labuche's son François Duchouquette had learned the trade while working for the American Fur Company. Duchouquette was hired as the agency blacksmith at a salary of two hundred dollars a year. He used his skills to mend muskets and repair and forge iron tools for the Ho-Chunk.

In 1819, the US Congress had passed the Civilization Fund Act "providing against the further decline and final extinction of the Indian tribes, adjoining the frontier settlements of the United States, and for introducing among them the habits and arts of civilization." Part of the funding was intended to "instruct [the American Indians] in the mode of agriculture suited to their situation."[30] Native people had raised crops on the land long before Europeans came to North America, but Congress wanted the tribes taught crop cultivation as practiced by the white citizens of the country. To this end, blacksmiths made and repaired axes, hoes, and plows for them. A few of the blacksmiths, like Duchouquette, also repaired locks and firing mechanisms on the guns that the Ho-Chunk and other Native people received as presents from the US government or in trade for furs.[31]

Around the same time Duchouquette was hired at the smithy, a man who would play an important role in Patsey's life came to Prairie du Chien to work as a laborer at the Indian agency. James Triplett was Black, and he may have been free. Several white families with the last name Triplett owned plantations along the tidewaters of North Carolina and Virginia. Records show that a James Triplett was emancipated by Moses Green in Culpeper County, Virginia, in 1801. The Triplett and Green families were related by marriage. This James Triplett, who may have been the same man who later came to Prairie du Chien, was described as a "negro man slave."[32]

At some point before Patsey moved with the Street family to Prairie du Chien, Triplett had come in contact with her. James and Patsey had a son, James, who had been born in June 1827.[33] Whether James had remained in Illinois or moved to the prairie with Patsey and Mrs. Street is not known. But James was at Prairie du Chien by October 1829, and Joseph Street employed him as a laborer at the Prairie du Chien agency from 1829 into 1831, for which James was paid an annual salary of $266.

By 1831, James and Patsey had another son, London, and James began working at the agency smithy. He may have developed an interest in learning the trade from watching Duchouquette and Oliver Cherrier, who later replaced Duchouquette as the agency smith, working at the forge. Beginning in October 1831, Triplett became the striker working with Samuel Gilbert, the new agency blacksmith. Triplett's annual salary of $196 was less than he had earned as an unskilled laborer, but his new position was an improvement because he was learning a trade. He held this position for at least two years.[34] On August 29, 1833, another son, Henry Harrison, was born to Patsey and James.[35]

Between 1828 and 1830, the Street family had also been growing. Joseph and Eliza had another son, John. They also adopted Elizabeth Cross, the child of friends who had died. All were enumerated in the federal census of 1830. Under the classification "Free Coloured" were five individuals: a woman between the ages of twenty-four and thirty-five, which was Patsey; a man between the ages of twenty-three and thirty-six; and three young men—one between the ages of ten and sixteen and two under age ten.[36] The young man listed as over age ten was probably Patsey's son Charles Forrester, though he was only eight. Charles would go on to serve Street for many years. One of the boys under ten was Patsey's son James. The other boy was Patsey's third son, London Triplett. The older man could have been either the elder London, who had signed an indenture alongside Patsey in 1818, or James Triplett, the father of young James and London. After this date, no records can be found mentioning the adult London. It is not known what happened to him, but he must have left a lasting impression on Patsey, for she named her third son London.[37]

The distance from the Street home to Fort Crawford soon became too great. The Winnebago War had caused the United States to believe that it still needed a military post at Prairie du Chien, especially with its planned treaties to commandeer Ho-Chunk lands. But the Fort Crawford barracks had deteriorated beyond repair.[38] At the end of 1829, troops began to be relocated to new barracks constructed on high ground on the mainland. The agency house Street had used to meet with representatives of American Indian nations was adjacent to the old post. The 1786 Ordinance for the Regulation of Indian Affairs stipulated that "all councils, treaties, communications and official transactions" between the agent and the Indian Nations were "to be held, transacted and done at the Outpost occupied by the troops of the United States." Street and the Prairie du Chien agency buildings needed to be closer to the new Fort Crawford.

On June 1, 1832, Joseph Street signed a deed of lease with John Dowling of Galena, Illinois. Dowling had built a house in the Village of St. Friole at Prairie du Chien, and Street agreed to rent the property for four hundred dollars a year for a term of five years. Dowling and Street also agreed "that inasmuch as the said buildings have not been completed by the said Dowling agreeably to his original stipulation and the said Street being about to move into them in their present and unfinished state that the said Street shall have the buildings completed at the proper cost and charges of the said Dowling."[39] The rooms in the house still needed to be plastered,

The southern portion of the Village of St. Friole in 1873. The photograph was taken to record damage from a fire. Beyond the damaged buildings are the homes that once fronted the thoroughfare. To the east (on the left, facing the road) is the house once owned by Alexis Bailly where Courtney lived. The arrow points to the buildings of the US Indian Agency where Patsey and her family lived and worked. COURTESY OF MARY ELISE ANTOINE

after which tin troughs and downspouts would be attached to the eaves of the house and venetian shutters, painted green, would be placed at all the windows. The Street family, along with London or James Triplett, Patsey, and her children, moved to the property. The location of the house was ideal—at the south end of a village, located above the river so as not to be flooded, and having a fine view of the waters of the Mississippi River.[40] Besides the house, there were several outbuildings on the property. No records have been found mentioning the size of the house, but Joseph's later correspondence indicates that Patsey and her sons were relegated to the kitchen, located in one of the outbuildings, where they slept on pallets next to the fireplace.[41]

Patsey and her family now lived and worked in a house much closer to the free Black people who lived at Prairie du Chien as well as to the Black enslaved servants who came and went as their officers were transferred to and from the new Fort Crawford. During the time that Patsey lived in this house, an enslaved Black woman named Courtney and her two sons came to Prairie du Chien with Alexis Bailly. Alexis's house stood two lots to the north of the agency house, and Courtney's son Joseph and Patsey's son Charles were about the same age.

Before her arrival at Prairie du Chien, Courtney and her sons had lived in the Bailly household at Mendota on the Minnesota River, isolated from any companionship. Courtney likely would have welcomed a neighbor who shared the same living conditions, as would have Patsey. Patsey's young sons, who had only the Street boys as possible playmates, now had Joseph, Courtney's eldest, with whom to play, share, and grow.

In 1831, a twelfth child was born to Eliza Street. Her children later recalled that while at Prairie du Chien, Eliza "was a frail little woman never weighing more than ninety pounds." The move to the new house did not improve her health. She was extremely fond of her children and overwhelmed by their number as well as by her constant pregnant state, so she rarely punished them, even though "they were a turbulent lot," according to son Joseph. In his position as agent, Street traveled often, and so the responsibilities for care of the Street children must have fallen to Patsey. She may even have been a wet nurse for the younger Street children, given that Eliza was frail from continual child-bearing and Patsey's sons would have been nursing when Eliza's youngest children were born.[42] In her enslavement, Patsey likely struggled to provide the attention to her own children that she desired, as Harriet Jacobs did while caring for a white child who was not her own. Years later, in her 1861 autobiographical narrative, Jacobs recalled: "I longed to be entirely free to act a mother's part towards my children."[43]

A remembrance of Joseph Trotter Mills, who visited the Street home in 1834, gives an indication of the constant chaos in the household. Mills was a student at Illinois College in Jacksonville—a fellow student of Joseph Hamilton Davies Street, Joseph and Eliza's son. When Street sent a message to his son, wondering whether someone would like to come to Prairie du Chien to teach the younger Street children, Mills agreed to take on the responsibilities. Mills traveled on the steamboat *Warrior* to the prairie, where he was "cast suddenly among men who wore epaulettes upon their shoulders and silken sashes and sword belts around their waists." He found himself boarding in a house "which had several rooms in it, some of which were occupied by the Indian agents and General Street and his family." He was a bit disconcerted to find "the floors and passages occupied and covered by natives, large and small, dogs and children."[44] But when he opened a narrow door, he found comfort in the family rooms. Still, these spaces would have been crowded. Thomas P. Burnett, who had been appointed the subagent to the Prairie du Chien agency, also lived in the agency house. In addition to serving the Street family, Patsey may have been attendant upon Burnett as well.

A grandson and a granddaughter of Joseph Street recalled years later that the Street children called Patsey "Aunt Patsey."[45] While many Black children were taught by their parents to address other Black adults as *aunt* or *uncle* to show respect, white people in the early nineteenth century began to attach *aunt* and *uncle* to the names of the adults they enslaved, usually those who worked in the house. White people used these kin terms to make themselves feel that they had established a special relationship with the Black person they called *aunt* and *uncle*. But a difference in status still existed between the enslaved adults and their enslavers. No matter the name, the Black men and women were still enslaved. And the enslaved adults could never address their enslavers with similar terms of kinship.[46]

Patsey was surely quite busy in the Street household throughout the 1830s as the children grew older, adding to the commotion caused by the duties of an Indian agent. The five eldest Street children left Prairie du Chien to attend Cumberland College in Princeton, Kentucky, and schools in Jacksonville, Illinois, returning to the prairie in the summer months. When daughters Mary and Lucy were present in the new Street home, the house was filled with young officers vying for their attention. Sarah Knox Taylor and Mary Street were "devoted friends," and around 1832, each had caught the attention of a particular officer. If Lieutenant Jefferson Davis called at the Streets' house to visit the family, Sarah would be found spending the evening with Mary. And when Lieutenant George Wilson called at the Taylor residence, Mary always happened to be there visiting Sarah.[47]

Neither Sarah's father, the future president Colonel Zachary Taylor, nor Mary's father, Joseph Street, wanted his daughter to marry an army officer. Zachary's efforts to dissuade his daughter proved to be in vain, as Sarah married Jefferson Davis in 1835. (Sarah died three months later of malaria; Jefferson recovered from the disease and went on to become president of the Confederate States of America in 1861.) Joseph escorted Mary back to school in Jacksonville, hoping the absence would break the relationship developing between her and Lieutenant Wilson. But a lack of finances did not allow Joseph to continue sending his children to Illinois College and

Jacksonville Female Academy. Joseph wrote to his son Thomas in November of 1833, "[I must] give my children what education I can there [in Prairie du Chien], and not attempt to send off another to school."[48]

Along with his children's education, Joseph was concerned about the lack of religious instruction to be found in Prairie du Chien. While living in Kentucky and Illinois, Joseph had been a member of the Cumberland Presbyterian Church. With no Protestant minister present at the prairie, Joseph started a prayer meeting. He held the service each Sunday in his house. In addition to reading from the Bible and singing hymns, Joseph always read a sermon. Employees of the Indian agency and officers of Fort Crawford attended his prayer meetings.[49]

As Joseph Street endeavored to provide an education and religious instruction to his children, perhaps Patsey's sons derived something from Mills's tutoring and Street's Sunday sermons. Patsey could not read or write, but later census records indicate that her sons London, Henry, Lewis, and Isaac Newton could all read and write.[50]

The lives of Patsey, her children, and the rest of the Street household changed in 1834 as the eastern portion of Michigan Territory prepared to become a state and the region west of Lake Michigan prepared to become a new territory called Wisconsin. The US government had forced the Oneida out of New York in 1822 and onto lands that had once been the home of the Ho-Chunk and Menominee. This removal, along with treaties with the American Indian nations living along the upper Mississippi, had greatly reduced the area in which the Native nations could live. The US government, therefore, believed it no longer needed the current number of Indian agencies.

At the close of the 1833–1834 session, Congress passed a bill reorganizing the Indian agencies in what would be Wisconsin Territory. A directive of the bill called for the annexation of the Sac and Fox (Meskwaki) Nation and its land to the Prairie du Chien agency. Street would now be responsible for the Ho-Chunk and the Sac and Fox Nations. Street was ordered to move to Rock Island, about 150 miles down the Mississippi from Prairie du Chien, in order to be closer to the Sac and Fox. Street vigorously opposed the move, as he did not want to leave his family. Also, the Winnebago School and pattern farm on the Yellow River had just opened through Street's efforts. If he left the prairie, he would be abandoning the school

and the Ho-Chunk. Street asked Colonel Taylor to write the superintendent of the Indian Department to request that Street remain at the prairie.
Instead, Lewis Cass moved Street to the agency on Rock Island and made
Prairie du Chien a subagency. Thomas Boyd was selected to oversee the
subagency at Prairie du Chien. When Thomas visited Prairie du Chien, he
roomed in the Street house in which Eliza Street and her family remained
and likely was waited on by Patsey.

Though the Prairie du Chien Indian agency had lessened in importance
to the US military, officers and volunteers at Fort Winnebago, just north
of Portage, had much work to do to prepare for the relocation of the
Ho-Chunk. There was need for more workers at the portage. To meet this
need, Joseph had James Triplett transferred to the Fort Winnebago subagency in October 1832, fracturing and separating Patsey's family.[51]

Once the waters opened in the spring of 1834, Joseph moved his possessions to Rock Island. Charles Forrester, Patsey's eldest son, also left
Prairie du Chien, continuing to serve Joseph. The building selected for the
agency house at Rock Island provided no comforts, so Eliza, Patsey, and
the children remained at Prairie du Chien. Any time Joseph was absent,
Eliza's health, mental and physical, declined. Though Lucy was still living
at home, most of the care for Eliza became Patsey's responsibility. During
the summer of 1835, Eliza was so ill that Joseph took her to Henderson,
Kentucky, so her brother, Dr. Alexander Posey, could care for her. Patsey
and her younger boys almost certainly accompanied Eliza on the trip, for
Ida Street, a granddaughter, stated years later that Patsey was Eliza's "body
servant."[52] For the next couple of years, Joseph spent the spring and summer months at Rock Island, returning to Prairie du Chien in the fall.

During this time of upheaval within the family, while Joseph's daughters resided permanently at Prairie du Chien, the young officers stationed
at Fort Crawford had continued to court Mary and Lucy Street. There were
few young white Protestant women living in the community, and therefore
the Street women received much attention from the unmarried officers.
In time, Joseph gave his permission for Mary and then for Lucy to each
marry one of the eligible officers.

Mary Street was united in marriage to Lieutenant George Wilson on
April 15, 1835. They were married by Reverend David Lowry of the Cumberland Presbyterian Church. On the recommendation of Joseph Street,

Reverend Lowry had been appointed the head of the Winnebago School being constructed along the Yellow River within the Neutral Grounds across the Mississippi River from Prairie du Chien. The United States planned to relocate the Ho-Chunk to land west of the Mississippi. As part of the treaty signed on September 15, 1832, in which the Ho-Chunk surrendered their traditional lands, the United States agreed to "erect a suitable building, or buildings, with a garden and field attached, . . . and establish and maintain, therein, for the term of twenty-seven years, a school for the education . . . of such [Ho-Chunk] children as may be voluntarily sent to it." For as long he was at the Prairie du Chien agency, Joseph advocated for the school and encouraged the Ho-Chunk leaders to arrange to send their children to the school to be taught reading, writing, arithmetic, gardening, agriculture, carding, spinning, weaving, and sewing."[53]

Joseph's new son-in-law, George Wilson, had been born in Steubenville, Ohio. He had graduated from the US Military Academy at West Point, New York, in July 1830 and had been immediately posted to frontier duty. Like other young officers stationed at Fort Crawford and other military posts, George claimed allowance on his pay vouchers for a domestic servant. Between April 1831 and December 1837, he claimed pay for ten different men and one woman, whom he listed as servants. The woman and eight of the men were Black. Before his marriage to Mary Street, George had claimed Etheldred, whom he described as a "Negro," on his pay account for July and August of 1834. According to Street family accounts, George, while posted for a few months at Fort Armstrong, met Dr. John Emerson, who had arrived at Fort Armstrong in December 1833. With Dr. Emerson was Etheldred, also known as Dred, whom Emerson had purchased from the estate of Peter Blow. This Etheldred, whom George claimed as his servant for two months, was most likely Dred Scott, whom Dr. Emerson would claim as a "Slave" and take to Fort Snelling in 1836.[54] In 1846, Dred Scott and his wife, Harriet, would file separate suits for freedom, claiming their freedom based upon the years they had resided in Illinois and Minnesota. The final result, which was not reached until 1858, was a decision by the US Supreme Court to deny their freedom and uphold the institution of slavery.

By the time of their marriage, both Lieutenant George Wilson and Mary Street were accustomed to being waited on by enslaved Black men

Dr. The United States, to *Lieut. Geo. Wilson* United Sta

ON WHAT ACCOUNT.	COMMENCEMENT & EXPIRATION.		TERM OF SERVICE CHARGED.		PAY PER MONTH.		AMOUNT.	
	FROM.	TO.	Months.	Days.	Dollars.	Cents.	DOLLARS.	CENTS.
Pay, for myself	1st July 1834	31st Aug. 1834	2	—	25	—	50	—
Ditto for private Servant not soldier	1st July 1834	31st Aug. 1834	2	—	6	—	12	—
Forage for Horse	18	18						
Clothing for private Servant not soldier	1st July 1834	31st Aug. 1834	2	—	2	50	5	—
Extra Services { 1st July 1834	5 Aug. 1834	1	18	10	—	15	80	Commanded 5 Aug. 1834
{ 18th Aug. 1834	31st Aug. 1834							from 18th

	No. of days.	No. of rations per day	Total No. of rations	Post or place, where due.	Price of rations. CENTS.	
Subsistence for myself	1st July 1834 31st Aug. 1834	62	4	248	Fort Crawford	20	49	60
Ditto for private Servant not soldier	1st July 1834 31st Aug. 1834	62	1	62		20	12	40
						144	80

I hereby Certify, Upon the word and honor of a Gentleman, that the foregoing account is accurate and just; that I have not received pay, nor drawn rations, forage or clothing, in kind, or received money in lieu of any part thereof, for any part service, the horse and private servant, for the whole of the time charged, and that I did not, during the time so charged, or any part thereof, keep or employ, as waiter or servant, soldier from the line of the army; that the annexed is an charged for my staff appointment, I actually and legally held the appointment; that I was the actual and only commanding officer at the double ration post charged for and that no officer, within my knowledge, has a right to claim, or does claim, for the period for which I have charged Brevet pay, I exercised my Brevet rank agreeable to law and regulations; that I am not in arrears with the United States, on any account whatsoever, that I was actually in command of a company for the whole time of any staff duties for which I claim, or have received extra compensation; and that the last payment I received was from PAYMASTER *Thomas Wright* and to the *thirtieth* day of *Aug. 1834* the sum of

I at the same time acknowledge that I have Received or *Thomas Wright* Paymaster U. S. Army, this *thirty first* day of *Aug.* 1834

forty four — 100 Dollars, being the amount, and in full, of said account.

(SIGNED DUPLICATES.)

DESCRIPTION OF SERVANT.					
NAME.	Complexion.	HEIGHT. Ft. Inches.	Eyes.	Hair.	
Etheldred	Negro				

Pay.......... 78.80
Subsistence, 61.00
Forage,.......
Clothing.... 5.00
AMOUNT.... $144.80

Pay voucher filed by Lieutenant George Wilson on August 31, 1834. Wilson had rented Etheldred from Dr. John Emerson from July 1 to August 31 of that year. Etheldred would come to be known as Dred Scott. NATIONAL ARCHIVES AND RECORDS ADMINISTRATION

and women. As a wedding gift, Joseph Street presented them with Henry, Patsey's son, who was less than two years old at the time. As an indentured servant, Patsey had no say in the "gifting" of Henry, who, as Patsey's child, was also indentured to Joseph, but she made a request, which Joseph honored. With the gift, Joseph insisted that Henry was to be taught a trade before he obtained his freedom at the age of twenty-one according to the law.[55]

The Wilsons lived in the officers' quarters while he was posted at Fort Crawford. In the two years after his marriage, George claimed another "Negro" servant on his pay reports. This servant was a woman named America, described as five feet tall. Her age was not listed. America was probably retained to help young Mary during a pregnancy, for within a year of their marriage, a daughter named Eliza Frances was born at Fort Crawford. Two years later, the couple had a second daughter, Lucy Montford. America would work for the Wilson family until December 1837.[56]

On March 10, 1834, Joseph M. Street purchased America. Street rented America to his son-in-law Lieutenant George Wilson, who claimed her on his pay vouchers from June 1834 through December 1837. YALE UNIVERSITY LIBRARY MANUSCRIPTS AND ARCHIVES, STREET FAMILY PAPERS, BOX 3, FOLDER 50

The woman named America listed on George's pay voucher may have been the same woman whom Joseph had purchased from John B. Cabanne of St. Louis a few years earlier. This purchase indicates that Joseph, like other representatives of the United States, had little regard for the government's prohibition of slavery. On March 10, 1834, Joseph paid Cabanne $265 for "a Negro girl slave named America." The bill of sale was witnessed by Joseph's brother-in-law, John Posey.[57]

Being a member of the Street family may have advanced George's position at Fort Crawford. When Lieutenant Thomas Stockton resigned his position as assistant quartermaster at the end of 1835, George received the appointment to replace Stockton. Perhaps at Joseph's behest, George also began to learn the Sac language because Joseph's position within the Indian Department had changed.[58]

At the time of her sister Mary's marriage in April 1835, Lucy Street was being courted by two young officers: Lieutenant John Beach and Captain Ethan Allen Hitchcock. Joseph Street worked regularly with Hitchcock, who was the disbursing Indian agent at the fort, responsible for the distribution of gifts and annuities to the Indian nations of the upper Mississippi. Beach commanded a company. In time, Lucy chose to marry Beach.

Eliza's granddaughter Ida recounted Patsey's thoughts on this courtship and Lucy's subsequent marriage to John Beach. Patsey did not approve of the marriage. In a stereotypical dialect that white people of the era commonly used when attempting to imitate Black speech, Ida recorded Patsey as saying, "Chile, your poah Aunt Lucy never should have married Major Beach, he wrecked her life; she ought to a married Major Hitchcock." When Ida questioned her father about it, he agreed with Patsey. He explained to Ida that "when his sister Lucy came back from school at Jacksonville, both men courted her for nearly two years." But John was younger and talkative and suave, whereas Ethan Allen Hitchcock was older, quiet, and serious.[59]

Joseph's reassignment to Rock Island brought an end to any tranquility that may have existed in the Street household. The new duties that forced Joseph to be absent from Prairie du Chien were likely one cause of Eliza's fragility, but other factors contributed to her ill health. In March 1836, Eliza gave birth to their fourth daughter, Sarah Eleanor. And then, about the time of Lucy's marriage in 1837, another son was born to Joseph and Eliza. They named him David.

At the same time that Patsey took on the increased workload of caring for the two infants, she was pregnant. In the same year that Sarah Eleanor was born, Patsey gave birth to another son and named him Lewis. Then, in the same year that David was born, Patsey and James had a fifth son, whom they named Isaac Newton. So, by 1837, Patsey had four infants to nurse and care for, along with the older Street and Triplett children, in addition to her household duties.

Other changes occurred in the Triplett family in addition to the births of Lewis and Isaac. On the last day of 1837, George Wilson resigned from the army. George and Mary, with their two daughters, continued to live at Prairie du Chien for a while, but soon they left the prairie for Cassville. As Henry Triplett was enslaved by Mary Wilson, she told Patsey to pack his belongings and prepare him to travel with the Wilson family. At about four years of age, Henry was forced to leave his parents and brothers. For the time being, James, Patsey, and their sons London, Lewis, and Isaac remained at Prairie du Chien.

With his resignation from the army, George Wilson sold America to Lieutenant William R. Jouett, who was stationed at Fort Crawford. William took America with him to his future postings. On his pay vouchers, Jouett listed America as a "Slave."[60]

The army had abandoned Fort Armstrong once the government had decided to move the Sac to the Des Moines River. The commanding officer's house at the post was cleared out, cleaned, and offered to Joseph. With a comfortable, though temporary, place to reside, Eliza joined her husband during the summer and fall of 1836.

The status of Patsey's children was dictated by the whims and movement of Joseph and Eliza. Charles, now in his teens, lived off and on at Rock Island serving and attending to Joseph. James, London, about six, and Lewis and Isaac, still infants, stayed with Patsey.

The decision to close the agency at Rock Island forced Joseph, if he wished to retain his position as Indian agent, to reside at the agency along the Des Moines River created for the Sac and Fox (Meskwaki) Nation. According to the 1837 treaty, the US government would force the Sauk and Meskwaki to move to a 140-square-mile reservation along the east bank of the Des Moines River. The treaty also stipulated that a saw mill and a grist mill were to be constructed and two millers employed, in hopes that the Sauk and Meskwaki would settle on the reservation and learn to farm and operate the mills. Joseph was to be the agent at the new location and oversee the enterprise.

Lambert Lapierre had been hired as the blacksmith for the Sac and Fox agency. Lapierre needed a striker to assist him, for it was expected that there would be much work for the blacksmith at the new agency. Therefore, in 1836, Joseph transferred James Triplett from Fort Winnebago to the agency on the Des Moines River. He was once again the striker to the blacksmith, but he now earned slightly less than he had at Prairie du Chien: $240 a year. But at least James was to be reunited with Patsey and some of his sons.[61]

Joseph chose to move his family to the Des Moines agency. The agent's house was to be ready by May 1839, so the family's possessions were packed up. Joseph directed the move of his wife, their younger children, Patsey, and her five sons to the agency that spring, leaving Prairie du Chien for the last time. Patsey, with her sons Charles, James, London, Lewis, and newly born Isaac Newton, boarded the steamboat with Eliza for the trip

Joseph Street and his family lived in the Des Moines Agency house, pictured here, built in 1839. Patsey and her sons resided in a cabin located on the property until she gained her freedom with the death of Eliza Posey Street. LIBRARY OF CONGRESS, PRINTS & PHOTO-GRAPHS DIVISION, HABS IA-30-31

down the Mississippi River. All, with their baggage, would disembark at the mouth of the Des Moines River.

With the treaty signed by the Sauk and Meskwaki after the Black Hawk War in 1832, the United States had appropriated a tract of land on the west bank of the Mississippi River from Missouri to the Neutral Grounds, which was called the Black Hawk Tract. The Sac and Fox were forced onto a nar-row tract to the west named the Keokuk Reserve. Four years later, Keokuk and the Sac and Fox were coerced into signing another treaty, which ceded all the land in the reserve to the United States government, and they were pushed farther west. By 1837, all Sauk and Meskwaki people had been forcibly relocated to the reservation where Joseph was to serve. With the reserve open, white people were beginning to settle on the Des Moines River, and whiskey sellers came in force. To supply these new settlers and bring goods to the reservation, steamboats had commenced making trips up the Des Moines River in 1837. By 1839, the steamboats had navigated the waters as far as Iowaville, Iowa Territory. Joseph, his family, and Patsey and her sons would have had to transfer to one of these smaller steam-boats to continue their journey. Even so, part of the trip would have been overland, for the agency buildings stood about fifteen miles from the river. For this part of the trip, Eliza and her young children rode in a carriage driven by her son Alexander, while the others walked, as William drove the small wagon carrying luggage and supplies. When all arrived, they found that the house was still under construction.

Joseph, though, found the positive side of the inconvenience and praised his wife's ability to make the best of the situation. He wrote to his son Thomas, who had remained at Prairie du Chien:

> I left your mother and all the family well and we have got into our new house and somewhat comfortably established once more. I am even surprised to see with what ease your dear mother accommodates herself to difficulties. . . . She has mastered them. . . . Your mother will move into the four rooms on the first floor [while the halls are being painted], which all can be used through the back piazza without going into the passage at all.[62]

The United States had contracted with a man from Clarksville, Missouri, to build not only the house but also other structures in the agency complex. The crew, which included enslaved Black men, first erected temporary shelters where they would live while building the council house, Street family home, barns, and outbuildings. The temporary housing included "board sheds close to the council house."[63] When the Street family and Patsey and her sons arrived at the agency on the Des Moines River, at least one of the temporary shelters still stood. In a letter to his son, Joseph described the structure as "a good log Cabbin" with a "nailed roof & brick chimney." Joseph directed Patsey and her sons to live in this structure. For the first time, Patsey had space for herself and her sons Charles, James, London, Lewis, and Isaac that was not also inhabited by the Street family. Joseph may have seen the cabin as more of a benefit to him than Patsey, for he wrote to Thomas, with "Patsey & all her family living in the house, [the kitchen] is alone used for a Kitchen."[64]

Patsey and her boys may have had their own living space, but she was not happy that Joseph made her sons work in the fields. At the Des Moines agency, Joseph and his family lived on a large tract of land and were required to be more self-sufficient than they had been when living in Prairie du Chien. One hundred sixty acres lying behind the house had been plowed and fenced. Of this acreage, about one hundred acres had been planted in oats, pease, corn, and potatoes. Joseph had ordered his sons William, Alexander, and Washington to assist with the planting. Joseph had also insisted that Patsey's sons Charles, James, and London help with the farm work. Joseph found his sons' work very satisfactory, but he recounted that he "had to speak to Charles, James & London, who are inclined to be idle." Patsey apparently demonstrated her displeasure with Joseph's order and, as he described it, "once or twice lagged and laid up," remaining within her house. With Patsey self-indisposed, Eliza was forced to prepare the meals, including bringing breakfast to Patsey. Rather than confront Patsey, Joseph and Eliza "took no notice of it but to wait on [Patsey] & make her comfortable." He said Patsey "soon came out to her usual duties." Patsey had also been responsible for milking the five cows at the farm, and while she stayed in the cabin, Charles did the milking. He continued to help Patsey after she returned to work.[65]

Though Patsey now slept in private living quarters rather than on a pallet next to the kitchen fireplace as she had been forced to do at Prairie du Chien, she soon had cause to consider the possibility of a larger change in her future. During the winter of 1838–1839, as the Street household had prepared for their move from Prairie du Chien to the Des Moines River, Joseph had suffered a slight stroke. As a result, he began having difficulty communicating. Often, he could not speak the words he wanted to say.[66]

Though slightly impaired, Joseph continued to maintain his duties as Indian agent, often traveling with his son William, who worked as his clerk and bookkeeper. In November 1839, Joseph had another attack, and the family sent for Dr. Alexander Posey, Eliza's brother. During the winter, Joseph was confined to his room. His son ordered one of Patsey's younger sons to be in the room with him at all times, to watch him and see to any of his needs. By May, Joseph seemed to have regained his health, and on May 5, he met in council with some of the Sauk. After the council, Joseph returned to his room. He ate dinner, and then his son Alexander roasted an apple for him. "After giving father the glass of water," Alexander later reported, "and waiting till he drank, I walked through the dining room into the garden, but had only reached the stile when the negro boy who was in the room when I left ran after me calling 'old master is dying.'"

Joseph's son ran back into the house to find Joseph lying dead on the floor in front of the fireplace, presumably the result of a stroke.[67]

Joseph M. Street was buried in a small plot at the Sac and Fox agency. As they had done after Joseph's first stroke at Prairie du Chien, the entire family of Street children had traveled home to be with their father during his illness that spring. With his death, the status of Patsey and her children was called into question. One family member believed that upon Joseph's death, all of the people he had enslaved gained their freedom. Another suggested that only Charles Forrester had gained his freedom.[68]

But Eliza Street proceeded as though Patsey remained indentured to her. Patsey had come along with Eliza when she married and moved to her new home with Joseph. Patsey had also signed an indenture in 1828, in which she agreed to travel with Eliza to Prairie du Chien and serve her "during the full period for which the aforesaid indentures were taken." Therefore, according to the documents Patsey had signed, she was bound to Eliza Street until 1868—twenty-eight more years.[69]

Joseph senior's son Joseph H. D. Street and his wife, Emily Street, and George and Mary Wilson had their homes in Cassville at the time of the elder Joseph's death. Patsey's son Henry was still with the Wilson family, and he may have also helped Joseph junior and his family. George had been appointed to represent Crawford County in the Wisconsin territorial legislature. He attended the first session of the Second Legislative Assembly in 1838 and the second session in 1839, and Henry may have traveled with him. Partway through the second session, George resigned his position and was replaced by Joseph Brisbois.[70]

When George resigned his position in the territorial assembly in 1839 to move his family to Dubuque, his brother, Thomas, was a justice in the court for Dubuque County, and George secured the position as clerk of court. He purchased some land outside of Dubuque and commenced farming. With the death of Joseph senior, George moved his family once again, this time to the Indian agency on the Des Moines River. Each time George moved his family, young Henry Triplett also moved. With the last move, Henry was reunited with Patsey and his brothers.

As he had done in Prairie du Chien, Joseph Street oversaw the beginning of a pattern farm at the Des Moines agency. The government's plan was to teach the Sauk and Meskwaki the basics of European agriculture.

In 1842, George took over the operation of the pattern farm. Henry was about nine years old. After five years, he could regularly see his mother again. As Mary Wilson began to teach her children their prayers, she also taught them to Henry. Later, she taught Henry to read, spell, and write.[71]

Henry was not the only Black person George Wilson enslaved. He had previously enslaved Etheldred and America, and at some point, when he began to farm in Iowa Territory, he brought an enslaved woman named Mary to work for the family. Years later, George's son recalled that George "owned a negro woman on his farm near Agency, or in Dubuque county" who became "so unruly that he traded her for a pair of mules." George's lack of regard for this Black person probably made an impression on Henry, reinforcing the premise that an enslaved person considered by their enslaver to be unruly could always be sold away.[72]

During this time, Patsey and her sons remained in Iowa as it progressed from territory to statehood. Article 23 of the Constitution for the State of Iowa adopted in 1846 stated, "Neither slavery nor involuntary servitude, unless for the punishment of crimes, shall ever be tolerated in this state." Iowa was admitted to the Union on December 28, 1846. By Iowa law, Patsey and her sons were free. Yet, as at Prairie du Chien, Patsey and her sons remained under the control of the Street family, in particular, Eliza. That is, until Eliza Posey Street died on February 2, 1847. She was only fifty-five years old but after giving birth to fourteen children, her health was fragile. Eliza was buried next to her husband, Joseph. The indenture Patsey had signed in 1828 in which she agreed to "remain with Mrs. Street as her servant" was cancelled with the death of Eliza.[73] Eliza's heirs may have decided that, with the deaths of the two people who had signed Patsey's indentures and the illegality of slavery in Iowa, giving Patsey her freedom was the pragmatic action to take.

In 1842, two years after Joseph's death, the Sac and Fox had signed another treaty with the United States. The Sauk and Meskwaki people agreed to relocate to land west of the Missouri River in three years' time. As the villages began to move westward, the Des Moines agency was closed and reestablished on the Raccoon River. By 1846, the US government had removed the Sauk and Meskwaki to a reservation in "unorganized" territory west of the Missouri River, and Congress admitted Iowa to the Union. The land on which the Des Moines agency buildings and farm had stood was surveyed into blocks and lots; the town of Agency City was founded. Joseph Street's two sons-in-law, George Wilson and John Beach, acquired much of the land. On November 27, 1847, eight months after the death of Eliza Street, George and Mary granted to Patsey Triplett Lot 12, Block 6, Agency Tract.[74] Patsey was now free, and she owned property.

Charles Forrester, Patsey's eldest son, had gained his freedom with the death of Joseph Street in 1840. Records do not indicate the circumstances under which this occurred. However, Charles left the Des Moines agency and in 1843 settled at Fairfield, about twenty miles east of the agency. Fairfield had been designated the seat of government for Jefferson County and offered many opportunities, and Charles opened a barber shop there. Many white people who lived in the southeastern part of Iowa had migrated to the state from Missouri, where slavery was legal. The presence of a free Black man owning a business in their community upset some Fairfield residents. Some white men made a complaint to the county commissioners. The commissioners, in turn, applied to the county prosecutor to have Charles arrested and "hired out" based on the statutes governing the Territory of Iowa. However, the prosecutor refused to judge Charles in any way. He stated that Charles had come to the territory before many of the commissioners had and that he was as much entitled to the freedom of the country as "any other man." So, Charles continued to operate his barber shop, though no record of him after 1845 has been found.[75]

Charles's experience may have caused George Wilson to consider the status of Henry Triplett, who was thirteen in 1846. Henry still lived with the Wilsons in Agency, Iowa. Though Black residents of Iowa were free as of 1846, in 1838, the Iowa territorial legislature had passed "Black Codes" to discourage Black people from moving to Iowa. These regulations were strengthened the following year when the legislature passed "An Act Regulating Blacks and Mulattoes" restricting Black people living in the territory. It stated that "no black or mulatto person shall be permitted to settle or reside in this Territory, unless he or she shall present a fair certificate . . . of his or her actual freedom, and give bond."[76]

In January 1846, just before Iowa became a state, George drew up a document that complied with the 1839 act. George may have presented the document to Henry as a way to protect him. In reality, by signing the document, Henry indentured himself to George.

Henry Harrison Triplett, the son of James and Patsey Triplett, was born at Prairie du Chien on August 29, 1833. At a young age, Henry was "given" to George and Mary Street Wilson. After obtaining his freedom, he worked as a blacksmith and studied to become a minister in the African Methodist Episcopal Church. He died January 26, 1906, in Horton, Kansas. ANNALS OF IOWA 4, NO. 8 (1901)

In a letter dated December 15, 1890, from Henry to George's son, Henry remembered what George had told him: "The Law of the State demanded [Henry have a guardian]. The Law did not know me as a sidesan [citizen]. All free negroes must have a gardean. Without that any one could abuse me and no law to protect me." The document that George wrote stated: "Henry Harrison Triplett, son of Aunt Patsey Triplett, being the age of 13 has of his own accord chosen George Wilson to be his guardian, and has Bound himself to me until twenty-one years of age."[77] While the certificate proved that Henry could reside in Iowa, it did not give him his freedom.

The document also stated that George would teach Henry to read and write, though by Henry's statement it was Mary Street, George's wife, who taught him to read and write. As part of the contract, Henry would stay in Iowa until he "came of age" at twenty-one. With his signature, George agreed to fulfill the request Patsey had made when Joseph "gave" two-year-old Henry to George and Mary in 1835: that Henry be taught a trade. George arranged for Henry to apprentice with James Stephens, the blacksmith for the Indian agency.[78]

Patsey's son London had remained with her since his birth, but that changed around 1850. One of Joseph and Eliza's sons, Washington Posey Street, had entered the US Military Academy at West Point in 1843. Upon his graduation in 1847, he had been posted to Jefferson Barracks and then posted to frontier duty in Texas. He served at San Antonio under Brigadier General John Spotswood Garland and then had scouting duty out of Fort Worth. While Washington was posted in Texas in 1850, London Triplett traveled to Fort Worth with him. Though legally free by the Iowa Constitution of 1846, Triplett served Washington as his servant. When Washington died in September 1852, London returned to Iowa to live with Patsey.[79]

After London's return, Patsey, London, Lewis, and Isaac continued to live in what was called District 13 in Wapello County, Iowa. They were the only Black family in the area. Since the mid-1840s, Henry Triplett had been apprenticed to John Stephens, the blacksmith for the agency. By 1854, Henry had reached the age of twenty-one. The guardianship certificate had been fulfilled, and Henry joined the rest of his family in District 13. James Triplett, father and son, may have died, as neither is listed as part of Patsey's family in census records.[80]

Patsey had taught each of her boys the necessity of learning a skill. This desire for her children had driven her to request that Henry be taught a trade when Joseph Street had given the boy away when he was less than two years old. Each son respected Patsey and heeded his mother's words, and as Patsey aged, they took care of their mother. By 1856, Patsey had asserted her independence. Patsey was now a free woman, and she chose a name for herself. She became Martha Triplett.[81]

Living in the household of Joseph Street, Patsey (now Martha) had been exposed to the teachings of the Cumberland Presbyterian Church. Street regularly professed his Christianity and often spoke of the Lord's will in the letters he wrote to family members and political acquaintances. And he had lobbied for the appointment of Reverend Lowry of the Cumberland Presbyterian Church to head the Winnebago school. Patsey had almost certainly been required to listen to Joseph read from the Bible, either in the Street family home or in the Sunday services he conducted. Over the years, she would have heard the story of Martha and Mary from the Gospel of Luke. Martha had busily prepared food for Jesus as Mary sat at

Jesus's feet and listened. Though Jesus praised Mary, Patsey may have seen herself as the person who always worked as others sat and therefore saw herself as Martha.

Over the years, the four youngest Triplett sons each married, started a home, and found employment, moving to the city of Keokuk, Iowa, where many Black people lived and worked. Henry established a smithy, London worked on steamboats, and Lewis and Isaac found employment as laborers. Martha sold her land in Wapello County, and by 1860, she lived with Henry and his family in Keokuk.[82]

When the Emancipation Proclamation was issued on January 1, 1863, the Union began the recruitment of African American men to serve in the army. London Triplett enlisted on August 18, 1863. He was immediately made a fourth sergeant of Company I, First Regiment Iowa African Infantry, and mustered in on November 27. In the course of his service, London received promotions, eventually rising to first sergeant.

Lewis and Isaac Triplett, only a year apart in age, enlisted before their older brother did: Lewis on August 15, 1863, and Isaac two days later. Lewis assumed the rank of fifth corporal, and Isaac was made first sergeant. Both were assigned to Company C, First Regiment Iowa African Infantry. Lewis never returned to Iowa. He died of disease at Helena, Arkansas, on August 31, 1864. At the end of the war, both London and Isaac mustered out at Devall's Bluff, Arkansas, on the same day in October 1865.[83]

Henry, along with his brothers, had registered for service in 1863. Six companies of the First Regiment Iowa African Infantry were mustered at Keokuk, where the Triplett brothers lived. Henry may have remained in Keokuk, where his skill as a blacksmith was greatly needed, as there are no details of his service.[84]

Once again a civilian, London returned to Keokuk and his family. Both Henry and Isaac, though, decided to move. Isaac had begun studies to be a minister. Upon his return, he was admitted to the Missouri Conference of the African Methodist Episcopal Church. He became pastor of St. Paul's A.M.E. Church in Columbia, Missouri, and dedicated the new building in 1871. He was given a parish in Macon, Missouri, and this became his new home. Martha became part of Isaac's household, which included Isaac's wife, Susan; their sons, Isaac and Ulysses; and Margaret Sarah Lewis.

Martha lived with the family until Isaac was transferred to the California Conference.[85]

When Isaac and his family moved to California, Henry again invited Martha to live with him and his family. Henry had moved to Memphis, Missouri. He too had become a minister, and by 1880, Henry's family resided in Chillicothe, Missouri. Martha joined Henry's household, which had grown to include his wife, Kate; their four sons, Henry, Edgar, Isaac, and James; and their daughter, May. At eighty years old, Martha made her final home in Missouri.[86]

Martha never returned to Prairie du Chien after gaining her freedom. Unlike Mariah, Martha had not acquired a house and property in the community. Connections, family or personal, seemed to determine where Mariah, and then Martha, decided to make their homes when they became free. Mariah had no children and seemingly no family ties to her place of birth, where slavery was still practiced. In Prairie du Chien, Mariah owned a home and farmed her small tract of land. She also had Helene Galarneau as a friend and neighbor, so she stayed in the community. Martha, on the other hand, chose to live with her sons and, in time, her grandchildren, no matter where they moved.

Family and personal connections would also be factors in determining where Courtney chose to live once she had gained her freedom.

CHAPTER 4

COURTNEY, 1812–1835

A woman named Courtney arrived in Prairie du Chien toward the end of 1829, a little more than a year after Patsey had arrived with her two sons and the Street family. As an enslaved person, Courtney was forced to accompany the family of Major John Spotswood Garland, with whom she had been living at Fort Snelling and other military posts since the young age of six or seven. John had been transferred to Prairie du Chien in late 1829 to oversee the construction of the new barracks of Fort Crawford, where the First Infantry were being relocated from Fort Snelling.

Mariah (along with Henry and two other enslaved people) had come to Prairie du Chien fourteen years earlier, in 1816, with John W. Johnson, who had then been appointed as the first US factor at Prairie du Chien. Since that time, only a few other enslaved people associated with the US Army or the US War Department had lived at Prairie du Chien. There is no indication that Black people in any condition of enslavement or freedom worked in the household of the US Indian agent Nicolas Boilvin. As to the officers stationed at the old barracks of Fort Crawford, the staff rotated between ten and twenty officers. Many of these men claimed servants on their pay vouchers. Most of these servants, though, were described as "White" men or women, or as having a "fair" complexion.[1] Willoughby Morgan, who commanded the post for stretches between 1823 and 1826, claimed Black and white servants on his pay vouchers. He did not note whether any of the men were enslaved. During the same period, only Lieutenant Henry Clark, who had used Mariah as his servant for a short period, and Lieutenants John Anderson, Joseph M. Baxley, and Anthony Drane claimed Black people on their vouchers. None elaborated on the status of their servants.[2]

However, the exact opposite was true at Fort Snelling during the years between 1819 and 1830. It was common practice for officers and other War Department personnel to keep enslaved individuals at that post. The permissive attitude toward slavery that existed at Fort Snelling, at the mouth of the Minnesota River, arrived at Prairie du Chien just as Courtney did, due to the federal government's reinvestiture in the post in 1827 and the change in command at Fort Crawford in 1829.

—｜｜—

Courtney was born into slavery around 1812 in the household of the Garland family of Albemarle County, Virginia. John Spotswood Garland's grandfather, James Garland, worked as a lawyer, but he also raised tobacco and purchased enslaved people to work his land and tend his crops in Albemarle County. James enslaved eleven individuals at the time of his grandson John's birth in 1793. As of 1810, John's father, Martin Hudson Garland, also enslaved eleven people on his property. Courtney's mother may have been enslaved by either James or Martin Garland.[3]

John Spotswood Garland was born on November 15, 1793, on the family's plantation in Albemarle County. He enlisted in the US Army in 1813 and was commissioned first lieutenant. At the end of the conflict with Great Britain, John remained in the military. He was posted to Detroit and, while stationed there, met Harriet Margaretta Smith, the daughter of fur trader Jacob Smith. In 1816, John married Harriet Margaretta. After his marriage, he continued to serve at Detroit until he was promoted to captain. He was then transferred to Fort Howard at Green Bay, where he commanded a company of men who were completing the construction of the barracks.[4]

When Courtney was six or seven, Captain John Garland visited his brother James. During the visit, James gave Courtney to John, perhaps because of his marriage or the recent death of John and Harriet's first child. James made a present of Courtney, thinking Harriet would need help living so far from family and on what was then the frontier. Like other enslaved young girls, Courtney had probably begun to serve the Garland family by tending to the Garland children, helping the enslaved women in the kitchen and dining room, and tending the kitchen garden. James Garland must have believed that Courtney, having gained some experience

Brigadier General John Spotswood Garland (1793–1861) was a native Virginian and an officer in the US Army. In 1820, he acquired Courtney from his brother and held her in slavery until 1832, when he sold her to Alexis Bailly. CIVIL WAR PHOTOGRAPHS, 1861–1865, LIBRARY OF CONGRESS, PRINTS AND PHOTOGRAPHS DIVISION

and training, could ably perform tasks that would make John and Harriet's life more comfortable. John then left Virginia with Courtney to return to his posting.

At the age when most white children would be beginning their formal schooling, Courtney was removed from her family, given to a twenty-five-year-old stranger, and transported with John's baggage from the Piedmont of Virginia across mountains and water to the frontier and life at a military post on Lake Erie. On his pay voucher for October and November 1820, John noted "Courtney A Negro" as a servant.[5]

The pay for an officer in the US Army was based on rank. In addition to a salary, each officer received three rations a day. But the pay was low, and the rations were basic. Congress realized that in the course of their duties, officers who were assigned to posts far from their homes would incur expenses and personal requirements that could not be covered by the supplies and provisions they procured through the quartermaster's office at a post. Beginning in 1818, Congress authorized emoluments and allowances for which officers could request additional pay. Officers could also request certain services of the enlisted men. The details of what was allowed an officer, plus many other rules, were laid out in *General Regulations for the Army; or, Military Institutes.*

The regulations detailed, in exact minutiae, all aspects of military life for enlisted men and officers, whether at an institute for instruction, on duty at a post, or in preparation for and during battle. Officers had benefits, but these benefits were dictated by rank. Section 148 allowed each

Pay voucher filed by Captain John Garland on June 30, 1826, claiming subsistence and clothing for Courtney, whom he listed as "Slave." NATIONAL ARCHIVES AND RECORDS ADMINISTRATION

Though John's status and pay had increased, he still claimed pay of only five dollars a month for Courtney and one ration per day at twenty cents. On this voucher, John's description of Courtney reflected several changes. Now about fourteen, Courtney had grown to five feet four inches. John still listed Courtney as having a black complexion, black eyes, and black hair. But he changed Courtney's status. She was no longer a servant or a waiter. John recorded that Courtney was a "Slave."[16]

Though Courtney was an enslaved person, John may not have wished to disclose this fact when he was in Detroit. The Jay Treaty of 1796, signed between the United States and Great Britain, defined enslaved people as property. After the treaty's passage, enslaved individuals living in the Northwest Territory in 1796 continued to be enslaved for life; their children born before this date were allowed to be held in bondage for twenty-five years. But according to the treaty, children born of enslaved women after July 11, 1796, were free from birth. Then, in 1807, Michigan Territory justice Augustus Woodward wrote the decision *In re Richard Pattinson* and "held that because the Ordinance of 1787 forbade slavery in the territory, no right of property existed in humans."[17] In this and a subsequent case, Woodward refused to allow the return of enslaved individuals to their enslavers. His decision "was widely acclaimed throughout the northern states and was popular in Detroit," where an abolition movement had already begun. By 1820 in Detroit, the antislavery sentiment had grown even stronger; not one enslaved person was recorded in either the Ste. Anne church register or the census for Detroit.[18] It is likely John had preferred to keep Courtney's enslavement to himself. But now living along the Minnesota River, John likely realized he had no need to use the euphemism "servant" to describe Courtney's enslavement. Officers at Fort Snelling were generally proslavery.[19]

At Fort Snelling, John and his family were assigned rooms in the officers' quarters, where Lieutenant Nathan and Charlotte Clark and their two children had been residing for nine years. The officers' quarters existed in a long wood-framed structure covered in clapboards. The building had been constructed with a roofed gallery running the length of the rear of the structure and wrapping around the ends to face the parade ground. The front of the main floor faced the enclosed parade ground. The quarters were divided into fourteen sets, with each set comprising two apartments. One entrance provided access to the two apartments. Each apartment had a sixteen-by-fourteen-foot front room and an eight-by-fifteen-and-a-half-foot rear room. In each set's cellar was a kitchen spanning the width of the two apartments. A fireplace on each floor heated the spaces, and meals were prepared using the cellar fireplace.[20]

John's family was probably allocated one of the quarters. Such allocations were based on rank and available space. The quarter, divided into two rooms, was about thirty feet long and twenty feet wide. An exterior stairway led from the living quarters to the cellar. An officer and his family would live, sleep, and eat within the two main floor rooms. Courtney and the other men and women serving the officers and their families likely resided in the cellar of each unit.[21]

John Garland and Nathan Clark each had a family of young children.

Fort Snelling, circa 1850, painted by Edward K. Thomas, a sergeant stationed at Fort Snelling. To the far left below the horizon are the two stone houses built for Lieutenant Nathan Clark and Captain John Spotswood Garland. MINNEAPOLIS INSTITUTE OF ART, THE JULIA B. BIGELOW FUND

The two men quickly formed a friendship and decided they wanted better and roomier living accommodations for their wives and children. They requested permission from Colonel Snelling to build "more commodious quarters" outside the walled compound. With permission granted, each officer directed military staff in the construction of a small stone house almost opposite the Indian agency. The two houses stood next to each other facing the Minnesota River. Harriet Garland and Charlotte Clark had soldiers plant shrubs and gardens to make a surrounding that was more pleasant than the crowded officers' quarters. They had a chicken coop erected and raised hens for a source of fresh eggs for the children and for desserts. The two families became close, and the daughters became "fast friends."[22]

Each new stone house was two rooms deep, with second stories tucked under the sloping roofs to provide additional space for sleeping. A small frame structure stood behind one house. This building may have housed a kitchen where Courtney prepared meals for both of the families. Nathan seems to have never filed a pay voucher requesting reimbursement for pay for a servant, so Courtney may have served the Garlands and the Clarks. She also may have slept in the outbuilding.[23]

The officers and their families at Fort Snelling had to provide their own society, and Courtney would have been responsible for the cooking, cleaning, and childcare that made their amusements pleasurable and possible. Charlotte Ouisconsin Clark Van Cleve, the daughter of Nathan and Charlotte Clark, later stated, "The only white people within three hundred miles were shut within that hollow square [Fort Snelling], a community dependent largely upon each other for all the little every-day kindnesses and amenities, which make life enjoyable."[24]

In the winter, the officers sometimes dressed up and presented skits, "impersonating all the characters while the women and children looked on." In the summer, the families with children, as well as single men and young women, would ride to Little Falls (now called Minnehaha Falls) or one of the lakes (Lakes Harriet and Bde Maka Ska/Calhoun). The children rambled about gathering flowers and playing games while the adults fished and picked strawberries. Then they went to the government mill, where the miller's wife prepared a meal.[25] Though Charlotte Van Cleve did not mention the assistance of any servants on these trips, it can be assumed that Courtney and the other Black servants and enslaved people at Fort Snelling were involved in the preparations for excursions into the countryside.

The household of John Garland also included a young white woman, Maria Smith, the youngest sister of Harriet Smith Garland. Maria had been born in Detroit in 1813. Her mother died in 1817, and soon after they married, the Garlands took Maria into their household. When John was transferred to Fort Snelling in 1826, Maria traveled with the captain and his family. Fulfilling Maria's wishes would have also been part of Courtney's duties.

For Courtney, there would have been no light social life. She waited on the needs of the three adults and five children that composed the Garland family and possibly those of the Clark family, too. Courtney would have prepared the meals when John entertained other officers, and then she would have remained in the kitchen, ready to be responsive to their wants. Enlisted men served as the waiters who cleared the table and filled glasses with wine and brandy.

Even if Courtney had a few minutes to herself after a day of cooking, cleaning, and tending to the children's needs, as a fourteen-year-old she had very few other Black women her age with whom to form friendships. Eliza, who was enslaved by Major Lawrence Taliaferro, would have been about Courtney's age, as would have Louisa, who was enslaved by Colonel Josiah Snelling, post commander. But the majority of the enslaved people at Fort Snelling were men serving unmarried officers. James Jetty was claimed on pay vouchers of Captain Robert McCabe, who had rented Mariah from John W. Johnson. Jetty may also have been rented out to Lieutenant Henry Clark. When Henry received orders to transfer to Fort Crawford in 1825, he took Jetty with him. At Fort Crawford, Lieutenant Colonel Willoughby Morgan and Major John Fowle also rented

Major Lawrence Taliaferro (1794–1871) was from King George County, Virginia. In 1819, he left the US Army and was appointed the US Indian agent for the St. Peters Agency at Fort Snelling. He held the post for twenty years. In 1836, Taliaferro officiated at the marriage of Harriet Robinson, a woman enslaved by him, to Dred Scott, enslaved by Dr. John Emerson. MINNESOTA HISTORICAL SOCIETY

James Jetty. William, who was claimed on pay vouchers at various times by Lieutenant Nathaniel S. Harris, Lieutenant Alexander Johnston, and others while at Fort Snelling, may have been William Thompson, who was enslaved by Lawrence Taliaferro.[26]

Lawrence had begun his posting at Fort Snelling in 1820 as Indian agent to the Ojibwe and Dakota. The Indian agency stood outside the walls of the fort, not far from the homes built for John Garland and Nathan Clark. Lawrence was not married when he arrived at Fort Snelling, but he had not traveled alone. He brought with him enslaved people who had lived on his family's lands in Virginia. The major had inherited these enslaved individuals from his father.[27]

Lawrence had served with Josiah Snelling in the battle of Fort Erie in September 1814, and the two had become close friends. They were

Lawrence Taliaferro compiled a list of the men and women whom he enslaved during the twenty years he was Indian agent at the St. Peters Agency at Fort Snelling. At the bottom, he noted that all twenty-one were "freed from slavery," listing the years 1839, 1840, and 1843. The line and arrow in the middle of the image are bleed-through from the other side of the paper. MINNESOTA HISTORICAL SOCIETY

reunited when Josiah was placed in command of the new post on the Minnesota River in 1820. By his own admission, Lawrence held twenty-one individuals in slavery during the years of his residence at Fort Snelling.[28] It is not known whether they all lived at the agency buildings located below Fort Snelling, but given that Lawrence left the military reserve only on short furloughs, it seems likely that over the course of his twenty-year appointment, all twenty-one enslaved individuals resided at Fort Snelling at some time in that span. On the back of a letter, Lawrence listed the names of the twenty-one individuals he enslaved as "Eliza, Frederick, William, Horace, Thomas, Samuel, Jerry, Armistead, John, Horace 2d, Lizzie, Bittie, Harriet, Susan, William E, Turner, Turner 2sd, Wyatt, Phillis, Lucy, Charlotte."[29]

Lawrence rented some of these enslaved people to officers stationed at the post. Eliza served Captain Joseph Plympton for fourteen months between April 1825 and May 1826. At the end of May, Joseph offered to purchase Eliza. Summarizing his response, Lawrence later wrote, "I informed him that it was my intention to give her freedom after a limited time but that Mrs. P. could keep her for two years and perhaps three." During the years Eliza was held at Fort Snelling, she gave birth to a daughter, Susan, who became Lawrence's property. While Eliza worked for the Plymptons, Lawrence rented William to Josiah Snelling for "Victuals & Clothes." Josiah claimed William on his pay reports so as to be reimbursed for the cost of the rations and clothing given to William. Lawrence also rented Frederick to assistant Indian agent Elias T. Langham Jr., and Lawrence hired out Horace (either Horace or Horace 2d) periodically to officers stationed at the post, including Lieutenant Seth Eastman, Lieutenant T. B. W. Stockton, and Captain Jefferson Vail. Lawrence later sold Horace to A. S. Mirie, the sutler at Fort Snelling.[30]

Both Lawrence and John Garland had been born in Virginia, where slavery was legal, and had been raised in an environment where the presence of enslaved Black people was a part of their everyday lives. They would have seen nothing unusual in using enslaved people to make their lives more comfortable at a military post where few comforts could be found. When confronted with what white Southerners sometimes euphemistically called this "peculiar institution," even many officers who did not come from enslaving families seemingly accepted the presence of slavery within the Fort Snelling community and took advantage of the availability of enslaved individuals.

For example, Josiah Snelling had been born into a family of successful bankers in Boston, Massachusetts. Instead of working for the family business, he had chosen a military career and, by 1811, was a captain in the US Army. Massachusetts had abolished slavery through a series of court decisions in 1783, the year after Josiah was born, and the 1790 census for Massachusetts showed that no enslaved people lived in the state. So, Josiah would likely not have come in contact with enslaved people until he was posted on the western frontier and then, in 1811, served under the command of William Henry Harrison, who held enslaved men and women at his home "Grouselands" near Vincennes.[31]

In his military service on the western frontier, where there were so few amenities, Josiah must have believed the benefits of having an enslaved person in one's household to assist with daily living outweighed the moral and ethical downsides of participating in slavery. After renting William from Lawrence Taliaferro, Josiah decided to purchase an enslaved person for himself. On May 14, 1827, Josiah noted in his journal, "Negro woman (Mary) and the child Louisa bt. of Mr. Bostwick of St. Louis for $400.00."[32] O. N. Bostwick, with his business partner and brother-in-law William H. Savage, operated Savage and Bostwick Auction Rooms, in which enslaved people were offered to the highest bidder. Besides William, Mary, and Louisa, Josiah also claimed ownership of a man named John Tully.[33]

While Josiah became an active participant in the institution of slavery, a reorganization of the US Army brought many more enslaved people to the upper Mississippi River Valley. The presence of enslaved men and women serving officers demonstrated that, though slavery was not technically legal in the Northwest Territory, the officers maintained a conviction that the prohibition against slavery in the Northwest Territory did not apply to men serving in the military. Nonmilitary white residents of the territory also seem to have accepted this belief.[34]

In 1825, the headquarters of the Fifth Regiment of Infantry had been placed at Fort Snelling. Officers and enlisted men of the Fifth Infantry were stationed at Forts Snelling, Crawford, and Armstrong. Then in 1828, the War Department decided to relocate the First Infantry to the upper Mississippi and return the Fifth Infantry to the posts around the Great Lakes. This change may have been in response to Josiah Snelling's failing health and the poor judgment he showed in allowing a duel at the post. Or the change may have been in response to the events of the Winnebago War of 1827, which led the US government to once again post a military force at Prairie du Chien. Whatever the reason, the change in command not only reinvested the military at Prairie du Chien but also increased the presence of enslaved people in the upper Mississippi River Valley.

Previous to this, the headquarters of the First Infantry had been at Baton Rouge, Louisiana, with Colonel Zachary Taylor in command. Taylor had been born in Virginia and, like Lawrence Taliaferro and John Garland, was raised around enslaved Black men and women who worked in their family homes and on their land. Zachary assumed command of Fort Snelling on May 24, 1828, which increased the Black population at the post. Traveling with him were his wife, some of his children, and at least two enslaved people, Jane and Glasco.[35]

With the First Infantry now assigned to the three posts in Michigan Territory, a change in the officer staff at all three posts occurred. Slightly more than thirty officers had had postings at Fort Crawford since 1817, and only two are documented as possessing enslaved men. Of the fifty officers who rotated through Fort Snelling between 1819 and 1828, John Garland and Josiah Snelling were two of just eight who declared enslaved people on their pay claims. However, the percentage of officers stationed at the two posts possessing enslaved men and women greatly increased with the arrival of the First Infantry.[36]

Taylor, Snelling, Taliaferro, Garland, Clark, and other officers stationed at Fort Crawford and Fort Snelling had gained military knowledge and experience by enlisting and participating in battles during the War of 1812. Afterward, they had chosen to enlist in the US Army as a profession and had been commissioned officers. But now, a new class of officer was permeating the US Army, men who had attended the US Military Academy at West Point and upon graduation had been commissioned second lieutenants. Fort Snelling and Fort Crawford would be the first assignment for many of these young graduates. Their first posting, before arriving at Prairie du Chien or Fort Snelling, would be Jefferson Barracks, just north of St. Louis.

Arriving at the Barracks, some of the young men from Northern states were likely exposed to slavery in a new way. They came in contact with officers who kept Black men and women enslaved to wait upon them and their families. Jefferson Barracks was in Missouri, a slave state, and officers could easily purchase a Black person from another enslaver or from slave dealers who operated slave markets in St. Louis.

By 1828, slavery had been forbidden in the northern states. Very few enslaved people were enumerated in the northern states' censuses after that date, although due to gradual emancipation, there were legally enslaved people in the North until 1865. The US Military Academy at West Point was in New York State, which had freed enslaved people by gradual emancipation. According to the US Federal Census for New York, a total of seventy-five enslaved people lived in the state in 1830, but none were enumerated as residing at the academy. The commanding officers at West Point did not allow cadets to bring enslaved individuals to the academy. It seems that no officer brought an enslaved person to his posting at the academy until 1842. In the years from 1842 until Robert E. Lee became superintendent of the academy in 1854, four short-term visiting officers claimed Black people—enslaved, indentured, or free—on their pay vouchers.[37]

So, arriving at Jefferson Barracks, young officers who had been appointed to West Point from the New England states, New York, Pennsylvania, and Ohio witnessed slavery in practice. Although these men were moving to the Northwest Territory and not the South, some of their behavior soon mirrored what Harriet Jacobs observed in her 1861 autobiographical narrative: "When northerners go to the south to reside, they prove very apt scholars. They soon imbibe the sentiments and disposition of their neighbors. . . . They seem to satisfy their consciences with the doctrine that God created the Africans to be slaves."[38]

The population of enslaved people on the Minnesota River had increased by July 1826 when Courtney arrived with the Garland family at Fort Snelling. About nine months later, another daughter, Maria Louise, was born to the Garlands. Courtney, at fourteen or fifteen years old, now served the needs of Harriet Garland and four young children.[39]

Then in 1827, Jack arrived at the post with his enslaver, Lieutenant Martin Scott. Martin had been born in Vermont and enlisted in the US Army at the beginning of the War of 1812. After the war, he received a commission in the Fifth Infantry and was posted to Fort Smith in Indiana Territory. Promoted to First Lieutenant, Martin was posted to Fort Crawford in May 1823. By the time Martin was transferred to Fort Snelling, he had, in Jacobs's words, "imbibed the sentiments and disposition" of Southerners on the enslavement of Black people. On his October 1826 pay voucher, Martin requested pay for Jack, whom he described as "a negro boy and slave." Jack was in charge of the many dogs Martin kept, as he was a marksman and avid hunter.[40]

Lieutenant Martin Scott and Captain Robert McCabe had been posted together at Fort Crawford, and in 1825, Lieutenant Henry Clark had joined the staff, all under the command of Lieutenant Colonel Willoughby Morgan. Willoughby traveled from posting to posting with two to three men whom he had enslaved since their youth. Martin Scott from Vermont, Robert McCabe from Pennsylvania, and Henry Clark from Connecticut witnessed Willoughby's enslavement of the Black men, as well as Mariah, who was still indentured to John W. Johnson. Robert and then Henry "rented" Mariah, and Martin acquired Jack, probably in St. Louis. Like Josiah Snelling, they had willingly chosen to participate in the system of slavery.

In 1827, Martin was transferred to Fort Snelling and traveled up the Mississippi River with Jack and his hunting dogs. Courtney must have met

Jack at this time, because Martin became a close friend of the Nathan Clark and Garland families. He often brought the bounty of his hunts to the families, contributing food to the meals Courtney prepared, and he taught young Malcolm Clark how to shoot. It is likely that Courtney and Jack encountered each other often.[41]

In 1828, another young graduate of the military academy arrived on the remote Mississippi frontier. At his first posting and then after he joined the social life in the Garland household, he too began to enslave Black people to do his bidding. Thomas Stockton was the last of thirteen children born to Charles and Elizabeth Stockton of Delaware County, New York. He entered West Point Academy in 1823 at the age of eighteen, received a second lieutenant's commission in the First Infantry, and was then ordered to Jefferson Barracks, Missouri.[42]

Thomas Stockton had spent his entire life in upstate New York. His uncle, Erastus Root, who publicly spoke in favor of the emancipation of Black people, had nominated Thomas to the US Military Academy. Thomas had not been raised with Black servants or enslaved people, and he must have known his uncle's position on slavery. In St. Louis, some Black men and women were free, but most Black people at Jefferson Barracks and in the city were enslaved. In the officers' barrack, Thomas saw Black men and women preparing and serving the officers' meals. Enslaved women cleaned the officers' quarters and washed their clothes. If Thomas purchased an enslaved Black person, he would not have to pay to have his clothes laundered. Walking on Market Street, Thomas would have seen the pens where enslavers held captive men, women, and children before selling them at various slave markets in the city. After observing other officers at Jefferson Barracks with servants and enslaved people, Thomas either bought or rented Jack, whom he described as "Black" and a "Boy."[43]

After a year at Jefferson Barracks, Thomas was ordered to Fort Snelling, arriving in August 1828. The fall of 1829 found him at Jefferson Barracks again, this time to await the arrival of presents and provisions destined for Fort Snelling. When they arrived, the goods and presents were placed on boats and Thomas proceeded with them up the Mississippi River. Thomas and the supplies reached Prairie du Chien. Though Thomas expected to continue northward, Major Stephen Watts Kearney, who was in charge of Fort Crawford, ordered Thomas to remain at that post. There too, he had

Colonel Thomas Bayliss Whitmarsh Stockton (1805–1890) graduated from the US Military Academy at West Point in 1827 and was posted to Fort Snelling. There, John Garland loaned Courtney to Stockton for several months. Then Stockton purchased Rachel in 1830 and enslaved her as his servant until 1834. In June of 1834, Stockton took Rachel to St. Louis and sold her to Joseph Klunk. HS11503, JOHN DEWEY PAPERS, BENTLEY HISTORICAL LIBRARY, UNIVERSITY OF MICHIGAN

to await the arrival of goods destined for Fort Snelling. While at Prairie du Chien, Thomas would have witnessed slavery in practice at military posts in the North as Jake or Andrew, the men Stephen Kearney enslaved, waited on Thomas and Stephen.[44]

The residents living along both sides of the Minnesota River welcomed Thomas's arrival, as he brought fresh provisions after a long winter. The opening of the river had also brought news to the post. Orders had reached Colonel Zachary Taylor that he was to move the command of the First Infantry from Fort Snelling to Fort Crawford.

Thomas Stockton had also welcomed his return to Fort Snelling. Like Martin Scott, Thomas had had many a glass of wine seated at the Garland table. Unlike Martin, Thomas had been enchanted by Harriet Garland's sister, Maria. Their courtship continued upon his return and reached a point where commitment was expected. Then Thomas received orders to travel down the Mississippi to the New Barracks under construction at Prairie du Chien.

John Garland, as an assistant quartermaster, had made trips to Jefferson Barracks and back and forth between Fort Snelling and Fort Crawford. When the US government decided to build new barracks at Fort Crawford, John assumed the quartermaster duties at Prairie du Chien, becoming responsible for ordering and maintaining all supplies needed for the construction of the post. He arrived at Prairie du Chien in October 1828. As John and the other troops had to occupy a portion of the old rotting barracks, John's family and Courtney remained in the stone cottage at Fort Snelling.[45]

In November 1829, John was promoted to major and permanently transferred to Prairie du Chien. But, as John continued to live in the old barracks, his family remained at Fort Snelling, as did Courtney. John, who still desired a servant, employed Martin Gregorich at this time.[46] Then, by December 1829, some of the men living in the old Fort Crawford moved into the completed north quarters of the New Barracks, and John must have been among them. That month, John claimed Courtney on his vouchers again, which suggests that Courtney and his family joined him on the prairie.[47]

With Major John Garland transferred to Prairie du Chien, Zachary Taylor appointed Thomas Stockton assistant adjutant for Fort Snelling. Thomas had valued having Jack present while he was at Jefferson Barracks, and with additional duties placed on him, Thomas approached Major Lawrence Taliaferro and asked to rent Horace from the major. On February 28, 1830, Thomas was not present at roll call, and Captain Gale reported Thomas as absent without leave on the March post return. There was no minister residing along the Minnesota River, and Thomas and Maria wished to marry, so they had slipped away to Prairie du Chien. On March 3, 1830, Reverend Rivers Cormack, a traveling Methodist minister, presided at the marriage of Lieutenant Thomas B. W. Stockton and Maria Smith.[48]

After Thomas's marriage to Maria, John offered to loan Courtney to Thomas. The Garlands may have considered it more appropriate for the Stocktons to have a woman servant in their household rather than just Horace. Courtney had been given to John soon after his marriage to Harriet Smith. Because Thomas was now part of the Garland family through his marriage to Maria, John did as his father had and "gave" Courtney to Thomas. From July through October 1830, Thomas claimed Courtney as his "servant" on his pay vouchers. John also claimed Courtney for the months of August and September, suggesting either that she worked for both families during those months or that John requested compensation for her pay during a time when she was serving someone else.[49]

By December 1830, enough of the New Barracks had been completed that the buildings could be occupied by the troops. With the transfer of Colonel Taylor and his command to Prairie du Chien, the New Barracks came to be called Fort Crawford. Quartermaster Garland ordered the remaining subsistence stores moved to the barracks, followed by "the baggage of the command." Living conditions at the new Fort Crawford, with barracks constructed from locally quarried limestone, provided much more comfort than the leaking and warped hewn-log structures at the old post. Based on John's rank and position as quartermaster, the Garland family were allocated the best housing in the north officers' barracks.[50]

Whether or not Courtney and Mariah had met at Fort Snelling, the two women could now grow a friendship at Prairie du Chien. When Mariah had been at Fort Snelling, she was already married to Jacob Faschnacht but was still indentured. Although enslaved and indentured women like Courtney and Mariah surely did not have much leisure time, they could, and did, establish bonds with one another. Tara Bynum's analysis of the friendship between Phillis Wheatley and Obour Tanner, two Black enslaved women living in New England in the late 1700s, proves this point. "That slaves had friendships with each other," Bynum writes, "presumes a kind of leisure that may be misconstrued as a moniker for 'happy slave' or a kind of normalcy that should not make sense in the midst of the horrors of enslavement. But here are two women [Wheatley and Tanner] who understand that their mutual fellowship is a friendship between one another and with God."[51]

When Courtney encountered Mariah at Prairie du Chien in 1830, she would have learned that Mariah had purchased her freedom just months earlier. And Mariah must have introduced Courtney to her friend and neighbor Helene Gagnier Galarneau and Helene's mother, Marianne, two more free Black women. For the first time since arriving in the upper Mississippi River Valley, Courtney met Black women who were free. Based on future events, it is clear that Mariah, Helene, and Marianne left a deep impression on young Courtney. But Courtney had little time to deepen her friendships with the women.

Major John Garland had not been well throughout the fall and winter of 1830–1831 and had postponed a furlough. In 1831, he received orders to report to duty at the nation's capital, Washington City, on the East Coast. The quartermaster general's office had received reports about how competently John had handled his duties as assistant quartermaster for the construction of the New Barracks at Prairie du Chien. John was therefore considered capable of greater responsibilities. Explaining he needed time to gain good health, John was allowed a short furlough. Then on March 14, 1832, John received orders from the War Department to report to the War Office in Washington City where he would assume charge of the Clothing Bureau.[52]

Courtney had been living at Prairie du Chien in service to John and his family for only a few months after the several months at the end of 1830 she spent waiting on the Stocktons. When John had received permission to go on furlough, he chose not to take Courtney with him. With this decision made, John had several options. He could give Courtney her freedom. He could change Courtney's status and allow her to become an indentured servant. As an indentured servant, she might have been able to purchase her freedom if she had the funds, as Mariah had done. Or John could sell Courtney to another person. He selected the last option.

It is not known whether John spread the news that he wished to sell Courtney or if he already knew someone who was interested in acquiring an enslaved woman for a servant, but he quickly found a buyer in Alexis Bailly.[53] No document recording the sale has been found, but there is an entry in one of Alexis's account books for 1831: "To Cash Paid Major John Garland: $450.00."[54] This amount was the going price for a young enslaved woman, and Colonel Josiah Snelling had paid four hundred dollars for Mary four years earlier. It is possible that this entry in Alexis's account book was made after purchasing Courtney.

Courtney, having been sold to a new owner, immediately traveled back to the Minnesota River with Alexis Bailly and his family, who lived across the river from Fort Snelling. Just around the time Courtney was sold to the Bailly family, she gave birth to a baby boy. Her pregnancy or the presence of a new baby may have influenced John Garland's decision to sell her. Either condition would have been an encumbrance on a trip to Washington City. And John would have known that another enslaved person could easily be purchased in the nation's capital, where slavery was legal.

Courtney named her baby boy Joseph after his father, Joseph Godfroy. Little is known of the elder Joseph. The younger Joseph later stated that his father was "a Canadian Frenchman." He may have been one of the young men recruited to work as voyageurs for the American Fur Company after

Sketch of Fort Snelling and the mouth of the Minnesota or St. Peter's River by Adolf Johann Hoeffler, 1852. In the foreground are the houses that constituted the small settlement of Mendota. These included the home of Alexis Bailly, where Courtney and her son Joseph were enslaved. WHI IMAGE ID 81527

the end of the War of 1812. In the Wisconsin census records of 1836, 1838, and 1842, a Joseph Godfroy lived at Prairie du Chien. In 1850, a Joseph Godfroy was working as a lumberman on the Chippewa River. He gave his age as forty, meaning he was born about 1810, so he and Courtney would have been the same age. Courtney and Joseph never married; perhaps they wished to but were not given permission. Their son Joseph later stated he had visited his father in Prairie du Chien in about 1855.[55] Joseph Godfrey (likely the same man with a differently spelled last name) had at some point returned to the prairie. He may have been the same Joseph Godfrey who died in 1879 and was buried in St. Gabriel's Cemetery in Prairie du Chien.[56]

Courtney served the Baillys for five years, living at New Hope, which is now called Mendota. She was a house servant and maid for Alexis's wife, Lucy Faribault Bailly.[57] Lucy had a temper and often took out her frustrations and anger on people over whom she had dominance. For example, Lucy wanted a young woman—one of the daughters of Philander Prescott, a white man from Ontario—to live with the Bailly family and help with the Bailly children. Philander was married to a Dakota woman, and he had served as a government interpreter to the Dakota at Fort Snelling. According to Philander, his daughter "had not been there only a short while before

Alexis C. Bailly (1798–1861), painted by Theophile Hamel in 1858. Alexis was born in Canada and migrated to the Mississippi Valley to engage in the fur trade. From 1823 to 1835, he traded for the American Fur Company. Alexis purchased Courtney from John Spotswood Garland in 1832. In 1836, he sold Courtney and her son William to Samuel Rayburn. Alexis continued to enslave Courtney's older son, Joseph. MINNESOTA HISTORICAL SOCIETY, PHOTO LAB

Lucy Anne Faribault Bailly (1808–1855) was the daughter of Jean Baptiste and Pelagie Faribault. In 1826, she married Alexis Bailly. Lucy was known for her bad temper and mistreatment of the servants and enslaved people in her household. MINNESOTA HISTORICAL SOCIETY, PHOTO LAB

she got a whipping. Mrs. B. was remarkably fond of whipping other people's children, so my wife took her daughter away."[58]

Courtney's son Joseph also raised Lucy's ire before he was even four years old. Philander recalled, "And whilst I am speaking about the whipping business—Mrs. Bailly had a little black child raised in the family and a young Sioux girl. These two children, I actually believe, would get from 25 to 50 lashes a day and sometimes more, every day almost. I frequently would leave the house to get away from the miserable crying of those children when she was cowhiding them."[59] That "little black child" may have been Joseph. As an older man, he confirmed Lucy's terrible mistreatment of him, recalling that "he had been beaten and abused."[60] As an enslaved person, Courtney would have been unable to protect her son.

During these years at Mendota, Alexis was the representative of the

American Fur Company. However, contrary to directives issued by Lawrence Taliaferro, Alexis sold liquor to the Dakota people and had been caught making these illicit sales. When Ramsey Crooks purchased John Jacob Astor's interests in the American Fur Company in the summer of 1834, Ramsey decided the company needed someone less controversial than Alexis to direct the outfit that operated among the Dakota. Ramsey chose Henry Sibley to replace Bailly. In the spring of 1835, Henry had a stone house built close to the Bailly home and either enslaved or employed Joe Robinson, a Black man, to cook and clean for him.[61]

With Alexis having lost his position, the Bailly family left Mendota and moved back to Prairie du Chien when spring arrived. Courtney accompanied them. Her son Joseph seems to have traveled with her, and Courtney also carried her infant baby boy, whom she had named William. He was about three months old.[62]

Arriving at the prairie, the family moved into a new house Alexis had commissioned James H. Lockwood to build in the fall of 1834. Lockwood had signed an agreement "to build and complete for the said Bailly a dwelling house and other out buildings." Payments were to be made in installments, the total being twenty-five hundred dollars. Alexis had already purchased from Lockwood a lot in the Village of St. Friole for $250. The dwelling house and other structures were to be erected on this lot. Upon arrival, Alexis decided he wanted more land, and Lockwood sold him a small piece south of the stable on Bailly's property.[63]

With the move to Prairie du Chien, Courtney finally had a neighbor who was like her in many ways: Patsey. Patsey lived with the family of Joseph M. Street, whose home was two lots south of the new Bailly home, as was the Indian agency building. With the proximity of the houses, Courtney and Patsey may have become friends. Like Courtney, Patsey was Black and enslaved. And like Courtney, Patsey had young sons; in 1835, James was seven, London was five, and Henry was two.[64]

For a few months, Courtney may have had a sense of community she had never before experienced. She met Patsey, and she reunited, once again, with Mariah. She came to learn more about Prairie du Chien, a vastly different community than all the other places she had lived. At Prairie du Chien, there were no plantations worked by many enslaved Black people, as there had been in her birthplace of Virginia. Prairie du Chien had a military post, but the prairie was also home to more than 450 people with no connection to the garrison, unlike Fort Snelling. Men who were engaged in the fur trade, such as Alexis Bailly, Jean Baptiste, and Alexander Faribault, lived at Prairie du Chien, but the community was larger than the three or four houses that stood at Mendota. A variety of people lived, worked, and socialized at Prairie du Chien. The community encompassed three villages with many houses, and the rest of the prairie was farmed by the residents; it was not a wilderness. Also, there were many Black people living at Prairie du Chien. And the vast majority of the Black people not associated with Fort Crawford and the War Department were free.

Mariah and Patsey knew the prairie and the people who lived there, and Mariah, if not also Patsey, taught Courtney what she knew. Courtney already knew the story of how Mariah had gained her freedom. But in 1835, Courtney would have learned from Patsey that, though she was still indentured, her children lived with her and knew their father and were going to learn a trade. A hope may have grown in Courtney that at Prairie du Chien she, too, could gain her freedom or at least manage to keep her sons with her. But that was not to be.

Courtney had lived just about four months at Prairie du Chien when Alexis Bailly decided to sell her. In October 1835, Alexis took Courtney down the Mississippi River to St. Louis, where he sold her and her seven-month-old son William to Samuel S. Rayburn.[65] Young Joseph remained with the Bailly family and would remain enslaved by them until he escaped at the age of seventeen to live among the Dakota. In the control of yet another strange man, Courtney would have despaired for her future and that of William. But perhaps she shared some of Harriet Jacobs's sentiments as she prepared for herself and her son to be sold by her enslaver to a plantation owner: "I had a woman's pride, and a mother's love for my children; and I resolved that out of the darkness of this hour a brighter dawn should rise for them. My master had power and law on his side; I had a determined will. There is might in each."[66] Indeed, Courtney's future was about to be dramatically changed for the better, thanks in part to this move to St. Louis where enslaved people could petition for their freedom and thanks in part to the similar efforts of a woman she had never met: Rachel.

CHAPTER 5

RACHEL, 1814–1834

R achel arrived at Prairie du Chien in October 1832, just a little more than a year after Courtney had been sold to Alexis and Lucy Bailly and relocated to Mendota. Very little is known about Rachel's early life. Unfortunately, no census record or documentation has been found from which to ascertain her place of birth. We do know, however, that she was in St. Louis in 1830 when she was purchased by Lieutenant Thomas B. W. Stockton.

After their marriage at Prairie du Chien in March 1830, Thomas and Maria Stockton had returned to Fort Snelling to begin their married life. Major John Garland, Maria's brother-in-law, had loaned Courtney to the Stocktons between July and October of 1830. When Thomas returned Courtney to John so she could serve the Garland family at Prairie du Chien, the Stocktons considered all the tasks Courtney had performed. Faced with the prospect of living with no domestic help, the couple decided to purchase an enslaved person to do their household work, especially as Maria was pregnant with their first child.

In the fall of 1830, Thomas called upon Elias T. Langham Jr., who was employed in the Fort Snelling Indian agency with Major Lawrence Taliaferro, to request a favor. Before the Mississippi iced over for the winter and water travel ceased, Elias planned to travel to St. Louis. Several slave markets existed in St. Louis, so Thomas asked Elias to purchase an enslaved person on his behalf. This person would work in the Stockton household, as Courtney had. Thomas suggested that once Elias arrived in St. Louis, he should contact Lieutenant Joshua B. Brant, who knew where and how to purchase an enslaved person.[1]

Both John Garland and Thomas Stockton, who held positions in the quartermaster's department, knew Joshua Brant, who had once been an assistant quartermaster. Joshua had since been promoted to the position of military disbursing agent in the Indian Department. In that role, he was responsible for acquiring and dispensing the goods requested not only by the military posts but also by the Indian agencies located near the posts on the upper Mississippi River. Owing to his connections and the fact that two enslaved men and an enslaved woman were part of his household, Joshua knew how to buy and sell adults and children just as he knew the best methods to procure material goods such as flour and beef. It is possible that Joshua had previously located and purchased enslaved people for other US Army officers.

In St. Louis in 1830, there were several avenues through which Joshua could purchase a young woman to work for Thomas Stockton. He could acquire her through a private purchase. Alternatively, he could make a purchase through the auction house of Savage and Bostwick, where Colonel Josiah Snelling had purchased a woman and child in 1827. This firm sold household goods and various commodities in addition to regularly conducting the auctions of enslaved people. Joshua could also visit the "slave pens" located in buildings along the main thoroughfares of St. Louis. Also, auctions of enslaved people were held about once a week on the steps of the St. Louis courthouse, as part of the auctions of the estates of deceased enslavers. Though it is not known exactly how Joshua fulfilled Thomas's request, he did purchase a young mixed-race woman for the lieutenant. The woman's name was Rachel. That same fall, Elias took Rachel with him when he returned to Fort Snelling.[2]

Elias and Rachel probably arrived at Fort Snelling in about mid-October. Fort Snelling, near today's cities of Minneapolis and St. Paul, was one of the northernmost posts maintained by the US Army, and Rachel disembarked from the steamboat to stand on a dock across which northwest winds blew. At Fort Snelling, her new home, Rachel would experience extreme cold and watch snow fall in a northern wilderness far different from urban St. Louis, Missouri.

Prairie du Chien had become the headquarters of the First Infantry by this time, so the officers posted to Fort Snelling rarely exceeded eight men, including the post surgeon. Only a captain commanded the post instead of a colonel, as at Fort Crawford, so Fort Snelling offered a small society in which to socialize. In addition, the residents who lived across the Minnesota River from the fort were rarely included in any social activities involving Fort Snelling's officers, Lawrence Taliaferro, his subagent Elias T. Langham Jr., and the post sutler. This small community across the river included Alexis and Lucy Bailly, who enslaved Courtney. Lawrence did not like Alexis and regularly accused him of selling liquor to the Dakota. So, because of their geographical separation and the social divisions between their enslavers, Courtney and Rachel may never have met, though they lived within shouting distance of each other.

Rachel, upon her arrival at Fort Snelling, was likely given a place to sleep within the quarters occupied by Thomas and Maria Stockton. Thomas was only a second lieutenant, and owing to the hierarchy that existed in the military, the Stocktons' quarters in the post officers' barracks were less pleasant than the rooms occupied by the officers of higher rank. Also, none of the officers' quarters had the comforts of the house that John and Harriet Garland had occupied outside the fort walls. The quarters assigned to Thomas were small and far from the center of the post. The Stocktons' apartment included a sitting room and a bedroom on the main level and a basement kitchen below the two rooms. This lower level was accessed by an exterior staircase. Rachel likely slept in the basement kitchen, close to the fireplace. In the basement, Rachel prepared meals for the family from the rations and other delicacies Thomas purchased at the sutler's store. Anytime Maria Stockton required Rachel's attendance or when Rachel brought the food she had prepared up to the Stocktons' table, she had to negotiate the exterior stairs and the occasional exposure to wind, rain, and snow.

In these new surroundings, Rachel surely met some of the enslaved men who worked for the officers, but as had been true for Courtney, Rachel had scant opportunity to meet other women servants at Fort Snelling. One exception may have been Eliza, whom Courtney also knew. Eliza was serving Lawrence Taliaferro in 1831. Lawrence had married Elizabeth Dillion in 1828 and brought his new wife to Fort Snelling. Upon his marriage, Lawrence may have taken one of the enslaved women from his family's plantation and brought her to the upper Mississippi to join Eliza. But on the whole, Rachel probably experienced a lonely life at Fort Snelling. At least in St. Louis, Rachel had had people like herself with whom she could have passed an evening after work was done or seen at Sunday church services in friendship.

Their shared status likely brought Rachel and Eliza, and Rachel and the other enslaved men and women at Fort Snelling, together. But any relationships Rachel may have established did not last long. After a certain length of stay at a frontier post, officers were granted furloughs. On August 2, 1831, Thomas Stockton received permission for a sixty-day furlough. He and Maria left the post, taking Rachel with them to care for their infant daughter, Harriet Abigail. It is not known where they traveled. Since Thomas and Maria had met and married while Thomas was stationed at Fort Snelling, they may have traveled to New York to visit his sister and her family. In 1817, the New York legislature had passed a law that would free all enslaved people by 1827. Consequently, if Thomas had brought Rachel to New York with a plan to live in the state, her status as a slave would have been illegal. But Thomas did not plan to live in New York State; he was only passing through. Rachel, therefore, according to New York State's laws, would have remained legally enslaved, even in a "free" state.

While on furlough, Thomas received orders from the adjutant general's office that he was to report to the office in Washington City. Rachel once again prepared the family and herself for travel. Rachel and the Stockton family remained in the nation's capital, where Maria gave birth to another child, Baylis Garland. According to his orders, Thomas was to return to Fort Snelling in February. When he did not return to the post, Captain Gale reported Thomas as away without official leave. Unknown to the captain, the adjutant general's department had ordered Thomas on detached service and placed him on duty at the quartermaster's office in Washington. It can be assumed that Rachel continued to serve Thomas and his family while he was stationed in Washington.[3]

After six to seven months at this posting, Thomas received orders to return to Michigan Territory. Once again, Captain Gale reported on the Fort Snelling post returns that Thomas was not at Fort Snelling; this time, however, Thomas was not listed as AWOL but rather as away on detached service. New orders required him to report to Colonel Zachary Taylor at Fort Crawford in Prairie du Chien. Presumably, during Thomas's time in Washington working in the Department of the Quartermaster General, he

THE UNITED STATES *Dr. to* 2nd *Lieut. T. B. W. Stockton A. Qr. M.*

ON WHAT ACCOUNT.	COMMENCEMENT AND EXPIRATION.		TERM OF SERVICE.		PAY PER MONTH.		AMOUNT.	
	FROM	TO	MONTHS.	DAYS.	DOLLARS.	CENTS.	DOLLARS.	CENTS.
PAY, for myself, ...	1st Novmbr 1832	31st Octr 1832	2	4	45	00	90	00
For private Servant not Soldier	do	do	do	do	2		5	00	10	00
FORAGE,								
For Horses (two) . . .	do	do	do	do	2	"	16		32	00
CLOTHING.								
For private Servant not Soldier	do	do	do	do	2		2	50	5	00
SUBSISTENCE,								

	No. of Days.	No. of Rations per day.	Total Number of Rations.	Post or Place where Due.	Price of Rations. Cents.		
For myself	41	3	183	Fort Crawford	20	36	60
For private Servant not Soldier	41	1	41	"	20	12	20

DOLLARS. 185 80

Description of Servants.

NAME.	COMPLEXION.	HEIGHT.		EYES.	HAIR.
		Feet.	Inches.		
Rachel	Black	5	5	Black	

I HEREBY CERTIFY, that the foregoing account is accurate and just; that I ha in kind, or received money in lieu of any part thereof, for any part of the time therei the horse and private servant for the whole of the time charged, and that I did no employ as waiter or servant soldier from the line of the army; that the annexed is period charged for my staff appointment, I actually and legally held the appointment, the double ration post charged for; and that no officer within my knowledge has a rig the period charged; that I was actually in command of my company; that I claim no ged; *that I am not in arrears with the* UNITED STATES, *on any account what*
Major Thos. Wright   Paymaster, Army of the United S
I AT THE SAME TIME ACKNOWLEDGE, That I have received of May & I M

Detail from pay voucher filed by 2nd Lieutenant T. B. W. Stockton on December 31, 1832, claiming subsistence and clothing for Rachel. Though she was enslaved by Stockton, she was listed as a "private servant." NATIONAL ARCHIVES AND RECORDS ADMINISTRATION

received training and experience in management and purchasing in preparation for his new assignment. Thomas had gained some experience when he assumed the duties of assistant quartermaster for Fort Snelling from his brother-in-law Captain John Garland. But Thomas would need greater knowledge for the responsibility he was about to undertake. Once he arrived at Prairie du Chien, Thomas assumed the duties of assistant quartermaster for Fort Crawford.[4]

—⊣⊢—

When Rachel arrived at Prairie du Chien in October 1832, the Stockton family included two infants. The post barracks were still under construction. The south officers' barracks had not yet been completed, as Colonel Zachary Taylor explained, "owing to the recent Indian [Black Hawk] War." We can presume that Stockton and his family found quarters in the north

Fort Crawford on Mississippi River at Mouth of Wisconsin River, painted in 1842. In the foreground is a skiff in which are seated Charles McDougall, post surgeon, and his orderly. PRAIRIE DU CHIEN HISTORICAL SOCIETY

officers' barracks, perhaps the same apartment in which the Garland family had lived as Thomas had replaced John as quartermaster.[5]

The new Fort Crawford had been planned as a rectangle. The east and west company barracks, each 170 feet long, composed two sides of the rectangle. A range of officers' barracks would compose the other two sides. Each building was constructed of locally quarried limestone, thirty feet deep and thirty feet high, two stories tall, with an attic space under the roof. The roofs were peaked and sloped, with each building's roof covering a piazza that connected all the quarters and rooms within each structure. Kitchens were located in the basement rooms. The men of each company had to prepare their meals and eat in mess, but each officer's apartment had its own kitchen with a fireplace for cooking meals. And the kitchen floor was paved with brick. As at Fort Snelling, servants and enslaved people worked in the kitchen spaces. Unlike at Fort Snelling, the stairs leading from the basements to the main floors had been constructed within each apartment. The thirty-by-eighteen-foot living spaces were relatively small, each including a main room, a bedroom, and a stairway to the basement.

At Fort Crawford, each officers' barracks had six apartments. Married officers had apartments to themselves, and unmarried officers shared quarters. As at Fort Snelling, the Fort Crawford barracks were constructed on raised ground. The front of the barracks faced the parade ground, and a covered, open piazza joined all the quarters within one structure. The basement rooms were partially below ground level. Each set of barracks, both officers' and company, had a full basement, and a door opened from each basement room onto the surrounding prairie.

In the 1830s, Fort Crawford had almost twice the number of officers as Fort Snelling. Therefore, Fort Crawford had a more a lively social scene. At Prairie du Chien, unlike at Fort Snelling, there resided several families who would be considered socially acceptable society to the officers. Joseph M. Street, the subagent Thomas P. Burnett, Reverend Alfred Brunson, Reverend David Lowry, attorney James Lockwood, justice Joseph Brisbois, and trader Joseph Rolette, along with all of their wives, would have been invited to social functions organized by the officers. They may have even received invitations to dine at the commanding officer's house.

The commanding officer at Fort Crawford did not live in the barracks of the post. When Zachary was ordered to take command of the "New Barracks," no accommodations existed for the commanding officer of the post. However, James Lockwood had built a house in the Village of St. Friole, which lay just north of the land purchased for the new post. James offered to sell his house to the US government, and his offer was accepted. The former Lockwood home became the Fort Crawford commanding officer's house. It stood between the post's barracks and the US Indian Agency house occupied by the Street family. Zachary regularly entertained the officers and their wives at his dining table. Rachel and the other Black people enslaved by officers may have assisted Jane, a woman enslaved by Zachary, in the preparation and serving of the dinners.[6]

The officers at Fort Crawford in the 1830s formed a closely knit community. As they were all part of the First Regiment of Infantry, many had served together at other posts and several had attended the US Military Academy in West Point, New York, at the same time. As Charles Fenno Hoffman, an American author and editor who visited the post in February

Fort Crawford's commanding officer's house, photographed by John Carbutt in 1863. The house stood north of the post barracks. COURTESY OF MARY ELISE ANTOINE

1834, stated, "The officers' families do indeed make a small circle." To pass the boring winter months, he wrote, they sometimes went into the Main Village and "amuse[d] themselves in getting up what is called a gumbo ball," which was described, not in a complimentary fashion, as a "harlequinade," because the ball included people of Canadian and American Indian heritage. Hoffman also wrote that the officers believed themselves to be men of superior quality and maintained "a great many high-bred dogs," which they used when they hunted, bringing back grouse, snipe, ducks, elk, and bear for their servants to clean and prepare.[7]

The visitor described the officers as well-read and educated gentleman. At the north end of the east barracks, the room above the basement prison cells had been designated a library and stocked by the officers. Some left books there after being transferred to another post. Willoughby Morgan, who commanded the first and second iterations of Fort Crawford several times, traveled with a personal library of more than 175 volumes. He read Greek and Latin, studied Napoleon and the art of war, and perhaps learned from the *Book of Common Prayer*. He also enslaved three men, who moved with him until they gained their freedom in 1833 as a result of Morgan's death the previous year.[8] Rachel may have met the men when she lived at Fort Snelling.

The officers created their own entertainment by transforming one of the vacant officers' apartments into a theater. Plays, such as *Who Wants a Guinea?* and Henry Fielding's *Don Quixote in England*, were primarily enacted for the garrison's own amusement, with the officers playing all the roles. Sometimes they invited the public. When that occurred, the officers printed playbills and had them distributed around the Prairie du Chien community. Seating at the performances open to the public depended on one's position in the community, explained Hoffman: "The seats, rising like the pit of a theatre, were so adjusted as to separate the audience into three divisions: the officers with their families furnished one, the soldiers another, and 'gumbos [French Canadians],' Indians, and a negro servant or two made up the third."[9]

By 1834, the south range of officers' barracks was completed, and with additional space to accommodate more men, the population of the garrison, free and enslaved, increased. The post was given two new assignments. Some soldiers were to be tasked with the construction of the western section of the military road that would connect Forts Crawford, Winnebago, and Howard. Other men would be placed under the direction of officers handling the forced removal of the Ho-Chunk to the Neutral Grounds and the construction of a school primarily intended for the assimilation of Ho-Chunk children to the United States' Protestant culture. More officers arrived at Fort Crawford to oversee these duties, and they took up quarters in the south barracks, housing the people they enslaved in the quarters.

As a captain, Thomas Gwynne commandeered the corner room. Then Lieutenants Wilson, Hill, Beall, Pegram, Harris, and LaMotte chose their apartments. These officers' servants and enslaved people may have resided in the attics or in the basement kitchens. The kitchens were heated by large fireplaces, so the rooms would have had warmth, but the kitchens also had rats.[10]

Unlike at Fort Snelling, where a few officers held many enslaved people, there were many officers at Fort Crawford, mostly lieutenants, and many of them each held one enslaved person. No one at the prairie post had great pool of servants, enslaved or free, as Lawrence Taliaferro did at

Fort Crawford's south officers' barracks, 1872. The hospital is located behind the barracks.
MINNESOTA HISTORICAL SOCIETY

Fort Snelling. Colonel Morgan enslaved three men, and when Colonel Taylor was at the post, a woman and man or two men from his plantation worked at the house reserved for the commanding officer. Because no one kept a large number of enslaved people at the post, the officers at Fort Crawford rarely rented enslaved people from one another. Each person listed as a servant on an officer's pay voucher was bound to that officer. The lieutenants and captains claimed only one person at a time on their paymaster reports.

Beginning with the arrival of Major Stephen Watts Kearney and Colonel Zachary Taylor, almost every officer stationed at Fort Crawford claimed a servant on his pay voucher at some time during his residency on the prairie, but the legal status of those listed as servants is difficult to determine. During the years that Rachel was held at Fort Crawford, from September 1832 through May 1834, according to extant pay vouchers, at least thirty-three officers submitted claims for maintaining servants. Aside from three servants who were described by their employers as either fair or white, all other officers described their servants as having complexions that were variously described as Black, dark, or yellow. A few of the officers described their servants as slaves.[11] Soon after her arrival at the prairie,

DESCRIPTION OF SERVANT.					
NAME.	Complexion.	HEIGTH.		Eyes.	Hair.
		Ft.	Inches.		
Wilkins	*Dark*	5	"	*Dark* *Dark*	
	My own Slave				

Detail from a pay voucher filed by Captain William R. Jouett on April 30, 1834, at Fort Crawford, in which he claimed subsistence and clothing for Wilkins, whom Jouett described as "My Own Slave." NATIONAL ARCHIVES AND RECORDS ADMINISTRATION

Rachel came to know some of the other Black men and women in service to the officers at Fort Crawford.

During the nearly two years that Rachel lived at Prairie du Chien, the Fort Crawford post returns listed the same officers month after month as "on station," with only an occasional variation. Rachel, therefore, likely met and came to know the men and women toiling in the same capacity as she. With seemingly no compunctions, some of the officers described the person for whom they claimed pay, clothing, and rations as a "Slave."[12]

Catherine was enslaved by Captain Jefferson Vail. Wiley and then Lucy were enslaved by Lieutenant Thomas P. Gwynne. Gwynne gave Lieutenant Thomas M. Hill the use of Lucy when he went on furlough in June 1834, and he claimed her once again when he returned to Fort Crawford. Captain William R. Jouett enslaved Wilkins and then, two years later, a new man named Moses. Polly was enslaved by Captain Samuel McKee, who later owned a man named William. Assistant Surgeon Robert C. Wood enslaved a man named Glasco who was owned by Colonel Zachary Taylor, Surgeon Wood's father-in-law. Brevet Second Lieutenant George H. Pegram enslaved Critty. Lieutenant G. W. Garry enslaved Abel. Captain Thomas Floyd Smith, in the course of his four-year posting, claimed pay and subsistence for multiple enslaved people: Eugene, Elomese, Ata, Horace, and Hetty. As no other officer claimed any of these men or women, they may have come on a rotating basis from Smith's home in Virginia. Stephen was enslaved by Lieutenant William L. Harris for the entire duration of Harris's posting at Prairie du Chien from August 1827 through October 1836. He must have been known by not just Rachel but also Courtney. Lieutenant Ingham Wood enslaved Abram. Charles was enslaved by Lieutenant E. A. Ogden.[13]

Additionally, a few men served many different officers during the course of Rachel's time at Fort Crawford, such as Charles, who was listed as a "Slave" and waited upon the wants of Lieutenants Beall, Covington, Dimon, Gale, Ogden, and Wilson.[14]

In April 1833, Lucy's enslaver, Lieutenant Thomas Hill, who would be given use of Lucy by Lieutenant Gwynne in 1834, signed an indenture with the mother of a five-year-old girl. Uk-see-har-kar, a Ho-Chunk woman, signed the agreement indenturing her daughter, Mary Ann Mitchel, to Thomas. According to the agreement, Mary Ann was to serve Thomas as an apprentice and obey "all his lawful commands" until she was eighteen. Thomas, in turn, agreed to teach Mary Ann "the arts of domestic industry and housewifery according to the improvements of civilized life . . . [and] give her good and sufficient meat, drink, washing, lodging, etc suitable to her condition." When Mary Ann turned eighteen, Thomas agreed to give her "a decent new suit of clothes and $25 in money."[15]

The pay vouchers document that other Black men and women worked for officers stationed at Fort Crawford during the years Rachel lived there, but those officers may have been reticent to state the status of the men and women they claimed on their pay vouchers. They may have been enslaved, indentured, or free. Demas worked for J. J. Abercrombie, a lieutenant and post adjutant. Lieutenant Lloyd Beall claimed Kritty, who may have been the same person whom Second Lieutenant Pegram listed as "Critty" on a voucher ten months later. Barker, and later Marcie, served Lieutenant J. Randolph B. Gardenier. Nicodemus worked for Captain R. B. Mason. Etheldred served Lieutenant George Wilson. Alexie served Lieutenant Joseph H. Pawling. And John worked for Lieutenant James Kingsbury.[16]

While Rachel was held at Prairie du Chien, she met John. A Black man who was five feet and six inches tall, John served Lieutenant James Wilkinson Kingsbury from September 1832 to March 1833. While Kingsbury did not describe John as a slave, Lieutenant Stockton did claim a Black man named John who was five-foot-six on his pay vouchers during the same time Stockton held Rachel. Because of the height description, he was probably the same man. It is also possible that this is the same John who, after Rachel found herself in St. Louis, would play an extremely important role in her life.

—⟶‖⟵—

On March 4, 1833, Thomas W. B. Stockton was promoted to first lieutenant—a cause for celebration in the Stockton family. But with the promotion came new responsibilities.

Thirteen years earlier, on May 15, 1820, Congress had authorized a massive extension of the Cumberland or National Road, hoping to extend the turnpike to St. Louis. Work had begun when, on March 3, 1825, Congress appropriated additional funding to build the road across the Mississippi and from St. Louis to Jefferson City, Missouri. Work on the extension between Wheeling, Virginia, and Zanesville, Ohio, was completed in 1833, leading to the new state capital of Columbus. Because Thomas had skills as a surveyor, he was ordered on extended duty to survey the route that would stretch from Columbus to Springfield, Ohio.

In the summer of 1833, anticipating that he would often be away from Fort Crawford, Thomas sent his family east. Rachel remained at Prairie du Chien and continued to serve Thomas. It was during the summer of 1833 that Rachel became pregnant. Rachel never identified the father of her son, whom she named James Henry.[17]

James Henry was born in early 1834. Rachel, about twenty years old, now had the shared responsibilities of waiting on Thomas and caring for her newborn son. If James Henry had been born on a plantation, his presence would have added to the assets owned by that enslaver, and James Henry would have become part of the enslaved population. On a plantation, there may have been older enslaved adults (either real or chosen kin) or older children who could have taken care of the baby while his mother worked. But at this military post, Rachel had no one to help her. Judging by a letter Thomas Stockton wrote to the quartermaster general Thomas Jesup, Stockton had moved to unmarried officers' quarters when Maria and the children had left Prairie du Chien. With Stockton and at least one other officer sharing the crowded two-room quarters, Rachel's new baby likely seemed to Stockton an inconvenience.[18]

After consideration, Thomas Stockton applied to Captain Jefferson Vail, the commanding officer at Fort Crawford, for a one-month furlough to travel to St. Louis. Thomas planned to sell Rachel and James Henry.[19]

Thomas received permission for the furlough, and Rachel, likely anxious and possibly expecting that Thomas would soon return her to St. Louis, prepared for the journey, packing what little she owned and any necessities for James Henry. The three boarded a steamboat on May 29, bound for St. Louis. At their destination, they disembarked. Thomas set about finding a means by which to sell Rachel and James Henry.

In addition to Savage and Bostwick, the slave market that would have been a place for Major Brant to purchase Rachel for Lieutenant Stockton, various other slave markets operated in St. Louis in the 1830s. Thomas may have gone to Savage and Bostwick to sell Rachel and her son, or he may have decided to have Rachel sold at one of the other slave markets that operated on various street corners. By whatever means, Thomas found a buyer for Rachel and James Henry in Joseph Klunk. On June 18, 1834, Joseph signed the paperwork making official his purchase of "Rachel & child. Slaves for life."[20] Joseph, who had been born in Germany, was twenty-two years old.

After having accomplished his purpose in St. Louis, Thomas boarded a steamboat bound for Prairie du Chien. By June 25, he had returned to his temporary duties at Fort Crawford.[21] In his decision to remove Rachel and James Henry from his household by selling them, Thomas was actively choosing to uphold and profit from slavery.

In the fall of 1834, Thomas requested permission to travel to Washington City. He had acquired land in Michigan, which was about to become a state, and he needed to ensure that his claim would be honored by Congress, requiring him to leave at "the utmost moment." Thomas received permission to present his claim and traveled to the capital. While there, he acquired an enslaved person named Janus. Janus traveled with Thomas and served him at Fort Crawford, remaining there as Thomas traveled between the post and Ohio to work on the Cumberland Road. While posted in Columbus, Ohio, and surveying for the National Road, Thomas claimed first Robert and then E. Smith on his pay vouchers. In neither instance did Thomas divulge the legal status of these two Black

Receipt stating that Thomas Stockton gave Joseph Klunk a bill of sale for the purchase of Rachel, dated June 18, 1834. MISSOURI PROBATE COURT, ST. LOUIS

men. By the end of 1836, Thomas had had enough of military life and resigned from the US Army.[22]

In the summer of 1834, Rachel found herself back in St. Louis, Missouri, exactly where she had been five years earlier and in a similar position: sold to an unknown white man, looking at an uncertain future. In the years since Rachel had left St. Louis, the city had doubled in population to more than thirty thousand people. The residents were a mix of white and Black men, women, and children. The population referred to as "coloured" on census records included enslaved and free Black and mixed-race people. Some of these free Black individuals were wealthy citizens. Added to the mix were many newly arrived immigrants from Germany for whom English was a second language.

Life for urban enslaved people was much less isolated than the life lived by enslaved people on plantations and in rural agricultural areas. As elsewhere, many people in St. Louis treated Sunday as a day of rest, and the opportunity to rest was sometimes extended to enslaved people. With their owners' permission, some enslaved people in the city could attend church. By 1827, the First African Baptist Church of St. Louis had been founded by John Berry Meachum, a free Black resident of Missouri. At this church, free and enslaved Black people could worship together. After services, they gathered, exchanged news and gossip, and listened to free, educated Black men read from newspapers. Many of the free Black men in St. Louis owned barber emporiums, where wealthy white men gathered. Many of the free Black women were seamstresses or laundresses, paid by white women for their skills. The Black community was generally well informed about local, regional, state, and national events through the sharing of gossip and newspapers, but also partly because white people spoke freely in front of (though not usually to) Black people. For this reason, the Black community also knew more about the white community than whites knew about the Black community. And life in a city offered a myriad of opportunities for information to be exchanged.[23]

Though owned by Joseph Klunk, Rachel was once again part of St. Louis's Black community, and she likely soon learned about the city's residents and happenings. What, if anything, Rachel did under Joseph's ownership is unknown. Joseph may have been working for William Walker, a well-known buyer and seller of enslaved people, for within a short time, Joseph sold Rachel and James Henry to Walker. By October 1, Rachel and James Henry were in Walker's possession.[24]

Among enslaved people, Walker was known as a "soul driver." For eight to nine weeks at a time, Walker would travel around St. Louis and the countryside purchasing enslaved individuals. He owned a farm just beyond the city line, and as he purchased enslaved people, he brought them to his farm. William Wells Brown, an enslaved man who had been hired out to Walker as a hand to take care of the people Walker purchased, described the house on the farm as a "domestic jail." Walker confined the men, women, and children to the house at night and forced them to work on his farm during the day. As Brown stated in his *Narrative*, "They were kept here until the gang was completed."[25]

As a small boy, William Wells Brown, along with his mother and siblings, had been brought to Missouri by his enslaver, a Dr. Young. In time, Dr. Young sold all the members of William's family, but he hired out William to various men who lived in St. Louis, including William Walker. Brown described the year he spent working for Walker as the "longest year I ever lived."[26] Brown lived in St. Louis for eight years, being hired out to other men after he left Walker. By 1834, the year Rachel and James Henry were sold to William Walker, Brown had left St. Louis and escaped to freedom.

When Walker had acquired what he felt to be enough enslaved people, he bound them in chains and herded them from his farm to St. Louis. Arriving in the city with a full "gang," Walker forced the captives to march to the levee, where they waited for a steamboat that would be traveling down the Mississippi to Natchez and then on to New Orleans. When the steamboat arrived, Walker made arrangements to have the enslaved people transported

Sketch of William Walker published in *My Southern Home: or, The South and Its People*, written by William Wells Brown, published in 1880. COURTESY OF THE LIBRARY COMPANY OF PHILADELPHIA

and then forced them onboard. Brown stated, "A drove of slaves on a Southern steamboat, bound for the cotton or sugar regions, is an occurrence so common, that no one, not even the passengers, appear to notice it, though they clank their chains at every step." The enslaved people were kept in a large room on the lower deck of the steamboat, all chained in pairs, and a white person was continually posted as a watch to ensure no one could escape. Brown remembered, "It was almost impossible to keep that part of the boat clean." Walker unloaded enslaved individuals at various ports along the Mississippi River, including Vicksburg, Natchez, and New Orleans, surely separating some people who had created bonds of friendship and support. Upon arrival, Walker compelled the slaves off of the boat and marched them to the city's "slave pen" where potential buyers could observe them.[27]

When the steamboat stopped at a port, it stayed at dock for several days. During these layovers, Walker stayed in each city's best hotel, and the enslaved people remained in the "slave pen" for viewing. At the hotel, Walker kept good wines in his room for the entertainment of the men who called upon him to negotiate the purchase of enslaved people. Brown recalled that Walker and the people he enslaved stayed at a port for one week, and then the people who had not been sold were driven onto another steamboat that would proceed down the river. New Orleans was the last stop.

Upon arrival at New Orleans, Walker forced the enslaved people into what William Wells Brown described as a "negro-pen, where those who wished to purchase a slave could call and examine them. The negro-pen [was] a small yard, surrounded by buildings, from fifteen to twenty feet wide, with the exception of a large gate with iron bars." At night, Walker and other enslavers would lock the enslaved people in the buildings. Since New Orleans was the end of the journey, those who had not been sold by Walker were led to the Exchange Coffee-House Auction Rooms and sold at public auction. The people sold at auction at the end of the trip often worked in the cotton or sugarcane fields until they died.[28]

Not all enslaved people sold "down river" were purchased to labor on plantations. Some enslavers were looking for "fancy maids": typically light-skinned Black or mixed-race women who were considered young, attractive, and adept at domestic service. They were subject to sexual violence at the hands of the men who purchased them in what was called the "fancy trade." Fancy maids were the only class of enslaved women who sold for higher prices than skilled men.[29]

In his *Narrative*, William Wells Brown wrote of a Black woman he knew named Cynthia, whom he described as a quadroon, a person who is one-quarter Black by descent, and "one of the most beautiful women I ever saw." Walker had purchased Cynthia to be sold at New Orleans but promised her that if she would "accept his vile proposals," he would take her back to St. Louis and establish her as "his mistress and housekeeper at his farm." Cynthia acquiesced and had four children by Walker. When Walker decided to marry, Brown recalled, he sold Cynthia and her children "into hopeless bondage."[30]

In *Slave Life in Georgia*, John Brown recorded his experiences in Freeman's slave pen in New Orleans in the 1830s, about the time Rachel was held enslaved by William Walker. John stated that enslaved people were brought to New Orleans "from all parts." "The men, the women, and the children of both sexes divided off all alike," he wrote. "In consequence of this arrangement, the various members of a family were of necessity separated, and would often see the last of one another in that dreadful show-room. . . . The youngest and handsomest females were set apart as the concubines of the masters, who generally changed mistresses every week." In his memoir, John Brown refused to detail "the dreadful fate which awaits the young slave women who are sold away South, where the slave-pen is only another name for a brothel."[31]

Rachel and her son James Henry were now held captive by William Walker, who planned to take them to New Orleans and sell them "down river."[32] Whether they would stay together or not depended on who purchased Rachel. If someone bought her to work in a house, James Henry may have gone with her, and Rachel may have been able to care for him until he was old enough to undertake tasks. On the other hand, if Rachel was purchased to be a field hand or a "fancy maid," James Henry might be taken from her immediately and sold to someone else.

Josiah Henson recalled his mother's grief when she was sold and separated from him in his 1858 autobiography, *Truth Stranger than Fiction*:

> My brothers and sisters were bid off first, and one by one, while my mother, paralyzed by grief, held me by the hand. Her turn came, and she was bought by Isaac Riley of Montgomery county. Then I was offered to the assembled purchasers. My mother, half distracted with the thought of parting forever from all her children, pushed through the crowd while the bidding for me was going on, to the spot where Riley was standing. She fell at his feet and clung to his knees, entreating him in tones that a mother only could command to buy her baby as well as herself.

Riley ignored her and disengaged "himself from her with such violent blows and kicks as to reduce her to the necessity of creeping out of his reach. . . . As she crawled away from the brutal man I heard her sob out, 'Oh, Lord Jesus, how long, how long shall I suffer this way!'"[33]

In the possession of William Walker, Rachel now faced a bleak future—separation from James Henry and a lifetime of enslavement until death. However, Rachel's current residence in Missouri, even before it had become a state in 1821, provided a means by which she—a person held in wrongful servitude—could file a petition and begin a suit for freedom.

CHAPTER 6

SUING FOR FREEDOM, 1834–1836

Having previously lived in St. Louis, Rachel must have heard of enslaved Black men and women who had filed suits for freedom in St. Louis Circuit Court, even before she had been sold to Lieutenant Thomas Stockton. While held by William Walker at his farm, Rachel was probably privy to discussions about Missouri's laws and the opportunities for escaping from slavery, which included fleeing to Illinois as well as suing for freedom in Missouri. Often, captives in a slave pen were required to run errands as part of their labor. An enslaved person on an errand for his or her enslaver might have the chance to approach a lawyer or a court clerk to begin a freedom suit.[1]

The narrative *From Darkness Cometh the Light; or, Struggles for Freedom*, written by Lucy Delaney, who sued for her freedom in 1842, suggests that enslaved people often learned about the existence of freedom suits from people who had gained their freedom or people who knew someone who was free. The person who informed Rachel of the legal means by which she could gain freedom for herself and James Henry may have been the man named John who would testify on her behalf.[2]

The John who helped Rachel may also have been the same man who worked for Lieutenant James Wilkinson Kingsbury. Kingsbury graduated from the US Military Academy and, after a couple of short postings, was assigned to the military posts of the upper Mississippi. How and when Kingsbury acquired John is not known. However, we do know that John served Kingsbury at Fort Snelling and Fort Crawford at the same time that Rachel was enslaved by Stockton at these posts. In 1833, Kingsbury became an assistant commissary in subsistence and was transferred to St. Louis.

John then became enslaved to Lieutenant Thomas Stockton, living at Fort Crawford at the same time Thomas held Rachel. When John testified on Rachel's behalf, he stated that he had known her for five or six years and offered details of her life and treatment by her enslavers at Prairie du Chien. He was listed on court documents as a "colored man" and not a "slave," which suggests that he was a free man. If so, by some means he had gained his freedom.[3] John may have been the person who explained to Rachel how she could obtain freedom for herself and her son.

In St. Louis, the first suit for freedom had been filed in 1806, and by 1834, when Rachel returned to the city, 102 petitions for freedom had been filed. Some of the suits had been filed against very prominent St. Louis families, so in the Black community, it would have been discussed in detail as to how, for example, Aspasia had gained her freedom from François Chouteau and Pierre Menard and how Winny and her children became free of Ephraim Musick. The majority of these freedom suits were based on the petitioner's prior residency in a free territory.[4] Only about one-third of the people who had attempted to gain their freedom had been successful. Filing suit for one's freedom was a risk; a positive outcome was not guaranteed.

The 1807 territorial statute, followed by an act enabling persons held in slavery to sue for freedom passed by the Missouri legislature in 1824, delineated the specific procedures for filing suits for freedom. First, a petitioner needed to file a petition in the circuit court explaining the circumstances of their preliminary argument for freedom. Then the petitioner awaited the court's response. If the petition contained sufficient evidence that the petitioner was being wrongfully held, the judge ordered that the petitioner be allowed to sue. The court then assigned an attorney to work for the person suing for freedom. Missouri law allowed enslaved people to sue as "poor persons." If the judge agreed that the person was "poor," court fees would be covered by the state. And if the judge determined that the enslaved person could bring suit as a poor person, the judge would order that the petitioner have liberty to attend to counsel and court and that the petitioner not be removed from the jurisdiction of the court or subjected to any severe punishment because of the freedom suit.[5]

The 1824 statute also stated that if the court found there were sufficient grounds for a person to sue for freedom, the court could then "direct an action of assault and battery and false imprisonment, to be instituted in the name of the person claiming freedom against the person who claims the petitioner as a slave." Most suits for freedom filed in Missouri were trespass cases, which could include assault and battery, or false imprisonment claims.[6]

Suing for freedom brought enormous risks for the person filing the suit, and deciding whether or not to file required careful consideration. If the court granted the petitioner his or her freedom, a new life would open up for the formerly enslaved person. But throughout the duration of the suit, the petitioner could be separated from family and friends. If the petitioner lost the suit, the individual would remain the property of the enslaver he or she had sued and would also become liable for the costs associated with the suit. In these cases, enslaved people could expect violent reprisals from their enslavers, including being sold "down river," a fate many petitioners attempted to prevent by suing for their freedom in the first place.[7]

An enslaved person could petition the court for freedom for one of four reasons:

- If one had been granted freedom by a former enslaver, but that freedom was not given

- If one had been held as an enslaved person and resided for a period of time in a state or territory where slavery was not allowed

- If one was free and had papers to prove one's freedom but was illegally returned to slavery

- If one had descended in the maternal line from a free woman of color

After making the decision to file suit, petitioners hoped the court would take their grievance seriously. White people dominated the legal system, and justices could capitulate to the power, position, and wealth of enslavers. The institution of slavery denied enslaved people many of their basic freedoms and aided enslavers in controlling and regaining their enslaved "property." But the laws that existed in Missouri also protected

enslaved people in some circumstances, such as the law that allowed enslaved individuals to sue for their freedom.[8]

Faced with the choice between a suit that could lead to freedom and the
likely separation from James Henry that would result if she did nothing,
Rachel chose to sue for freedom for James Henry and herself. Her argument
would be based on her having been held for more than two years as an
enslaved person in Michigan Territory, a territory in which slavery was
illegal. Rachel could not write and may not have been able to read, but by
some means or connections, she engaged the services of Josiah Spalding,
who prepared a petition for freedom for herself and James Henry.

To petition the court for her freedom, Rachel first had to prove to the
court that she was poor. Josiah submitted Rachel's petition to the judge
of the St. Louis Circuit Court, and it was filed on November 4, 1834. In
the petition, Rachel stated her case: that she was a "mulatto woman, about
twenty years of age" and that "about five years ago she was claimed and
possessed as a Slave by one Stockton." The petition explained that Thomas
Stockton "took the petitioner to Michigan Territory, first to Fort Snelling
and then resided at Prairie du Chien about two years [and] . . . held her
as a slave during that time . . . using her to work for & serve himself &
family at that place." After the birth of James Henry in Prairie du Chien,
Thomas brought Rachel "to St. Louis [and] sold her and her child to Joseph
Klunk . . . who has recently sold her and her child to William Walker, a
dealer in slaves . . . who is about to take her and her child down the Mississippi River for sale, claiming her as his slave." In the petition, Rachel
also requested that Walker be restrained from taking her and her child
out of the jurisdiction of the St. Louis Circuit Court. Rachel signed her
petition with an X.[9]

To support Rachel's petition, Josiah found a witness to testify on
Rachel's behalf. Either Josiah came in contact with John, or John learned
of Rachel's petition and contacted Josiah. John swore testimony to Daniel
Hough, a justice of the peace for St. Louis County, that he knew Rachel and
had known her for about five or six years. John also swore that he knew
Thomas Stockton had held Rachel in slavery "for more than one year" at
Prairie du Chien. In addition, John said he had seen Rachel at Prairie du
Chien while Thomas enslaved her. John continued his testimony by cor-
roborating everything Rachel had stated in her petition. Like Rachel, John

Rachel's petition, submitted to the judge of the St. Louis Circuit Court on November 4, 1834, requested that she be allowed to sue as a "poor person . . . for freedom & that the said Walker may be restrained from carrying her or said child out of the Jurisdiction."

CIRCUIT COURT RECORDS, UNIVERSITY LIBRARIES, WASHINGTON UNIVERSITY IN ST. LOUIS

Luke E. Lawless was justice of the St. Louis Circuit Court. Rachel and Courtney presented their suits for freedom in his courtroom. Lawless presided over several other suits for freedom and the grand jury that refused to indict the men who lynched Francis McIntosh in 1836. COURTESY OF THE MISSOURI HISTORICAL SOCIETY, ST. LOUIS

signed his testimony with an X. John's testimony was placed in evidence with Rachel's petition.[10]

The court accepted Rachel and James Henry's petition and decided that Rachel and James Henry had "sufficient matter to authorize the commencement of suits for freedom." There were to be two suits: one presented on behalf of Rachel and the second presented on behalf of James Henry. Justice Luke E. Lawless ordered that "they be permitted to sue as poor persons to establish their freedom." The justice then assigned Josiah Spalding Esq. as their counsel. As Rachel was still enslaved, and in accordance with the 1824 law, the judge also ordered that Rachel "have reasonable liberty to attend counsel and the Court when the occasion may require; & that said Rachel and James Henry shall not nor *shall* either of them be taken or removed out of the jurisdiction of the St. Louis Circuit Court, nor be subject to any severity because of their application for freedom."[11]

The Missouri statute required that freedom suits be brought to court as assault cases. Therefore, nearly every freedom suit filed in the St. Louis Circuit Court described an act of violence by the enslaver upon the person seeking freedom. In one case, the enslaved plaintiff stated that she had been "treated with great cruelty and severity and oppression" because of filing suit for her freedom.[12] Enslavers used violence to keep enslaved people subjected to their rule. So, while no instance was recorded of an enslaver taking the person suing for freedom out of the court's jurisdiction, violence against the petitioner did occur.

The majority of defendants in freedom suits did not deny the accusations of assault and violence leveled against them. When the court issued a summons for William Walker to appear and respond to the allegations made by Rachel, William responded through his attorney, who said he "defends the force and injury and says that he is not guilty of the said supposed wrongs and injuries above laid to his charge."[13]

Rachel's lawyer, Josiah Spalding, had relocated from Connecticut to St. Louis during the winter of 1819–1820. He had graduated from Yale University and then tutored at Columbia University as he studied law. For four years, Josiah had been the editor of the *Missouri Republican*. After resigning from the position in 1826, he practiced law full time. He was primarily known as a commercial lawyer, but he also filed suits for freedom. Because the court had determined that Rachel was a "poor person," the court would pay Josiah's fees to represent Rachel and James Henry. With the petition granted to sue for freedom as poor persons, Rachel's and James Henry's suits began.

The Missouri statute required that the action taken in the suit be an action of assault and battery, trespass, and/or false imprisonment. It went on to require that "the declaration shall be in the common form of a declaration for false imprisonment, and shall contain an averment, that the plaintiff, before and at the time of the committing of the grievances, was, and still is, a free person, and that the defendant held, and still holds, him in slavery."[14]

Josiah presented two separate complaints against William Walker. Rachel's complaint stated that on October 1, 1834, William "with force of arms &c" assaulted Rachel and that he "did beat & bruise & ill treat & strike & also then and there did imprison the said plaintiff & kept & detained her in confinement & restrained her liberty without any reasonable cause." Rachel averred that at the time this occurred, she was a free person. Josiah argued that William's actions were contrary to the laws of the State of Missouri. Rachel therefore requested five hundred dollars in damages.[15]

At the same time Rachel's petition was filed, Josiah filed a petition for James Henry, whom Josiah described on the court document as "a mulatto." On behalf of James Henry, Rachel, and those helping to prepare the petition, requested to file for his freedom and entered a charge of trespass against William Walker. The same charges made by Rachel were made on behalf of James Henry. Josiah claimed that at the time the charges occurred, James Henry was held in slavery but by right of law was free. Since

Portion of the complaint of James Henry against William Walker for a plea of trespass, submitted to the St. Louis Circuit Court for the November 1834 term. CIRCUIT COURT RECORDS, UNIVERSITY LIBRARIES, WASHINGTON UNIVERSITY IN ST. LOUIS

the suit *Rachel v. Walker* stated that Rachel was free based upon her residence in free territory, it would follow that James Henry, her son, was free as well, not only based on the law of matrilineally inherited enslavement, but also because he had been born in a free territory. On behalf of the plaintiff, the petition contained a request for two hundred dollars in damages. The judge approved James Henry's petition.[16]

Judge Lawless then issued a summons for William Walker to appear and answer to the charges made by Rachel and James Henry. Served with the summons, William retained H. R. Gamble as his counsel. The suits were set to be presented and argued in front of Lawless at the March 1835 term of the circuit court. That left four months for Rachel to await a determination on her and her son's freedom.

There is no information as to where Rachel and James Henry, still under a year old, awaited the date for their trial. Before Rachel filed her suit for freedom, Joseph Klunk's property and William Walker's farm were the only places she and James Henry had slept since Thomas Stockton had sold them. The petitioner could stay with the person who held them enslaved, but that person, who was the defendant in the case, could be dishonorable and attempt to sell the petitioner. Thus, the section of the statute stating that the petitioner "shall not be taken nor removed out of the jurisdiction of the courts, nor be subjected to any severity" because of

St. Louis City Jail, located at the corner of Sixth and Chestnut Streets, 1850. COURTESY OF
THE MISSOURI HISTORICAL SOCIETY, ST. LOUIS

the suit was an attempt by the court to keep the petitioner from harm,
though there is no evidence it was enforced.[17]

When deciding whether to initiate a freedom suit, an enslaved person
also had to consider how their protection would be secured in the lead-up
to a trial. The court understood this concern and therefore could order
that the petitioner be placed in jail for "safekeeping." This order was intended to protect petitioners from enslavers who might sell them or refuse
to feed or clothe them.

If Rachel and James Henry spent the months from November 1834 to
March 1835 in the St. Louis jail, they did not live in comfort. A February
1834 report found that the conditions of the jail "greatly jeopardized" the
health and safekeeping of the prisoners. The grand jury investigating the
jail recommended that a new building be constructed, adding that any
repairs made to the existing structure would be "a waste of public money."
The cells were only eight-foot square with ten-foot ceilings. Receipts for
board included in freedom suit records suggest that the enslaved petitioners housed in the jail received a low standard of care.[18]

The St. Louis County sheriff received funding to pay for the inmates living in the jail. In 1835, when Rachel and James Henry may have lived at the jail, Missouri law listed the sheriff's fee as 37.5 cents per day for "furnishing a prisoner with board." The 37.5 cents included the sheriff's pay and the jailer's pay, in addition to food and clothing for the inmate.

Also, an enslaved person who had been placed in the jail for safekeeping could legally be hired out by the sheriff. Since a petitioner in a freedom suit had been determined poor by a judge, the petitioner could be hired out to the highest bidder to help cover the cost of the suit. The petitioner would be led to the courthouse steps—the same steps on which an enslaved person could be sold to a new enslaver—and the sheriff would conduct an auction of the petitioner's labor. When the sheriff hired out an enslaved petitioner, the court required that the sheriff collect a bond from the hirer. The bond was to guarantee the safety of the petitioner, so that the hirer would not mistreat the petitioner or remove the petitioner from the court's jurisdiction. On the one hand, there was no guarantee that the bond would prevent mistreatment, and any wages earned by the petitioner were paid to the sheriff. But on the other hand, it must have been extremely unpleasant to spend day after day in a dark, poorly ventilated cell. Neither situation was desirable.[19]

It is not known whether Rachel knew people in St. Louis other than John, who may or may not have been free. If she had no connections where she could live while awaiting trial, it is possible that Rachel and James Henry were placed in the St. Louis jail during the months before their suit. Rachel may have then requested that she be hired out. In St. Louis, Rachel could have been hired out for domestic service in a private home or to work as a laundress, kitchen laborer, or cleaner in a hotel or other business. She could have lived on the property of the person who hired her or returned to the jail at night. Any wages earned and paid to the enslaved plaintiffs could offset costs owed to the sheriff.

When the appointed date arrived for the March 1835 term of the court to begin, Rachel walked to the St. Louis courthouse with James Henry in her arms. Perhaps they came alone, or maybe they were escorted by a sheriff's deputy or Josiah Spalding. We cannot know what Rachel was thinking as she walked up the courthouse steps. Perhaps Rachel herself had stood,

St. Louis Courthouse, 1850. The first St. Louis courthouse was built in 1828 and greatly enlarged in 1839 with four wings and a three-story cupola. The east wing, on the left, included the original courthouse. Slave auctions were held on the steps of the east wing until 1861. COURTESY OF THE MISSOURI HISTORICAL SOCIETY, ST. LOUIS

bound, upon these steps in 1830, as Elias T. Langham waited in the crowd and placed his bid for a young woman to serve Thomas Stockton.

It is possible that Rachel shared some of the same feelings as Lucy Ann Delaney, who mounted those steps in 1844 in hopes of gaining her freedom. Lucy later described her feelings in her autobiography, which was published sometime in the 1890s: "A bright, sunny day, a day which the happy and care-free would drink in with a keen sense of enjoyment. But my heart was full of bitterness; I could see only gloom which seemed to deepen and gather closer to me as I neared the courtroom. . . . I could not see one gleam of brightness in my future, as I was hurried on to hear my fate decided."[20]

As Rachel entered the courtroom, she would have seen William Walker and his attorney, Hamilton R. Gamble. When the case was called, William testified in response to Rachel's petition that he was "not guilty of the said supposed wrong, and injuries above laid to be his charge." He denied the charges brought against him by Rachel and James Henry.[21]

With William having made his plea, the judge ordered the cases to be continued at the next session of the circuit court scheduled for the end of July 1835. In preparation, the sheriff was ordered to summon Elias T. Langham Jr. and Frederick Ortley (former post sutler at Fort Snelling) to appear before the court in July "to testify and the truth to say in a certain matter of controversy now pending in said court" in *Rachel, a woman of color v. Walker, William* and *James Henry, a boy of color v. Walker, William*.[22] Rachel and James Henry were then returned to the jail or wherever they were living.

When the court reconvened on July 28, 1835, neither Elias nor Frederick appeared. The presiding justice therefore again ordered James Brotherton, sheriff of St. Louis County, to serve a summons for Elias and Frederick to appear in court during the November 1835 term. Court then convened on November 17, 1835. When once again neither Elias nor Frederick made an appearance, the case was continued until the March 1836 term.[23]

Elias, who was now employed as a government surveyor in Illinois and Missouri, and Frederick did not respond to the second summons, which the sheriff himself had read to them. And they again did not appear on March 23, 1836. The court had had enough of Elias's arrogance. The court ordered Sheriff Brotherton "to attach Elias T. Langham by his body and safely keep, so that you may have his body before the Judge of Circuit Court . . . to testify and the truth to say."[24]

Rachel had now climbed the steps of the St. Louis courthouse three times and presented herself and James Henry before the court with her counsel. Each time, because Elias and Frederick had refused to obey the summons, Rachel and James Henry had walked back down the steps not knowing whether they would be declared free or not, their long wait extended once more.

The following day, March 24, Sheriff Brotherton "had the body of Elias T. Langham in court." Faced with no other choice, Elias stood before the court and swore to tell the truth. He was to testify on behalf of Rachel. Elias stated that in the fall of 1830, he was residing near the mouth of the St. Peter's River and came to St. Louis. Lieutenant Thomas Stockton sent Elias to Major Joshua Brant to purchase an enslaved person on Thomas's behalf. Elias then purchased Rachel "for the said Stockton" and took her to Fort Snelling, "where Stockton held her as a Slave" until the fall of 1831. Thomas removed to Fort Crawford taking "the said Rachel with him as his Slave." There, Thomas "held her in slavery until the spring of the year 1834 until he took her to St. Louis." Elias stated that while Thomas was at the two posts, he was there as an officer in the US Army. During that time, Elias said, "Rachel was only employed in attendance upon said Stockton and his family."[25]

Elias may have been avoiding the summons while attempting to contact Thomas, who could have given him advice about what to say to the court. The purchase of an enslaved person had been Thomas's idea, and perhaps Elias did not want to face the court and be judged as the person who had acquired Rachel. Elias therefore may have been hoping for Thomas's testimony to back up his actions. And he may have initially had difficulty locating Thomas because of his work on the construction of the National Road. Then in November 1835, Thomas resigned his position as assistant quartermaster for Fort Crawford. He left Prairie du Chien to return to his family in Michigan, where they made their home.[26]

Thomas finally responded to the appeal from Elias in a written response, which may have been delayed because of the difficulty of travel during the winter months. Elias presented Thomas's letter to the court on March 24, 1836, and it was read into evidence. In the letter, Thomas stated, "Rachel the girl who has now sued for her freedom was purchased of Major Brant by my direction." He related that Rachel had lived at Fort Snelling and had been taken with his family when he went on furlough in the spring of 1832. She was with him and the family in Washington City and then accompanied them to Fort Crawford. He stated that he had remained at Fort Crawford "until June 1834 the period at which I sold Rachel, having taken her with me to St. Louis, Missouri for that purpose." He agreed that her son had been born at Prairie du Chien "sometime in the spring or summer of 1834." Then he offered a justification for his ownership of Rachel and James Henry, writing, "During all the time I owned her & her child I was an officer of the United States Army, stationed at those different posts by order of the proper authority. Rachel was never employed otherwise than as my very private servant and immediate attendance upon my family.[27]

Thomas also argued that Fort Snelling was "on the west side of the Mississippi River & north of Missouri" and therefore not part of the territory of the United States governed by the Northwest Ordinance.[28]

The court had also subpoenaed Elias T. Langham Jr. in the case of *James Henry v. Walker*. In James Henry's case, Elias repeated the statement he had made regarding the purchase of Rachel for Thomas. Thomas's written statement presented in *Rachel v. Walker* was again read into evidence in *James Henry v. Walker*. For James Henry, the court then concluded "it was further proved that the plaintiff James Henry is the same child, that was born of said Rachel at Prairie du Chien, while she was held a slave by said Stockton, as stated in Stockton's letter."[29]

After William Walker had been served with a notice in November 1834 of the charges against him, he went to Josiah Spalding's office, and Josiah transcribed what William said to him. Josiah read William's statement into the court record on March 24, 1836. William had told Josiah that he believed that he should not have been sued. He had purchased Rachel from Joseph Klunk and taken her to his farm. He claimed he did not know there was a claim for freedom. William claimed that as soon as he was served with the notice to attend court, he went to Joseph and canceled the sale. While Joseph returned the down payment, William said he had never received a receipt from Joseph to prove the deal.[30]

Listening to Thomas's letter and then William's testimony, Rachel may have been filled with conflicting emotions. Perhaps she felt similarly to Lucy Delaney, who described her enslaver's actions at her trial in detail:

> For one hour, he talked so bitterly against me and against my being
> in possession of my liberty that I was trembling, as if with ague, for
> I certainly thought everybody must believe him; indeed I almost be-
> lieved the dreadful things he said, myself, and as I listened I closed
> my eyes with sickening dread, for I could just see myself floating
> down the river, and my heart-throbs seemed to be the throbs of the

mighty engine which propelled me from my mother and freedom forever![31]

Rachel and especially Josiah may have realized that in Elias's and Thomas's testimony two arguments were presented, and their interpretation would determine the decisions in Rachel's and James Henry's suits for freedom.

When Elias's testimony and reading of Thomas's letter was presented, the document noted that the "Court sitting as a Jury" heard the testimony. All the freedom suits filed in Missouri were jury trials. And other freedom suit records indicate that after attorneys for each party presented their case, the attorneys requested that the judge give particular instructions to the jury: either points of law, specific arguments presented in the testimony, or other factors. Justices had great discretion as to the instructions they gave to juries. Without so stating, the instructions could reflect the justice's opinion and thereby influence the jury.[32]

Judge Lawless had now heard the testimony in *Rachel v. Walker*. He would base his instructions to the jury on arguments and decisions in previous suits for freedom with which he was familiar, including those filed in Missouri as well as in other states. And one particular suit that had occurred sixteen years earlier influenced his thinking: *Rankin v. Lydia, a pauper*, an 1820 case heard by the Kentucky Court of Appeals. Lydia had sued for and been granted her freedom in *Lydia v. Rankin*. She had resided in Indiana Territory for a number of years and then had been taken to Kentucky, where she was enslaved. To attempt to prove that Lydia was not free, John W. Rankin filed suit to regain Lydia. John's lawyer questioned whether Lydia had been a resident of Indiana or a "sojourner." He argued

that if the [Northwest] ordinance could give freedom at all, it could and would do it in a moment when the slave touched the enchanted shore, and that consequence would be, that the slave of the traveler who attended his master; the slave of the officer who marched in the late armies of the United States; those sent of errands to the opposite shores; or attending their masters while removing beyond the Mississippi through the territory, would all have an equal right to freedom with Lydia; and that, by a decision in her favor, the right of such property would be much jeopardized.[33]

The court found in John Rankin's favor. Lydia had been born enslaved to John Warrick in Kentucky. He left Kentucky to settle in Indiana, where he held Lydia and then sold her. After being sold again, she returned to live in Kentucky. Therefore, the court claimed she had never been a permanent resident of Indiana, but simply a "sojourner" in the state. A person enslaved by a traveler or an officer in the military who had lived for a time in the Northwest Territory was not necessarily free if their enslaver could prove that they were a visitor to, rather than a resident of, the territory.

After all testimony had been presented in *Rachel v. Walker*, Judge Lawless used the decision in *Rankin v. Lydia* to pointedly instruct the jury hearing Rachel's suit:

> If said Stockton was an officer of the army of the United States while he held the plaintiff in slavery stationed at Fort Snelling and Fort Crawford by the proper authority; and if he employed the plaintiff during that time only in personal attendance on himself and family, that such residence of the plaintiff at those places as has been proved, does not entitle her to her freedom.

The judge's instruction encouraged the St. Louis jury to interpret the law as sanctioning Thomas's decision to keep Rachel enslaved during their time in the Northwest Territory because he and his family were considered "sojourners" in the territory. With testimony presented and instructions given, the court took a short recess and then made its ruling.

Rachel had lived for almost four combined years in the Northwest Territory and in Michigan Territory, where slavery was not legal. Yet, the court determined she was not free because she had been in the employ of a US Army officer during that time and had only been a "private servant and in immediate attendance" on Thomas's family. The jury unanimously decided that Rachel and James Henry were the property of William Walker, who could do with them as he wished.[34]

As soon as the verdict was read, Rachel's counsel, Josiah Spalding, requested that the court set aside its decision and grant a new trial "because

the finding of the issues by the court is against laws & against evidence."
The court overruled the motion.

With the St. Louis Circuit Court having reached a decision, two options
existed for Rachel. She could consent to herself and James Henry being
returned to William Walker as his property, or she could continue the
pursuit of her freedom through a higher court.

When courts did not grant new trials to lawyers who requested them
as Josiah had for Rachel, Missouri law allowed the court's decision to be
stayed with a bill of exemption presented to the Supreme Court of the
Third District. If Rachel chose to make an appeal, in the appeal she could
request that the circuit court's decision be overturned and then present
legal precedent to support the argument. Josiah needed to file the appeal
within the time allowed by the court, but he would need to consult with
Rachel first. Would she be willing to appeal the decision or accept that she
and James Henry were the property of William Walker?

This was Rachel's last chance for freedom. She had nothing more to lose.
Rachel decided to attempt an appeal of the circuit court's decision. Josiah
filed a response stating that he found exemption to the judge's refusal to
grant a new trial. He requested that the court sign Rachel's bill of exemption
and remove the case to the supreme court. Judge Lawless signed the bill.[35]
If the supreme court chose to hear Rachel's case, the court would meet and
decide the future of Rachel and James Henry at the July term.

While waiting to learn if the supreme court would hear her case, Rachel
and James Henry were returned to their living quarters, wherever they
were located. Josiah, however, had another suit for freedom that he needed
to prepare to present before Judge Lawless. Between the November 1835
and March 1836 terms of the circuit court, as he had prepared to argue
Rachel's and James Henry's cases, Josiah had also been retained as counsel
in another case of a young Black woman seeking freedom for herself and
her young son. Before Josiah wrote the appeal to the supreme court for
Rachel's case, he needed to represent his client in *Courtney, a woman of color
v. Rayburn, Samuel.*

—||—

Courtney had lived at Prairie du Chien for just four months when Alexis
Bailly decided to sell her. Alexis, using the same method Thomas Stockton

Charles D. Drake practiced law in St. Louis from 1834 to 1847. Drake represented Courtney in her suit for freedom for herself and her son William, heard in the March 1836 term of the St. Louis Circuit Court. Drake later assisted in Dred and Harriet Scott's suit for freedom. BRADY-HANDY PHOTOGRAPH COLLECTION, LIBRARY OF CONGRESS, PRINTS AND PHOTOGRAPHS DIVISION

had used to sell Rachel in 1834, took Courtney down the Mississippi River to St. Louis. Once they arrived, Alexis sold Courtney and her seven-month-old son William to Samuel S. Rayburn.[36]

As Rachel had done just a year earlier, Courtney looked at her future and that of her son, William. Rayburn was not a slave driver like William Walker, so her immediate concern may not have been the prospect of being sold "down the river." But Courtney had been born into slavery, been enslaved by two men and rented out to another, and she wanted to be free. How she learned that residing in Missouri offered her a means by which to gain her freedom cannot be determined. She may have heard people discussing freedom suits, or someone who knew of Rachel's suit and the similarity between Rachel and Courtney's situations may have suggested that Courtney seek a lawyer to begin a suit for freedom. In any case, the lawyer who agreed to help Courtney was Charles Daniel Drake. Charles had just arrived in St. Louis from Cincinnati and was newly admitted to the bar. Though he was not an abolitionist, Charles did consider slavery "a sore evil and a vast misfortune for the country, and was ready to help its removal by proper means."[37]

Almost exactly one year after Rachel filed her petition for freedom as a poor person, Charles filed a petition for Courtney to sue for her own and her son William's freedom as a poor person. Charles submitted her petition to the same justice who had heard Rachel's petition, Luke E. Lawless. In her petition, Courtney stated that she was about twenty-three years old and had been born in Virginia. She explained that at a "quite young" age, she was sold by a man named Garland to his brother Major John Garland, taken to Detroit, "kept there in slavery as nearly as she can recollect for two years," then taken to Fort Howard on Green Bay, "where she was kept some time, but how long she does not remember, still held in service by Major Garland." Then she was taken to Prairie du Chien, "where she was kept about five years in the family of Major Garland." At Prairie du Chien, John Garland sold her to Alexis Bailly. Alexis took her to the "St. Peter's River," a name used in the eighteenth and the first half of the nineteenth centuries to encompass the mouth of the Minnesota River; the settlement of Mendota, where Bailly and Sibley lived; and the Fort Snelling military tract. Courtney lived there for five years. Then, about four months before Courtney's petition was filed, Alexis took her to Prairie du Chien. During this entire time, she had been held in slavery. Finally, Alexis took her to St. Louis and sold her to Samuel S. Rayburn "as a slave." In addition to Courtney, Alexis sold to Samuel "an infant child of hers, a boy, about seven months old, named William, who was born at St. Peters."[38]

As had been similarly stated in Rachel's petition, Courtney considered herself and her child "to be legally entitled to their freedom." Courtney concluded her petition with the request to "sue as a poor person for her freedom." Justice Lawless granted Courtney's request to bring a suit for freedom and sue as a poor person. Lawless appointed Charles Drake as attorney for Courtney and William.[39]

Courtney's case was placed on the docket for the March 1836 term, and a summons was issued for Samuel Rayburn to appear in court at that time to answer Courtney on her charges.[40] Justice Lawless had adjourned Rachel's petition until the same term, so he would hear both petitions within the same session of his court.

Rayburn was a successful St. Louis businessman. Like Joseph M. Street, he had been born in Montgomery County, Virginia. He left Virginia to explore business possibilities in the newly admitted states. He relocated to Bedford County, Tennessee, purchased a partnership in the Cumberland Iron Works, became involved in banking, and married. He purchased an enslaved Black woman, whom he and his wife held and forced to do their household chores. In 1833, Samuel moved to St. Louis to manage an outlet

To the Hon Luke E. Lawless Judge of the
Circuit Court of St Louis County.

Your petitioner, Courtney, a woman
of color, about twenty three years of
age, respectfully represents, that she
was born in the State of Virginia and
belonged to a man named Garland; that
when quite young she was sold by him
to his brother Major John Garland of
the United States Army, who took
her to Detroit in Michigan; that
she was kept there in slavery as nearly
as she can recollect about two years;
that from there she was taken by
Major Garland, to Green Bay, she believes to Fort Howard on Green Bay in
Michigan Territory, where she was kept
some time, but how long she does not
remember, still held in service by Major
Garland; that from there she was taken
to Prairie du Chien in Michigan Territory, where she was kept about five
years in the family of Major Garland;
that about five years since she was
sold by Major Garland to Mr Alexis
Bay at Prairie du Chien; that she
lived with Mr Bay about five years
at St Peters on the Mississippi River;
that somewhere about four months
since Mr Bay removed to Prairie du
Chien and brought her with him,
and that she has been there with

On November 2, 1835, Courtney filed a petition in front of Justice Luke E. Lawless requesting she be allowed to sue as a poor person for her freedom and that of her son
based upon her residency in the upper Mississippi River Valley. CIRCUIT COURT RECORDS,
UNIVERSITY LIBRARIES, WASHINGTON UNIVERSITY IN ST. LOUIS

since until a short time ago, when she was brought by him to the city of St Louis, and there sold by him to Mr Samuel S. Rayburn as a slave, and that said Rayburn now holds her in custody as a slave.

Your petitioner also represents that the said Alexi Bay at the time of selling her sold also to the said Samuel S. Rayburn, an infant child of hers, a boy, about seven months old, named William, who was born at St Peters, while she was there in the service of Mr Bay.

Your petitioner further states that she believes herself and her child to be legally entitled to their freedom; and she therefore prays that she may be permitted to sue as a poor person for her freedom and that of her son, and that your honor will make such other & further order in the premises as will secure to her, her legal rights.

                              Courtney her mark X

State of Missouri } ss
County of St Louis } Before me Wilson Primm a justice of the peace within & for the county aforesaid personally came Courtney a woman of color, who being sworn on her oath says that the facts stated in the above petition are true.   Courtney her mark X

Sworn to & subscribed before me this 2d Nov. 1835   Wilson Primm J. P.

for the sale of products from the iron works. He then founded Bridge, Rayburn & Company, which manufactured plows and other implements. Samuel was then appointed a director of the State Bank of Missouri.[41] He probably purchased Courtney in 1835 to supply the labor needed for entertaining clientele. By 1840, Samuel enslaved four people.[42]

On March 24, 1836, soon after the court had made its decision in *Rachel v. Walker*, denying Rachel's suit for freedom, the court clerk called the court into session for *Courtney v. Rayburn*. Acting on behalf of the plaintiff, Charles presented Courtney's charges against Samuel: trespass, assault and battery, and false imprisonment. She averred that "with force and arms and assault he [Samuel Rayburn] did make," and that he did "beat, wound, and ill treat" her. Charles also stated that Samuel "did imprison without any lawful or probable cause whatever kept & detained her in prison there from the day last aforesaid [October 1, 1835] to this day." Courtney therefore sued Samuel for five hundred dollars in damages as well as freedom for William and herself.[43]

Counsel for the defendant then presented Samuel's rebuttal. Samuel had retained Josiah Spalding as his attorney. For a year and a half, Josiah had appeared before the court representing Rachel in her suit for freedom. Now, he stood as counsel arguing against the same position that he had argued for in *Rachel v. Walker*. Josiah stated that Samuel was not guilty of the charges presented by Courtney.[44]

While it is impossible to know exactly what Josiah Spalding was thinking as he stood to represent the enslaver Samuel Rayburn the same day he had the enslaved Rachel and James Henry, he seems to have avoided letting his personal politics affect his work. If he had been proslavery, Josiah might have accepted the verdict that Rachel and James Henry were not free. But in response to the verdict, Josiah questioned the legality of the court's decision, fulfilling his duty as a lawyer. Josiah was known to have spoken publicly against slavery, but he also believed in the tenets of the American Colonization Society, which argued that all African Americans should be sent back to Africa. In fact, he was an officer within the St. Louis chapter of the Society. After the trials of William Walker and Samuel Rayburn, Josiah would go on to represent twice as many enslavers in freedom suits than plaintiffs.[45]

Samuel, with Josiah as his counsel, stated he was "not guilty of the said trespass nor any of therein in said declaration mentioned in manner & form."[46] With the petition and response placed before Judge Lawless, both Courtney and Samuel placed themselves before the court for a decision.

Earlier that day, the judge had determined that Rachel and James Henry were not free on the basis of Thomas Stockton's position as an officer in the US Army and the fact that he had employed Rachel only for his personal use. Josiah had protested the decision, and Lawless had given Josiah an appropriate amount of time to decide whether to appeal the decision in *Rachel v Walker* to the Supreme Court of the Third District. If Josiah submitted an appeal on behalf of Rachel and James Henry, and the supreme court chose to review the lower court decision, the supreme court ruling would have bearing on *Courtney v. Rayburn*. Josiah was particularly aware of this because he would be the person to write the brief arguing Rachel's and James Henry's cases, which would be placed before the supreme court.

Although there are no records of the judge's instruction to the jury or the court's decision on *Courtney v. Rayburn* on March 24, 1836, it seems that Judge Lawless stayed a decision on *Courtney v. Rayburn* until the supreme court made a decision in Rachel's case. The women's situations were so similar that the decision in *Rachel v. Walker* would dictate the decision in *Courtney v. Rayburn*.

Rachel had filed her suit for freedom in November 1834. It was now March 1836. James Henry, who had been only a few months old at the beginning of her suit, was now almost two years old. He had grown from a nursing infant to a child who had learned to crawl and then walk, to eat and then talk.

Although Courtney had not waited quite as long as Rachel for her petition to be heard in front of the circuit court, she had still been waiting five months. As they awaited the proceedings, Courtney and William, who was approaching his first birthday, might have continued living with Samuel Rayburn, or they may have been quartered in the St. Louis jail for protection and hired out by the sheriff. If the latter supposition is true, Rachel and Courtney likely came to know each other and raise their sons together while residing in jail. They would have shared their stories of enslavement and soon come to realize how similar their situations had been. Both had been under the control of US Army officers stationed first at Fort Snelling and then at Fort Crawford. And astoundingly, these officers were brothers-in-law. Also, both women had been brought down to St. Louis with an infant son. They may have drawn comfort from each other. They would have waited together after the March 1836 term of the circuit court wondering about the course of their future and that of their sons. Courtney and William's future depended on Rachel and James Henry's future, which would be determined by the decision of the Supreme Court of the Third District.

—‖—

After the March 24, 1836, decision in *Courtney v. Rayburn*, Josiah Spalding filed bills of exemption for Rachel and James Henry on April 6. With the bills filed, Josiah wrote a brief appealing the decision in *Rachel v. Walker* and presented it to the Supreme Court of the Third District. The justices would impart their decision in July. Until the final decision was rendered, the court ruled that William Walker could not have contact with Rachel and James Henry.[47]

In June, the appeal of *Rachel, a woman of color v. Walker, William* was heard at the supreme court. All of the documents from the lower court (St. Louis Circuit Court) trial and the judgment rendered were submitted to the supreme court. Both Josiah, attorney for Rachel (the appellant), and Hamilton R. Gamble, attorney for William (the defendant), had written briefs, which were also presented to the court.

Josiah presented the same position that he had argued in the circuit court as to why Rachel and James Henry were free. He stated that in the proceedings of the lower court and in the rendition of the judgment "there is manifest error." He claimed that the judge in the lower court "incorrectly laid down and declared law." Therefore, he continued, "Rachel prays that said judgment may be reversed & that she may be entitled to all that she has lost by said judgment."[48]

In his brief to support Walker, Hamilton began by stating that in previous cases it was decided that residence in the Northwest Territory amounted to forfeiture of the ownership of enslaved people. But he argued that "exceptions are allowed to exist"; for example, "if a person be passing through the Country with slave property, which he has a right to do, if high waters detain him with his slave and he resumes his journey as soon as may be, his slave shall not be considered as a resident so as to work a loss of the slave."[49]

Hamilton then contended that Rachel's case constituted an exception and stated his reasons:

> In this case Stockton was a Soldier of the American Army and as such was bound to be and remain wherever his superior officer should command him to be,
> [T]hat the slave was only with him as a servant not a slave
> [As a] being obliged by law to be and remain in a country where slavery is forbidden he had a right to have his servant there also.[50]

Josiah addressed Hamilton's argument by saying, "Although this officer was bound by law and authority, to be and remain in a country where slavery is not allowed, yet no law nor public authority, required nor compelled him to take this person there as a slave nor as a servant."[51]

Having listened to the arguments and spent time reading the briefs and reviewing the laws and cases cited by Josiah, the court delivered its opinion. The three justices reviewed the facts of the case and began their written opinion with this statement: "It may not be unprofitable to state again the principles on which this Court has heretofore rested in the many decisions heretofore made in regard to this Ordinance."[52]

The justices in their opinion then cited previous court decisions, including that in the 1824 freedom suit of *Winny v. Whitesides*, in which the Missouri Supreme Court established the judicial precedent of "once free, always free."[53] They also cited *Merry v. Tiffin & Menard*, which held that an enslaved person who resided in any territory where slavery was prohibited by the Northwest Ordinance was free.[54] In addition, they cited the 1833 case of *Julia v. McKinney*, which reaffirmed the holdings of *Winny v. Whitesides* and *Merry v. Tiffin & Menard*, asserting that an enslaved person who resided (even temporarily) in a territory where slavery was prohibited should be free, even if the enslaver had no intent for the enslaved person to reside there.[55]

The justices thought the language in the case of *Julia* may have allowed Stockton to think he could keep Rachel as a slave in the territory but then stated in their opinion why the argument did not apply in *Rachel v Walker*:

> It is said the officer was under orders from the government to remain where he did, and therefore a necessity existed, which brings him within the reason of the decision.
>
> This plea of necessity, is well answered by Mr. Spalding for plaintiff, which answer is, that though it be that the officer was bound to remain where he did, during all the time he was there, yet no authority of law or the government compelled him to keep the plaintiff there as a slave. This answer is complete as we think; shall it be said, that because an officer of the army owns slaves in Virginia, that when as officer and soldier, he is required to take command of a post in the non-slave holding States or territories, he thereby has a right to take with him as many slaves, as will suit his interests or convenience? It surely cannot be the law; if this be true, then it is also true that the convenience or supposed convenience of the officer, repeals as to him and others who have the same character, the ordinance and the act of 1821 admitting Missouri into the Union, and also the prohibitions of the several laws and constitutions of the non-slave holding States.
>
> But it is said in this case that the plaintiff was only employed as a body servant, to induce the belief of the fact that the service she performed was necessary, or perhaps to establish the fact that the officer has a right to a family servant. We are yet to learn that the law, which gives to officers' servants of a certain sort, authorize such officers to hold slaves in lieu of such servants, and in places forbidden by the ordinance. In this case the officer lived in the Michigan territory at the time he bought the slave, he sent to a slave holding Country and procured her, this was his voluntary act, done without, any other reason than that of convenience, and he and those claiming under him must be beholden to abide the consequence of introducing slavery both in Missouri territory and Michigan, contrary to law.
>
> The judgment of the circuit court is reversed—the cause is remanded for a new trial.
>
> M. McGirk, George Tompkins, R. Wash[ington][56]

Justices Mathias McGirk and George Tompkins, the same justices who had issued the opinion in *Winny v. Whitesides* twelve years earlier, delivered the opinion. McGirk had also rendered the decision in *Julia v. McKinney*. The justices had reinforced the opinion "Once free, always free."

Rachel and James Henry returned to the circuit court in July. *Rachel v. Walker* was summarized, and the opinion of the supreme court was read into the record. The lower court accepted the opinion of the upper court, and the decision was recorded on August 16, 1836.

Rachel was finally free. And because of the decision in *Rachel v. Walker*, James Henry was free. This is confirmed by a small notation written at the end of the bill of exemption for James Henry, which states, "Remanded from Supreme Court submission & judgment for plaintiff."

The circumstances and arguments in *Rachel v. Walker* and *Courtney v. Rayburn* were so similar that the circuit court must have applied the decision in *Rachel v. Walker* to *Courtney v. Rayburn*. No records support this occurrence, but the remainder of Courtney's story supports the argument that Courtney and William also gained their freedom.

In initiating their suits, Rachel, James Henry, and Courtney had each declared that they had suffered ill treatment and been wrongfully imprisoned. Each claimed harm to their person and demanded payment of damages. Rachel and Courtney each requested five hundred dollars, and James Henry requested two hundred. Because all three plaintiffs won their suits, each defendant was required by law to pay these amounts. It is not known whether William Walker or Samuel Rayburn did pay restitution. If Rachel, James Henry, and Courtney received the amounts they claimed they were due, each acquired a great deal of money. In 1840, the average monthly wage for farmer laborers was $10.85.[57]

Prior to the decision being rendered in *Rachel v. Walker*, William Walker had demanded that Joseph Klunk return the down payment he had made for Rachel and James Henry, which it seems he did. Joseph had lost his investment. When he died in 1839, the attorney handling his estate wished to show the loss. Joseph Magehan traveled to Chicago and met with Thomas Stockton. Stockton gave Magehan the bill of sale for Rachel "dated 18th day of June 1834."[58]

Now that Rachel and Courtney were free, if they planned to remain in Missouri, they needed to obtain freedom licenses. While the *Rachel v.*

Walker case had been in process, the General Assembly of the State of Missouri had passed "An act concerning free negroes and mulattoes" on March 14, 1835. The act stated that all free persons of color had to apply to the court in the county in which they lived for a freedom license. The courts could, if they so chose, grant a license to "any free negro or mulatto, possessing the qualifications required by this act to reside within the state." In order to qualify for a freedom license, the person had to have been born in Missouri or prove that he or she was a "resident of this state on the seventh day of January, in the year eighteen hundred and twenty-five, and continue to be such residents at the effect of this act." If the person could "produce satisfactory evidence that he is of the class of person who may obtain such license, that he is of good character and behavior, and capable of supporting himself by lawful employment, the court may grant him a license to reside with the state."[59]

Rachel may have been born in Missouri, or she may have been living in Missouri on January 7, 1825. If either of these things were true, she would have been able to apply for a freedom license. A great number of Black people living in St. Louis applied for licenses in December 1835, but Rachel had not yet gained her freedom at that time. If Rachel applied at a later date, she did not do so in St. Louis County.[60] Rachel and James Henry may have left St. Louis after gaining their freedom, or they may have left Missouri to reside elsewhere. The only person she seems to have known from the time of her residence on the upper Mississippi was John, who may have been the father of James Henry. To be able to testify for Rachel, John must have been living in St. Louis at that time. After gaining their freedom, perhaps Rachel and James Henry began a life together with John. No records of Rachel and James Henry's lives after August 1836 have been found.

Courtney was born in Virginia, and she had not been a resident of Missouri as of January 7, 1825, so she could not obtain a freedom license. But as she awaited the court's decision in her case, she probably formed a plan for what she and her son would do if they were declared free. They would leave St. Louis and return to the community in which she had made friends—a community where Black people owned and farmed their land, earned and saved money, and married and raised their children without fear of being controlled or punished by an enslaver.

CHAPTER 7

LIVING FREE IN PRAIRIE DU CHIEN, 1836–1880

S oon after the decision in *Rachel v. Walker* ensured freedom for Court-ney and William, Courtney gathered her belongings from wherever they had been living and headed to the levee. Using money either from the settlement for damages the court required Samuel Rayburn to pay or gained by some other means, Courtney paid for passage on a steamboat traveling up the Mississippi River. As people of color, Courtney and William would have had access to only lower-quality accommodations on the vessel. But on this steamboat, Courtney and William were traveling as free people. They were not below deck and chained to others as they would have been if Courtney had been sold to a slave driver and transported down the Mississippi River. Courtney did not have to wait on a person who planned to sell her and her son to a new enslaver. She could watch the moving water, feel the wind on her face, and know that she controlled her own destiny. Stops at one river community after another lengthened their journey, but finally Courtney and William arrived at their destination.

As men stood on the prow watching for snags and casting the weight rope to determine water depth, the steamboat glided into Hunter Slough to dock at the steamboat landing at the south end of Prairie du Chien. Probably one of the last people to leave the steamboat, Courtney likely picked up William and their possessions, walked off the deck, onto the dock, and across the small bridge. At the end of the bridge, she may have gazed at the prairie as a free woman, then turned to the road that would lead her north into the Main Village. She likely followed the old trail and passed Fort Crawford. A bit farther up the trail, she would have come upon the Indian agency, maybe looking for Patsey amidst all the activity. Next, she would have come to the house set close to the road where she had worked for the Bailly family. Reaching Antoine Boisvert's house, she may have turned to check the level of the water in the *marais*, or slough. After discovering the water was low, she might have waded through the marshy slough to the opposite bank and maneuvered up the muddy incline and onto the island that was still the main village of the community. Here, she may have rested, moving her bare feet across the crispy grass. We can imagine Courtney shifting William's weight on her hip and taking the last steps toward what she hoped would be her new home. She must have knocked on the door of Mariah's little house at the south end of the Main Village with hope. When the door opened, Mariah surely welcomed Courtney and William into her home with arms flung wide.

Back at Prairie du Chien, Courtney reconnected with her friends Mariah and Helene Galarneau. They still lived next door to each other on their small farms. They probably looked just as they had when Alexis Bailly had taken Courtney and William from Prairie du Chien about a year earlier, but some changes had occurred in the lives of the men and women Courtney had met while living on the prairie.

Most of the changes had brought happiness to Courtney's friends. Helene's daughter Sophia had been a young bride when Courtney had first arrived in Prairie du Chien. Now, Helene was a grandmother, for Sophia and her husband, John Fonda, had given birth to a son named Henry. They were already expecting another child. They had moved from the prairie to Bloody Run Creek and then back to the prairie. Sophia and John continued their itinerant life until they and their four children found a permanent home on North Main Street in Prairie du Chien.

Mariah had no children and rarely saw her husband, Jacob Faschnacht, but it was obvious she enjoyed her freedom. In many ways, Mariah lived a single life and assumed all the chores demanded by her small farm. Mariah had been listed as the head of the household on the 1830 census. She had worked for the entire year of 1831 in the employ of Colonel Willoughby Morgan, who commanded the second Fort Crawford. Willoughby described Mariah as a "Free Negro" on his pay voucher.[1] And Mariah was again listed as the head of a household in the 1836 census of Wisconsin Territory.[2]

Courtney may have inquired about Patsey and her family. If so, she would have learned that Patsey was looking at an uncertain future. By this time, Patsey had attended Eliza Street on a trip to Henderson, nursed her through her illnesses and two childbirths, and raised her own children, but Patsey did not know if General Joseph Street would return permanently to the prairie or be relocated to Rock Island or a different posting. Having signed two documents indenturing herself to the Street family, Patsey would have no choice but to move wherever the Street family moved unless she gained her freedom. No one could have known, of course, that Patsey would be forced to leave Prairie du Chien in 1839 when the Street family relocated to the Des Moines agency or that she would eventually obtain her freedom in 1847 after the deaths of both Joseph and Eliza Street. Courtney may have visited the agency building in Prairie du Chien to see Patsey, not knowing how long she would remain in the area. At that meeting, Courtney may have also reconnected with London, the older enslaved man who lived in the Street household along with Patsey when Courtney first came to the prairie in 1830.

Courtney was surely relieved to learn that she would not have to face any of the three men who had held her in servitude. Major John Garland had been ordered first to Fort Jesup and then to Detroit for "Indian duty," where he would remain for several years. Lieutenant Thomas Stockton had left Prairie du Chien in November 1835 after submitting his resignation as assistant quartermaster. From the prairie, he too had journeyed to Detroit and for a while had been employed to survey roads in Michigan. Alexis and Lucy Bailly had borrowed money because Alexis wished to return to the fur trade and needed to purchase trade goods, and they used their house in the Village of St. Friole as security. Courtney would likely learn that they were unable to repay the loan. Gossip may have indicated that they had to sell the property to Hercules L. Dousman in lieu of payment.[3]

Courtney could have seen another man from her past. Alexander Faribault, Lucy Bailly's brother, had come to Prairie du Chien, perhaps working for his father and conducting fur trade business. Alexander operated several trading posts on the Minnesota River, and in 1834, he had established a new post at the confluence of the Cannon and Straight Rivers. Alexander was enumerated in the 1836 census as being at Prairie du Chien. With the freedom to move about the prairie, Courtney would have had many opportunities to meet Alexander upon her return. She may have sought him to ask about her son Joseph, who had remained with the Bailly family when Courtney and William were sold to Samuel Rayburn in St. Louis. She could have learned that Joseph still worked for Alexis Bailly and lived at Wabasha. Courtney could have asked Alexander to relay the message to Joseph that she was free and living again at the prairie.[4]

Courtney had been gone from the prairie for just a little over a year and therefore recognized many residents as she walked about the villages. But there were always new faces to be seen. Each fall, young men from French-speaking Canada converged on Montreal and signed engagements to work for a fur trading company as *milieux*, the voyageurs who sat in the middle of the large trade canoes. After signing a legal document called an *engagement*, the men paddled canoes filled with trade goods into a trading region. In the first third of the nineteenth century, the active trading regions were Michilimackinac and west into the upper Mississippi River and its tributaries. These young men would winter in a remote location where their trader had his wintering post. At the end of the trading season, the voyageurs converged at Prairie du Chien, and many found rooms at Brunet's tavern or in the upper floors of Joseph Rolette's stone store. They lived in Prairie du Chien until the fall when the trading season began again.

The lure of the fur trade brought Benjamin Boudrie to Prairie du Chien. Almost nothing is known about Benjamin. He arrived at Prairie du Chien just before the enumeration of the residents for the 1836 territorial census. Benjamin was listed as a single man and his age recorded as between twenty and twenty-nine. He must have been from Canada, for he was registered as an "alien." Soon after Courtney's arrival at Prairie du Chien, she either met or was reunited with Benjamin, and they fell in love.

On July 4, 1838, Benjamin and Courtney were joined in marriage by George W. Pine, justice of the peace. Courtney recorded her name as "Courtney London." Perhaps London, Joseph Street's indentured servant, had shown Courtney some kindness when she had lived in bondage at Prairie du Chien. With a first and last name to record on her marriage certificate, Courtney could proudly reinforce her status as a free woman. Courtney also wished for her young son to have a surname, and so after her marriage, William came to be known as William Boudrie.[5]

After the marriage, Mariah invited Benjamin, Courtney, and William to live on her land. Mariah's lot was small, only 50 feet wide by 376 feet long, but she produced an income from the land. In her generosity, Mariah reduced the amount of land available to her for raising animals and growing crops. Benjamin constructed a house not far from Mariah's for his family, and now Courtney had a house she could call her own.

On the land close to their house, Benjamin constructed a bakery. A baker and a bakery had always been an important part of the community at Prairie du Chien. One of the earliest crops grown on the prairie was barley, and many of the farmers operated horse-powered flouring mills. By the late 1730s, wheat was being grown in the Illinois Country, ground into flour, and shipped south to New Orleans and as far north as Detroit. Michel Brisbois and Strange Powers had previously been the bakers for Prairie du Chien, but by the time of Benjamin and Courtney's marriage, both men had died. Benjamin and Courtney's bakery therefore filled a community need.[6]

By this time, Mariah's marriage to Jacob Faschnacht had broken apart. When Courtney returned to Prairie du Chien in 1836, Jacob was no longer living there. In 1839, Mariah retained the services of William H. Banks, a lawyer residing in Mineral Point. On behalf of Mariah, Banks filed a petition for divorce in the chancery court of Crawford County. When the hearing opened in the October term, Jacob did not appear. Upon evidence presented by Banks, the court issued a decision "dissolving the bonds of marriage" between Mariah and Jacob.[7]

On the first day of January 1841, Mariah married Era Putnam. Era had been born in New York, but little else is known about him and his arrival in Prairie du Chien. He was enumerated as one of the single men living in the community in 1836. Once Era and Mariah married, they lived in Mariah's house and farmed the small plot of land. In 1845, Era purchased 160 acres in the Township of Prairie du Chien. Soon after acquiring the land, young William Boudrie became part of their household and helped with the farm work.

The small Black community at the south end of the Main Village expanded with the birth of Benjamin and Courtney's children. Margaret was born in 1841. Two years later, Courtney gave birth to a son, Benjamin. Their last child, Seraphina Catherine, was born in October 1845. All the children were baptized at St. Gabriel's Church.[8]

By the time of Seraphina's birth, Benjamin had saved enough money to purchase their home and a small tract of land surrounding the structure. On November 13, 1845, Era and Mariah Putnam sold Benjamin Boudrie "All that certain Lot or parcel of Land on which the Said Benjamin Boudrie now resides, being a part of the Lot which Francis Galeno and Hellene his wife . . . conveyed by Deed to Jacob Forsnat." Courtney must have felt even more secure in her freedom when she became a homeowner and was surrounded by her four children and good friends, Mariah and Helene.[9]

The free Black community at the lower end of the Main Village continued to grow beyond Mariah, Courtney, and Courtney's children. By 1842, Mary Antoine and her daughter and three sons lived at the prairie, as did Charles and Mrs. Jackson. Josiah and Mary Ann Smith had moved to the prairie a few years after Benjamin and Courtney had married, and they set up housekeeping on the south end of the Main Village. Josiah had been born in Virginia and Mary Ann in Missouri. Josiah worked as a butcher and supported their family of a boy and three daughters.[10]

Six months to the day after Benjamin and Courtney became owners of their small piece of property, the US Congress passed "An Act for the Prosecution of the existing War between the United States and the Republic of Mexico." The fighting between the two countries had officially become a war. The First Dragoons, which had replaced the First Infantry at Fort Crawford, were ordered into service in Texas. With the US military fully engaged in the conflict, President James Polk requested that each state and territory organize one regiment of volunteer infantry for service during the war with Mexico. Governor Henry Dodge informed the residents of Wisconsin Territory of this request. The response was swift, and the Crawford County Volunteers, or "Dodge Guards," were "mustered into the service of the United States at Prairie du Chien" on June 24, 1846. Their assignment was to garrison Fort Crawford while the regular army troops stationed at Prairie du Chien were sent to the seat of war. The company at Prairie du Chien was commanded by Captain Wiram Knowlton. Though the vast majority of the men who enlisted lived in Prairie du Chien, all enlistees were required to live in the barracks at Fort Crawford. The men were to serve for one year.[11]

On average, seventy-five privates plus officers of the volunteers manned Fort Crawford every month. They aided in the forced removal of the Ho-Chunk to west of the Mississippi River. If any Ho-Chunk

individuals returned to their ances-
tral lands, the guards were ordered
to find them and transport them
to the land the nation had been assigned west of the river. However,
many Ho-Chunk people continued
to return to their native land, even
in the face of these threats. John
Fonda, Sophia Galarneau's husband,
was appointed a sergeant in the
Dodge Guards. John had enlisted
in the US Army at Fort Crawford in
1829. Promoted to corporal, he had
been stationed at Fort Crawford for
the three years of his enlistment.
John may have convinced Benjamin
Boudrie to join the Dodge Guards.
Benjamin was forty-two years old,
but he enlisted in July 1846, leaving
Courtney to manage the bakery.[12]

John Henry Fonda was born in Water-
vliet, New York. He arrived at Prairie
du Chien in 1829 and enlisted, assisting
in the construction of the second Fort
Crawford. He married Sophie Galarneau,
the daughter of François and Helene
Galarneau and the granddaughter of
Marianne Labuche. WHI IMAGE ID 3476

Living conditions were poor at Fort Crawford. Captain Knowlton
contracted with a local physician to provide care for the men, but frequent
deaths occurred. While at the post, Benjamin passed away on October 16,
1846. Courtney was now a widow with four children—and Seraphina was
just a year old.[13]

Once again, Courtney relied on her friendship with Mariah for support. William, now more than ten years old, moved into the Putnam house
and assisted Era with farming chores. Courtney did have the security of
knowing that, in the future, she could use the land bounty certificate Benjamin had been given for enlisting in the Dodge Guards or sell it to raise
money. She took over the operation of the bakery and would be the only
baker in the community until the arrival of Charles Weidemer in 1850.

By 1850, the population of Prairie du Chien had greatly increased. The
forced removal of the Ho-Chunk and other American Indian nations had
opened Wisconsin lands for settlement by immigrants from Ireland, Germany, and Norway. One of the German immigrants who chose to make

Prairie du Chien his new home was Charles Weidemer. He was born about 1826 in the German state of Baden. Arriving in the community, Charles also worked as a baker. Tall and fair, Charles soon developed an attraction to the petite Courtney. They married about 1855, and Charles became part of the old Main Village neighborhood north of the road to the mainland of Prairie du Chien. By 1860, two sons—Jonas and Joseph—had been born to the couple. Courtney had given the name Joseph to her eldest and youngest sons.[14]

By 1860, Mariah and Era Putnam had left their house in Prairie du Chien and moved onto a farm east of the prairie in the Township of Eastman. Having no children, the couple brought William Hinson, a six-year-old boy of mixed race, into their family. William had been born in Illinois in 1854. In all but one census record, Mariah was listed as "Black" or "Mulatto." But in the last record of her life, the 1870 federal census, she is listed as "White."[15]

The population growth of Prairie du Chien encouraged the establishment of new businesses, and other Black people came to the settlement. Several people on the 1860 census were listed as "Mulatto," including Humphrey F. Dixon from Ohio, who opened a barber parlor, and his wife, Lucy; the saloon keeper Emmanuel Walker and his employees Francis McKinney, a barber, and Mary Johnson, a cleaner; the baker William Jenifer; and Edward Rice from Virginia who became employed as a cook. Edward married a white woman named Catherine, who had immigrated to the United States from Ireland.[16]

But by 1870, many of the Black people living at Prairie du Chien had moved elsewhere. Courtney and her family, however, stayed. Courtney's son William remained in Prairie du Chien and worked for some time as a barber. By 1870, William had changed his name to James Barr and married Martha Henry Glass. In 1880, he built a large house for his family that included two children, named Emma and John, about three blocks north of the small home in which he had been raised. He was employed first as a steam brakeman and then as a Pullman car porter, probably for the Milwaukee, Chicago, and St. Paul Railroad, since his home was only a block from the depot.[17] C. Perry Cole, a mixed-race man born in Kentucky, boarded in James's home for a time and worked, perhaps also for the railroad, as a cook. The only other Black residents of the community were William and Martha Rent, Robert Brown, and John D. Robert. All three men were barbers.[18]

James Barr, the son of James Barr (previously called William) and grandson of Courtney, owned and operated a tavern at 20th and Vliet Streets in Milwaukee, Wisconsin. James is pictured, second from left, with his wife, Babette; daughter Stella; and three unknown patrons, circa 1912. COURTESY OF DEBBIE FURMAN

By 1878, Charles and Courtney had left Prairie du Chien and moved to Perry Township in Plymouth County, Iowa. Their son Jonas had married Jennie Faith in 1873, and Courtney and Charles joined them on their farm. While working for the railroad, James decided to move his family to Milwaukee, and they made their home on Sixth Street. Years later, his son, also named James, would own and operate a saloon on West Vliet Street. When the elder James died in 1894, his remains were returned to Prairie du Chien and interred in Evergreen Cemetery next to a daughter who had died as an infant.[19]

Sadly, Courtney did not live to visit son James in his new house. She died of dropsy in 1879 at age sixty-seven, soon after she moved to Perry. Jonas and his wife were expecting at the time. When the little girl was born several months after Courtney's death, Jonas named her in memory of his mother.[20]

Marguerite Caya, a great-granddaughter of Marianne Labuche, was born August 14, 1843. She was the daughter of Rosalie Loyer and Michel Caya and married Acan Varo (Vereau). Her descendants continue to live in and around Prairie du Chien. COURTESY OF SUSAN CAYA-SLUSSER

No records for Marianne Labuche's death or burial have been located, but according to her family, she died in 1833. In the 1860 federal census for Prairie du Chien, a seventy-five-year-old "Mulatto" woman named Mary is listed in the household of William Logan. William was married to Lena Menard, who was Marianne's granddaughter. No other Black woman living at Prairie du Chien since Marianne's arrival there in the 1790s had the name Mary, except Mary Antoine and Mary Ann Smith. Mary Antoine had left the prairie by 1850, and Mary Ann lived with her husband, Josiah Smith. Since Lena Menard Logan was Marianne's granddaughter, it is possible that the Mary listed in the 1860 census was Marianne.

Marianne's grandchildren followed the culture of their parents and continued to marry into French Canadian families. Few of Marianne's grandchildren and great-grandchildren made their homes beyond Crawford County, except some who moved up the Mississippi River to Minnesota. Descendants of Marianne Labuche continue to reside in Crawford County and western Wisconsin, including Prairie du Chien.

Conclusion

Although Courtney's freedom suit was successful and she was able to return to Prairie du Chien as a free woman, the experience must have been bittersweet as she encountered friends and acquaintances in the village who were still enslaved or involuntarily indentured in this supposedly free territory. Patsey and her sons were still in service to the Street family. Many other Black men and women were forced to labor for the Fort Crawford officers and their families as enslaved individuals. Joseph, Courtney's eldest son, was still the legal property of Alexis Bailly, though he lived in the Northwest Territory just as Courtney and William did.

Based on the decisions handed down by the courts in *Winny v. Whitesides* and *Rachel v. Walker*, and the fact that he had been born in free territory, Joseph should have been free. But Joseph could not gain his freedom by legal means unless he traveled from Mendota to a state where one could file a freedom suit and resided in the state. The legislators of Wisconsin Territory, of which Mendota was a part in 1836, had not written a statute detailing the means by which a person illegally held in bondage could gain their freedom. Although Rachel and Courtney endured trips from Prairie du Chien to St. Louis that had at first seemed likely to end in a dreaded future, the women took advantage of the laws of Missouri and gained their freedom, despite the efforts of their enslavers. As stated in the laws passed in Missouri Territory and then the State of Missouri, one had to be living in Missouri to petition the circuit court for freedom. And Missouri law affected only Missouri residents. Consequently, Joseph remained enslaved to Alexis because he still resided in what had been Michigan Territory and now was Wisconsin Territory. Neither territory provided a means by which an enslaved person living in the territories could gain their legal freedom without the willing participation of their enslaver.

In the late 1840s, Joseph gained his freedom by escaping slavery at the age of seventeen. Having "been beaten and abused and [able to] stand it no longer," Joseph ran away from where he had been enslaved at Oliver Faribault's post to the home of Alexander Huggins at Traverse des Sioux on the lower Minnesota River. Alexander was a missionary to the Dakota and would later become an abolitionist. When Joseph arrived at his mission, Alexander wrote Oliver Faribault to tell him that he was harboring Joseph. In the letter, he stated that he "did not believe slavery was legal, and would not lend himself to any effort to take [Joseph] Godfrey."[1] Joseph continued on his freedom-seeking quest and lived the rest of his life with the Dakota.

Obtaining freedom would have been just as difficult for any enslaved Black man, woman, or child living at Prairie du Chien, Fort Crawford, Fort Snelling, Fort Howard, or Fort Winnebago in the early to mid-1800s. These people should have been free because slavery was immoral. But they also should have been legally free by virtue of their residence at Prairie du Chien and/or Fort Snelling or in the new Wisconsin territory.

Yet, in order to petition the court to file a suit for freedom, one had to reside in or travel to a state whose legislature had enacted a law allowing such suits. Missouri was not the only state in which an enslaved person could petition for freedom. Arkansas had adopted a freedom suit statute identical to that of Missouri in 1807. Virginia, South Carolina, Georgia, Florida, Tennessee, Kentucky, and other states that allowed slavery, including the District of Columbia, had freedom suit statutes in the 1830s.[2] Theoretically, when Lieutenant Thomas Stockton took Rachel with him while he worked for the quartermaster general in Washington City, Rachel could have filed a suit for her freedom.

Of course, enslaved people had to carefully weigh the pros and cons of initiating a suit. Filing a petition for freedom required great bravery, an ability to withstand trying conditions between the commencement of a trial and the rendering of a decision, and the acceptance that a trial could result in the person's circumstances actually worsening. Rachel and Courtney, as well as many others who sued for their freedom, must have decided that the possible rewards outweighed the risks. If they did not fight for their freedom, not only would they be "sold down river," but they were also likely to be separated from their young sons.

Some years after Rachel and Courtney had filed their suits for freedom, two other enslaved individuals sought to obtain their freedom through the Missouri court system. They would follow in Rachel's footsteps and use the success of Rachel's argument as the basis for their argument for freedom. But their suits, which led to one of the most infamous legal decisions in American history, would end quite differently.

—⊣⊢—

Etheldred (Dred) Scott was born into slavery in Virginia in about 1800 and was later purchased by Peter and Elizabeth Blow. Peter Blow was from Southampton County, Virginia, where several free Black people and a white family had the last name Scott, so the Blows may have purchased Dred from the Scott family. Peter and his family moved from Virginia to Huntsville, Alabama. When his attempt at farming there was not successful, the family moved to St. Louis. Peter had enslaved twelve Black people while living in Virginia, and six enslaved people worked for him at St. Louis in 1830. Dred was one of these enslaved people. Peter died in June 1832, but before his death, he sold Dred to Dr. John Emerson.[3]

John was of Irish heritage and had attended medical school in Philadelphia. He drifted westward until he arrived in St. Louis and began working as a civilian doctor at Jefferson Barracks. In the fall of 1833, he was appointed a US Army assistant surgeon. The Fort Armstrong surgeon had died of cholera, so soon after receiving his appointment, John was posted to Fort Armstrong. He arrived at Rock Island in late November; Dred Scott accompanied him as his enslaved servant, for whom John could now submit expenses on his pay vouchers. Throughout 1834, 1835, and the first half of 1836, John and Dred lived and worked at the hospital and surgeon's quarters located in the northern portion of the 270-foot-square fort. At this time, Dred was listed as Etheldred in the pay vouchers. In addition to serving John, he served three other officers stationed at Fort Armstrong. John made money by renting Dred, and one of the officers who benefited from Dred's labor was Lieutenant George Wilson, Joseph Street's son-in-law.[4]

In April 1836, John and Dred boarded a steamboat traveling up the Mississippi River, as John had been ordered to report to Fort Snelling.

About 140 officers and men of the Fifth Infantry had also boarded the vessel with their belongings. All disembarked at the Fort Snelling dock on May 8, 1836. Dr. Jarvis, the surgeon John was ordered to replace, had awaited the arrival of the steamship. He probably escorted John to the hospital and surgeon's quarters located in barracks adjacent to the main entrance of the post. Dred would also reside within the quarters. Jarvis recorded his impression of John: "The new doctor is no chicken, 6'4" in his stocking feet." At that height, John towered over Dred, who was five-foot-six and of slight frame.[5] For the next month, John busily organized the hospital, dealing with illnesses such as smallpox, which had broken out with the warm weather. On June 3, John had his first call upon Major Lawrence Taliaferro, the US Indian agent.[6]

Either through this meeting or in the course of daily life at Fort Snelling, Dred Scott met Harriet Robinson, who was enslaved by Lawrence Taliaferro. In 1835, Lawrence had brought Harriet from Virginia to Fort Snelling. Within a year, Lawrence sold Harriet to John Emerson.[7] In 1836, Dred and Harriet, while living at Fort Snelling, "with the consent of said Dr. Emerson, who then claimed to be their master and owner, intermarried, and took each other for husband and wife."[8]

When John left Fort Snelling for an assignment in St. Louis in 1837, the river had frozen and he could not transport his property, including Dred and Harriet. The couple were left at Fort Snelling and hired out until John sent for them. Harriet worked for Captain Plympton and Mrs. Anderson. When the river opened, the couple went on to St. Louis. There they stayed while John spent time at Fort Jesup in Louisiana. While in Louisiana, John met and married Eliza Irene Sanford. After the marriage, Dred and Harriet joined John and Eliza, but by October of 1838, all four were on their way back to Fort Snelling. While on board the *Gipsey*, as it steamed up the Mississippi River, Harriet gave birth to a girl, whom the couple named Eliza. Little Eliza had been born north of latitude 36 degrees, 30 minutes, and therefore was born a free person. The Emersons and Dred, Harriet, and Eliza Scott remained at Fort Snelling until May 1840.[9]

For the next six years, Dred and Harriet lived in St. Louis as John was moved from one post to another in Florida during the Seminole War. Harriet worked for Eliza, and Dred was hired out to Captain Henry Bainbridge, Irene Emerson's brother-in-law. John was discharged from the army in

September 1842. He returned to St. Louis but, unable to maintain a successful private practice in the city, he settled permanently in Davenport, Iowa, on land he had purchased in 1835. He began a medical practice there in the summer of 1843. Irene Emerson joined him and gave birth to their daughter, Henrietta, in November 1843. On December 29, 1843, John died at age forty.

There is no record of Dred and Harriet during the last two years of John's life. They may have remained in St. Louis or lived in Davenport, Iowa. But, as of March 1846, Dred and Harriet were living in St. Louis. Irene Emerson hired them out to Samuel Russell, the owner of Russell & Bennett, a wholesale grocery.[10]

Dred and Harriet must have been well aware of the opportunity for them to file petitions seeking freedom in St. Louis. They had lived in territory in which slavery was not permitted for two different periods, each lasting two years or more. Both could make the same argument for their freedom and their daughters' freedom that Rachel and Courtney had successfully made ten years earlier. On April 6, 1846, Dred and Harriet filed separate petitions for leave to sue for freedom with the St. Louis Circuit Court. Their petitions were granted.[11]

Peter Blow's children, who lived in St. Louis, learned of the petitions and became involved, providing legal and financial assistance to Dred and Harriet. Charles Drake, the lawyer who had been appointed to represent Courtney in her suit for freedom, had been married to Martha Ella Blow. Though a widower, Charles kept in close contact with the Blow family. So, when Charlotte Blow Charless asked Charles to assist Dred and Harriet, he agreed.

The case came to trial on June 30, 1847. Henry Taylor Blow testified that his father, Peter, had sold Dred to John Emerson. Witness depositions established that Dred and Harriet had resided at Fort Armstrong and Fort Snelling. *Winny v. Whitesides, Merry v. Tiffin & Menard*, and other cases supported Dred's claim to freedom based on residency in Illinois. It was argued that even though John resided at a military post, this did not prevent the emancipation of Dred and Harriet, according to the court's 1836 determination in *Rachel v. Walker*. Between the decision in Rachel's case and 1846, the Missouri Supreme Court had made no new decisions to overturn the clearly established doctrine of "once free, always free." There was no question as to the validity of the Northwest Ordinance slavery prohibition or the similar prohibition in the 1820 Missouri Compromise. However, the jury did not feel that they heard testimony sufficient to prove that Irene Emerson had claimed Dred and Harriet Scott as her "slaves," and the jury returned a verdict in her favor. The Scotts' lawyer moved for a new trial, and the motion was granted. But unforeseen circumstances delayed the case: the St. Louis courthouse had a fire, a cholera epidemic swept through the city, and both parties in the lawsuit retained new counsel. The case was finally heard in circuit court in January 1850. The jury found for the plaintiffs, proclaiming Dred and Harriet and their daughters, Eliza and Lizzie, free. But Irene Emerson was not happy with the verdict. Her attorneys appealed to the Missouri Supreme Court, and a hearing was granted.

At the supreme court level, Emerson's attorneys continued to maintain that military law was different from civil law when slave property was involved. They made this claim despite the court's ruling to the contrary in *Rachel v. Walker*.

By the time *Dred Scott v. Irene Emerson* was heard by the Missouri Supreme Court in 1852, sixteen years had elapsed since *Rachel v. William Walker* had been decided. The question of slavery in the United States had grown increasingly divisive among white people. Two of the justices sitting on the supreme court were proslavery, and the third, though not as staunchly in favor of slavery, was also not antislavery. On March 22, 1852, they made their decision. The long, complex decision questioned the legality of the Northwest Ordinance and redefined the Missouri Compromise. One justice concluded his opinion by stating that slavery was the will of God. He wrote, "Times now are not as they were, when the former decisions on this subject were made."[12]

With support from friends, Dred and Harriet Scott continued their fight for freedom, taking their case from the Circuit Court of the United States to the US Supreme Court. In December 1858, Chief Justice Roger B. Taney wrote the majority opinion of the court.

In his opinion, Taney stated that Black people were not and could not be citizens of the United States and therefore had no right to bring suit in a court. In addition, he ruled that Dred Scott had not become a free man as a result of his residence at Fort Snelling because the Missouri Compromise was unconstitutional, as Congress had no authority to prohibit slavery in the federal territories. This statement invalidated the Northwest Ordinance and the Missouri Compromise. Furthermore, he stated, Dred Scott did not become free on the basis of his residence at Fort Armstrong because his status, upon returning to Missouri, depended on Missouri law, as had been determined in *Scott v. Emerson*. Because Dred Scott was not free under the provisions of the Northwest Ordinance of 1787 or the 1820 Missouri Compromise, Taney ruled that Dred Scott was still an enslaved person.[13] The decision in *Scott v. Emerson* further divided the nation regarding the question of slavery, moving the United States closer to civil war.

Dred and Harriet Scott had used the same argument Rachel and Courtney had used in 1836 in their freedom suits—an argument supported by previous court decisions establishing "once free, always free." In addition, *Rachel v. Walker* made case law in the ruling that a person enslaved by an army officer residing in a territory in which slavery was prohibited was thereby free.

But by 1858, the disposition of the United States had changed. If Rachel and Courtney had filed suits for their freedom and the freedom of their sons on the basis of their residency in Prairie du Chien ten or twenty years later than they did, they may not have gained their freedom.

—‖—

In 1836, the year in which Courtney and Rachel gained their freedom, the US Congress formed the Territory of Wisconsin. Henry Dodge was commissioned governor. His first duty after his appointment was the organization of a territorial legislature. Until statehood occurred twelve years later in 1848, this legislature debated and passed laws that affected all the residents of the territory. The 1838–1839 legislature passed "An Act to Provide for the Punishment of Offences Against the Lives and Persons of Individuals." Section 20 stated that anyone who would

> confine or imprison any other person within this territory, against his will, or shall forcibly seize and confine . . . a person against his will . . . or to be sold as a slave, or in any way held to service against his will, and every person who shall sell, or in any manner transfer, for any term the service or labor of any negro, mulatto, or other person of color . . .

shall be punished by imprisonment in the county jail, not more than two years nor less than one year, or by fine, not exceeding one thousand dollar nor less than five hundred dollar.[14]

When the territorial statutes passed in 1836 were published in printed form, the publication included the text of the Northwest Ordinance, so the legislators must have assumed that the ordinance applied to Wisconsin Territory and, therefore, that slavery and involuntary servitude were against the law. Section 20 of the 1838–1839 legislature act only addressed the punishment if one was *found* holding someone against their will or selling their labor. In reality, many white enslavers living in Wisconsin continued to hold people of color in slavery and involuntary servitude without fear of punishment. Henry Dodge himself was a slave owner, and he did not manumit the people he enslaved until 1838, two years into his tenure as territorial governor. And the Wisconsin statutes, unlike the statutes of Louisiana, Missouri, and other Southern states, offered no recourse by which "negroes, mulattos, or persons of color" could obtain their freedom. By not addressing the issue of slavery in the Wisconsin Territory statutes, these early legislators allowed slavery to continue within the territory.

According to the 1836 Wisconsin Territorial Census for Crawford County, nineteen enslaved people lived at Fort Crawford. Other Black men and women were listed in the census as living in households with white families in the community, but they were not listed as "slaves."[15] In 1823, the Prairie du Chien fur trader Joseph Rolette had acknowledged that slavery was not allowed "here," and he refused Pierre Chouteau's offer to purchase an enslaved person for Rolette. Yet, Joseph Street's son Thomas held one enslaved woman in 1836, and James H. Lockwood held one enslaved man. Both James and Thomas knew the law. James was an associate justice of Crawford County and, in 1836, was serving as a territorial legislator. Thomas had been a town supervisor and, with the formation of Wisconsin Territory, became one of the Crawford County commissioners. They still held Black individuals in bondage.[16]

During Rachel's suit for freedom, Thomas Stockton and his counsel had argued that officers of the US Army and Navy could own and hold enslaved people wherever they were stationed, because they had been ordered to those locations. Thomas had stated, "During all the time I owned her & her child I was an officer of the United States Army, stationed at those different posts by order of the proper authority."[17]

The Missouri Supreme Court's decision in *Rachel v. Walker* specifically addressed this argument put forth by Thomas.

> This plea of necessity, is well answered by Mr. Spalding for plaintiff, which answer is, that though it be that the officer was bound to remain where he did, during all the time he was there, yet no authority of law or the government compelled him to keep the plaintiff there as a slave. . . .
>
> We are yet to learn that the law, which gives to officers' servants of a certain sort, authorize such officers to hold slaves in lieu of such servants, and in places forbidden by the ordinance.[18]

Perhaps the news of the decision in *Rachel v. Walker*, made by the Missouri Supreme Court in July 1836, had not arrived at the upper reaches of the Mississippi when the territorial census was conducted in August 1836. But several events indicate that even when the news of the *Rachel v. Walker* decision became known at Prairie du Chien, it was blatantly ignored by the officers stationed at Fort Crawford.

One example is Brevet Brigadier General George M. Brooke. In July 1837, as hostilities between the US Army and the Seminole Nation increased, Colonel Zachary Taylor departed Fort Crawford with a detachment of men. George assumed command of the post in mid-July. He found that the accommodations for the commanding officer had severely deteriorated, and he immediately requested funds from the War Department to repair the commanding officer's house. An inspection of the structure determined that the house was beyond repair. However, George refused to live in one of the apartments assigned to officers, finding the size of the rooms, fifteen feet square, entirely too small. In a letter to Major R. Cross, he wrote, "How is a man to set a Dinner Table in such a room, with a fire proportioned to the Cold of this Climate, & the necessary Furniture of a Parlour."[19]

As a brevet brigadier general, George was the highest-ranking officer to ever be posted to Fort Crawford. He was born at Mantipike in King and

Queen County, Virginia, and had received a commission into the US Army at an early age and risen quickly through the ranks. He was very aware of his position and rank, and he regularly entertained junior officers in his command. With his rank, George was allowed to maintain two private servants. During his time at Fort Crawford, these servants were Mrs. Mc-Laughlin, whom George described on his pay vouchers as having a "Dark" complexion, and Willie, whom George described as five feet nine inches tall and "Yellow" complected. At the officer gatherings, George's servants may have been assisted by Rosa Cook, Lieutenant McKissack's servant, or one of the enslaved people owned by Captain Alexander Hooe.[20]

Captain Thornton Alexander Seymour Hooe is another example of an officer who continued to hold a Black person in bondage in Prairie du Chien after the *Rachel v. Walker* decision. Alexander, as he was known, was born on the family plantation in King George County, Virginia, and after graduating from the US Military Academy in 1827, he was posted to frontier duty. While stationed at Fort Howard in Green Bay, Alexander met Joseph Rolette's daughter Emilie, and the two married on June 8, 1830. As a lieutenant, Alexander was allowed reimbursement for one servant. Unlike Thomas Stockton and other officers who had not been raised in slaveholding states, Alexander did not purchase or rent an enslaved person. Rather, he transported one of the enslaved people from his family's plantation to the military post, as Zachary Taylor, Lawrence Taliaferro, and John Garland had also done.

In May 1839, Joseph Rolette wrote a letter regarding a young man held in bondage by Hooe, which provides an example of how slavery flourished in the 1830s in a land where slavery was ostensibly forbidden. The letter also reflects the US military's continued practice of allowing officers to enslave people in free territory.

Earlier in the year, Major Thomas Floyd Smith, who had kept enslaved "servants" while posted at Fort Crawford, had written to Alexander from Jefferson Barracks asking if he wanted an enslaved young man back. The young man was not mentioned by name and referred to only as "the Boy." Thomas must have rented the young man from Alexander. But, apparently, the young man knew that because he had lived in a part of the country where slavery was illegal, he should be free. Because Alexander was on temporary duty to Fort Snelling, the letter was forwarded to his wife,

Emilie, who asked her father, Joseph, to handle the response to Thomas's inquiries.

In a letter written in May 1839, Joseph Rolette relayed Alexander and Emilie's response to Thomas:

> The Boy they do not want back—as they have written for another one.
>
> What Capt Alexr promised him, they are ignorant, but as to his claiming his freedom from he having lived in a free Country would not be sustained, it has been decided in Philadelphia and in this Territy [sic], that an officer was ordered to Such a Post, and that he had a right to take his servants with him as well as Baggage — that he had no right and this not acquire by his Staying the right of a Citizen of the State or Territy [sic] where he was Stationed.[21]

Joseph's 1839 letter reflects the attitude within the US military that officers could hold enslaved people in free territory with impunity. The 1836 decision stated in *Rachel v. Walker* was, apparently, of no consequence in this instance and many others.

—||—

With the close of the second Seminole War in 1842, troops were returned to Fort Crawford and other posts. By the end of 1839, the garrison at Prairie du Chien had decreased to two officers and a few enlisted men, as troops had been sent to Florida. With several companies reposted to Fort Crawford by 1842, construction of Fort Atkinson for the protection of the Ho-Chunk, who had been removed from the Neutral Ground and relocated on the Turkey River in Iowa, was completed. With the increase in men stationed at Fort Crawford, the number of enslaved people living at the post also increased.

Like the officers who had been stationed at Fort Crawford in the 1830s, these new men were all part of the First Infantry. The 1830s officers such as John Garland, Ethan Allen Hitchcock, William Jouett, and their contemporaries had all paid their dues at frontier forts. They had risen in the ranks, been given important responsibilities, and been posted to less isolated communities. The brevet and first lieutenants at Fort Crawford in the 1840s were more recent graduates of the US Military Academy.

Most of the new officers would soon be commanding men in charge of forcing the Ho-Chunk from the region around Fort Winnebago to Prairie du Chien and then across the Mississippi River to Fort Atkinson—a job that would involve a good deal of travel. Therefore, the majority of Fort Crawford's officers arrived as either single men or married men without family. Black enslaved women who had lived at Fort Snelling and Fort Crawford during the time Courtney and Rachel had been held at the posts were enslaved by married men whose wives and children also lived at the posts.[22] As a result, the Black servants and enslaved people living at Fort Crawford in the 1840s were almost exclusively men. A man named Nap was described as a "slave" on the pay vouchers of his enslaver, Captain Albert Miller from Tennessee. But Dan, Charles, Jackson, Isaac, Harrison, William, and Harry Bernard were listed simply as "Black" by the officers claiming their support."[23]

Lieutenant Colonel Charles McDougall, the post surgeon, had been transferred from duty in the Creek and Seminole Wars to Fort Crawford. His family accompanied him to Prairie du Chien. A daughter had been born while he was stationed at Fort Winnebago, and two more children were born at Prairie du Chien. Though he had been born in Chillicothe, Ohio, McDougall claimed pay for two Black people he described as "servants." Both had the last name Watkins and, based upon their heights, which McDougall listed at five-foot-two for M. Watkins and three feet for B. Watkins, they may have been mother and child.[24]

Very little information has been found describing how enslaved people and servants were treated by John W. Johnson, Joseph Street, and the officers of the US Army stationed at Fort Crawford in the 1840s, but one occurrence gives some indication of the officers' behavior toward the people who provided them service.

This incident, which took place in 1845, left a lasting impression on John Fonda. John was related to Marianne Labuche through his marriage to Sophia Galarneau, Marianne's granddaughter. He had probably heard firsthand accounts about the lives of enslaved people and may have been sensitive to the conditions of the enslaved Black population at Fort Crawford.

In 1840, John had been elected a constable for the village, and then in 1845, he assumed the additional duties of county coroner. While coroner, John was notified that a body had been found on the shore of Pig's Eye Slough on the south end of the prairie. This slough flowed south from the

Fort Crawford wharf to the steamboat landing. Arriving at the location, John removed the body from the slough and "recognized it as the body of a negro woman belonging to a certain Captain then in Fort Crawford." He examined the corpse and found "the body was cruelly cut and bruised." As coroner, John called an inquest to take evidence in the woman's death. At the inquest, the captain testified that he did not recognize the deceased person. "A verdict of 'Found Dead' was rendered," wrote John, "and I had the corpse buried." John had examined the woman and saw the evidence that the woman had been whipped to death and "thrown into the river during the night." The military did not investigate, even though people stationed at Fort Crawford knew the man to whom the woman "belonged," but, as John wrote, "the affair blew over."[25]

The letter about "the Boy" and the murder of the Black woman by an officer stationed at Fort Crawford demonstrate that officers in the US Army still held Black men and women enslaved as their servants. This practice would continue until the beginning of the Civil War. But at Prairie du Chien, perhaps because of *Rachel v. Walker*, a change had begun to occur. Officers posted to Fort Crawford still maintained private servants, but over 50 percent of the officers stationed at the fort in the 1840s described their servants as "White" or "Fair." In the 1830s, when Courtney and Rachel had been held at Prairie du Chien, almost all of the officers' servants had been described as "Black" and/or "Slave."[26]

By 1849, the post at Prairie du Chien no longer held importance to the US military. Troops had forced the Ho-Chunk west of the Mississippi River and would soon push them farther west into Minnesota Territory. The barracks and other buildings that were part of Fort Crawford were aging and in need of repair. On April 24, 1849, Company C marched down to the steamboat landing, boarded the *Senator*, and permanently departed for Fort Snelling. Companies B and F boarded the *Dr. Franklin* en route to Fort Leavenworth. A small detail remained at Fort Crawford to dispose of the government property and stores. After a sale of surplus material was held on May 30, the remaining troops left.

With the departure of the US Army officers from Fort Crawford, slavery ceased to exist at Prairie du Chien. And in less than fifteen years, the small community of free Black men and women began to dissolve. By 1860, Mariah and Era Putnam moved from Prairie du Chien to the Township of Eastman; by 1878, Courtney and Charles Weidemer moved to Perry Township in Iowa; and in the late 1880s, Courtney's son William moved his family to Milwaukee. Some of Marianne Labuche's descendants were the only exceptions, remaining in Crawford County and western Wisconsin up until the present day.

—⊩—

The lives of Marianne, Mariah, Patsey, Courtney, and Rachel tell a story of the early history of Wisconsin that few people know. We are fortunate to have information about the five women, though none of it was recorded by the women themselves.

Marianne was a free Black woman of many talents and a mother and grandmother to a large family. Her descendants have faithfully and proudly passed her history down from generation to generation. Through determination and savvy, Mariah was able to purchase her freedom from her enslaver. Through persistence and fortitude, Patsey gained her freedom with the deaths of her enslavers, and her descendants have preserved her story. And with astounding bravery and conviction, Courtney and Rachel each obtained their freedom by suing their enslavers.

The white men who enslaved Mariah, Patsey, Courtney, and Rachel—along with hundreds of US Army officers in the first seventy years of the nineteenth century—did so in a territory where Black people should have been free. Despite today's popular conception that slavery was never legal in Wisconsin, the truth is that from the acquisition of the Northwest Territory in 1787 to the Emancipation Proclamation of 1863, the various laws that governed the land we call Wisconsin allowed slavery to exist.

Enslaved Black men, women, and children lived at Prairie du Chien as early as the 1790s.[27] And as soon as the construction of Fort Crawford began in 1816, officers brought enslaved people with them to Prairie du Chien. The number of enslaved men and women on the prairie increased with the installation of the second Fort Crawford and continued until the US Army abandoned the post in 1856. Slavery also existed at Forts Howard and Winnebago, as well as in the US Mineral District that stretched from the Wisconsin River to the Fever River in Illinois, where men like Henry Dodge, the first governor of Wisconsin Territory, enslaved Black people.

The stories of Marianne, Mariah, Patsey, Courtney, and Rachel help to create a fuller picture of life in Wisconsin in the early 1800s. But, perhaps more importantly, they add five inspiring narratives of hope, perseverance, and triumph to this chapter of our state's, and nation's, history.

NOTES

Introduction

1. *Deeds A*, 229–230, Crawford County Register of Deeds, Prairie du Chien, Wisconsin.

2. Settled Accounts, Army Paymaster, National Archives, NA, RG 217, E516.

3. *An Ordinance for the Government of the Territory of the United States, North-west of the River Ohio* (New York: s.n., 1787), 2, www.loc.gov/resource/bdsdcc.22501/?sp=2.

4. *1820 United States Federal Census, Michigan Territory, Crawford County, Prairie du Chien*, Random Acts of Genealogical Kindness, https://raogk.org/census-records/wisconsin.

5. James H. Lockwood, "Early Times and Events in Wisconsin," in *Wisconsin Historical Collections*, vol. 2, Collections of the State Historical Society of Wisconsin (1856; repr., Madison: State Historical Society of Wisconsin, 1903), 125–126; Edgar Harlan and Ida M. Street, "Joseph M. Street's Last Fight with the Fur Traders," *Annals of Iowa* 17, no. 2 (1929): 105–148.

6. Henry Triplett to George Wilson, December 15, 1900, Joseph Montfort Street Papers, 1829–1840, State Historical Society of Iowa, Cedar Rapids, Iowa.

7. Congress of the Confederation, *An Ordinance for the Government of the Territory of the United States, North-west of the River Ohio*.

8. Paul Finkelman, "Slavery and the Northwest Ordinance: A Study in Ambiguity," *Journal of the Early Republic* 6, no. 4 (Winter 1986): 343–370.

9. Robert M. Taylor Jr., *The Northwest Ordinance, 1787: A Bicentennial Handbook* (Indianapolis: Indiana Historical Society, 1987), 72–76.

10. "(1724) Louisiana's Code Noir," Black Past, www.blackpast.org/african-american-history/louisianas-code-noir-1724/.

11. Kelly M. Kennington, *In the Shadow of Dred Scott: St. Louis Freedom Suits and the Legal Culture of Slavery in Antebellum America* (Athens: University of Georgia Press, 2017), 19–25.

12. *Acts Passed at the First Session of the First Legislature of the Territory of Orleans: Begun and Held in the City of New-Orleans, on Monday the Eighteenth Day of January, in the Year of Our Lord One Thousand Eight Hundred*

and Eight (New Orleans: Bradford and Anderson, 1807), 150. *The Laws of the Territory of Louisiana: Comprising All Those Which Are Now Actually in Force within the Same* (St. Louis: Joseph Charles, 1808), Missouri Digital Heritage, www.sos.mo.gov/archives/education/aahi/beforeDredScott/ 1807FreedomStatute.

13. David Thomas Konig, "The Long Road to *Dred Scott*: Personhood and the Rule of Law in the Trial Court Records of St. Louis Slave Freedom Suits," *UMKC Law Review* 75, no. 1 (2006): 53–80.

14. Lea S. VanderVelde, "The Dred Scott Case in Context," *Journal of Supreme Court History* 40, no. 3 (2015): 263–281.

15. Kelly M. Kennington, *St. Louis Freedom Suits and the Legal Culture of Slavery in Antebellum America* (Athens: University of Georgia Press, 2019), 17–40.

16. *Ohio Constitution of 1803*, Ohio History Central, https://ohiohistorycentral .org/w/Ohio_Constitution_of_1803.

17. O. W. Aldrich, "Slavery or Involuntary Servitude in Illinois Prior to and After Its Admission as a State," *Journal of the Illinois State Historical Society* 9, no. 2 (1916): 117–132.

18. Ethan A. Snively, "Slavery in Illinois," in *Transactions of the Illinois State Historical Society for the Year 1901* (Springfield, IL: Phillips Bros., 1901), www.museum.state.il.us/RiverWeb/landings/Ambot/Archives/trans actions/1901/IL-slavery.html.

19. Aldrich, "Slavery or Involuntary Servitude," 117–132.

20. Tiya Miles, *The Dawn of Detroit: A Chronicle of Slavery and Freedom in the City of the Straits* (New York: The New Press, 2017), 177–182; *Denison v. Tucker*, 2 Blume Sup. Ct. Trans. 134 (1807).

Chapter 1

1. James L. Hansen, "Prairie du Chien's Earliest Church Records, 1817," *Minnesota Journal of Genealogy* 4 (November 1985): 329–342.

2. James H. Lockwood, "Early Times and Events in Wisconsin," in *Wisconsin Historical Collections* 2, Collections of the State Historical Society of Wisconsin (1856; repr. Madison: State Historical Society of Wisconsin, 1903), 125–126.

3. Census of Louisiana, (New Orleans, September 2, 1771), in ed. Lawrence Kinnaird, *Spain in the Mississippi Valley, 1765–1794*, vol. 2, part 1 (Washington, DC: US Government Printing Office), 196.

4. Anne Ulentin, "Free Women of Color and Slaveholding in New Orleans, 1810–1830" (master's thesis, Louisiana State University, 2007), 13.

5. Ulentin, "Free Women of Color," 13–20.

6. Ulentin, "Free Women of Color," 34–35.

7. Carl J. Ekberg, *Colonial Ste. Genevieve: An Adventure on the Mississippi Frontier* (Carbondale: Southern Illinois University Press, 1996), 208.

8. Patricia Cleary, *The Word, the Flesh, and the Devil: History of Colonial St. Louis* (Columbia: University of Missouri Press, 2011), 263.

9. Ebony Jenkins, "Freedom Licenses in St. Louis City and County 1835–1865," *National Park Service*, October 8, 2008, www.nps.gov/jeff/learn/historyculture/loader.cfm?csModule=security/getfile&PageID=3120173.

10. Ebony Jenkins, *Freedom-Licenses-Database*, National Parks Service, October 22, 2008, www.nps.gov/jeff/historyculture/loader.cfm?csModule=security/getfile&PageID=3120522.

11. Louis Houck, *A History of Missouri: From the Earliest Explorations and Settlement until the Admission of the State into the Union* (Chicago: R. R. Donnelley & Sons, 1908), 54, 351.

12. Lockwood, "Early Times and Events."

13. "Collet's Index of Marriage Holy Family Parish, Cahokia, Illinois," 1740–1839, Diocese of Belleville, Illinois, Catholic Parish Records, 1729–1956, www.familysearch.org.

14. Clarence Walworth Alvord, *Cahokia Records, 1778–1790* (Springfield: Trustees of the Illinois State Library, 1907), 153.

15. Walter S. Franklin, *American State Papers* 4 (Washington, DC: Gales and Seaton, 1834), 863–865.

16. Franklin, *American State Papers*, 852.

17. Henri Duchouquette of Kaskaskia was known as Henri LaFleur. Claude may have had a connection of business or friendship to Pierre LaFleur, which again connects Marianne Labuche to this Duchouquette family from the Illinois Country; Franklin, *American State Papers*, 867, 869.

18. Lyon Lucius, *Plat of the Private Claims at Prairie du Chien*, Wisconsin Historical Society Manuscripts D GX9029 P89 MA.

19. Hansen, "Prairie du Chien's Earliest Church Records."

20. Lockwood, "Early Times and Events."

21. Lockwood, "Early Times and Events"; probate file of the estate of James Aird, Crawford County Register in Probate Office, Prairie du Chien, Wisconsin.

22. Franklin, *American State Papers*, 867, 869.

23. Lyon Lucius, *Plat of the Private Claims*.

24. Jean Barman, *French Canadians, Furs, and Indigenous Women in the Making of the Pacific Northwest* (Toronto: University of British Columbia Press, 2014), 19–22.

25. Wisconsin Census Records, *1820 US Federal Census, Michigan Territory, Crawford County, Prairie du Chien*, Random Acts of Genealogical Kindness, https://raogk.org/census-records/wisconsin.

26. Wisconsin Census Records, 1820–1860 federal census reports for Michigan Territory, Crawford County, and Prairie du Chien, Random Acts of Genealogical Kindness, https://raogk.org/census-records/wisconsin; *1834 Michigan Territorial Census, Crawford County*, www.ancestry.com.

27. Herbert G. Gutman, *The Black Family in Slavery and Freedom, 1750–1925* (New York: Vintage Books, 1976), 211–229.

28. *1834 and 1836 Michigan Territorial Census, Crawford County*, www.ancestry.com.

29. Franklin, *American State Papers*, 868–869.

Chapter 2

1. Walt Bachman, "Bachman Army Slave Database," shared with author October 2021. Bachman has created a database of US Army officers stationed at military posts throughout the United States, circa 1810–1863. The database is compiled from paymaster vouchers filed in Settled Accounts, Army Paymaster, National Archives, NA, RG 217, E516.

2. Rinaldo Johnson marriage contract, July 1, 1790, Early Colonial Settlers of Southern Maryland and Virginia's Northern Neck Counties Database, www.colonial-settlers-md-va.us.

3. John Mason to Joseph B. Varnum, Jr., June 21, 1815, in *Wisconsin Historical Collections*, vol. 19, Collections of the State Historical Society of Wisconsin (Madison: State Historical Society of Wisconsin, 1910), 382.

4. John Mason to John W. Johnson, August 7, 1815, in *Wisconsin Historical Collections*, vol. 19, 386–389.

5. *Deeds A*, 229–230, Crawford County Register of Deeds, Prairie du Chien, Wisconsin.

6. Office of the Illinois Secretary of State, *Illinois Servitude and Emancipation Records*, Illinois State Archives, https://apps.ilsos.gov/isa/servemansrch.jsp.

7. Wisconsin Census Records, *1820 US Federal Census, Michigan Territory, Crawford County, Prairie du Chien*, Random Acts of Genealogical Kindness, https://raogk.org/census-records/wisconsin.

8. John Mason to John W. Johnson, August 7, 1815, in *Wisconsin Historical Collections*, vol. 19, 386–389.

9. *Deeds A*, 229–230.

10. Walter S. Franklin, *American State Papers: Public Lands*, vol. 4 (Washington, DC: Gales and Seaton, 1834), 874.

11. Elizabeth Fox-Genovese, *Within the Plantation Household: Black and White Women of the Old South* (Chapel Hill: University of North Carolina Press, 1988), 152–167.

12. John W. Johnson to François Bouthellier, June 23, 1816, in *Wisconsin Historical Collections*, vol. 19, 424–425.

13. Franklin, *American State Papers: Public Lands*, 874. By his own testimony, John W. Johnson arrived at Prairie du Chien on May 26, 1816.

14. James H. Lockwood, "Early Times and Events in Wisconsin," in *Wisconsin Historical Collections*, vol. 2, Collections of the State Historical Society of Wisconsin (1856; repr. Madison: State Historical Society of Wisconsin, 1903), 122.

15. Colonel John Shaw, "Shaw's Narrative," in *Wisconsin Historical Collections*, vol. 2, 229–230.

16. Lockwood, "Early Times and Events," 129; Shaw, "Shaw's Narrative," in *Wisconsin Historical Collections*, vol. 2, 229–230.

17. Walter S. Franklin, *American State Papers: Indian Affairs*, vol. 2 (Washington, DC: Gales and Seaton, 1834), 356–357.

18. *1820 US Federal Population Census, Wisconsin, Crawford County*, ancestry.com.

19. Wisconsin Census Records, *1820 US Federal Census, Michigan Territory, Crawford County, Prairie du Chien*, Random Acts of Genealogical Kindness, https://raogk.org/census-records/wisconsin.

20. Franklin, *American State Papers: Indian Affairs*, 334.

21. Joseph Rolette to Pierre Chouteau, April 4, 1831, Chouteau Family Papers, Box 25, Missouri Historical Society, St. Louis, Missouri.

22. *1820 US Federal Census*.

23. "François Galarneau," Voyageur Database, https://archivesshsb.mb.ca; Augustin Grignon, "Seventy-two Years' Recollections of Wisconsin," in *Wisconsin Historical Collections*, vol. 3, Collections of the State Historical

Society of Wisconsin (1857; repr. Madison: State Historical Society of Wisconsin, 1857), 253.

24. Lockwood, "Early Times and Events," 147.

25. Royal B. Way, "The United States Factory System for Trading with the Indians, 1796–1822," *Mississippi Valley Historical Review* 6, no. 2 (September 1919): 220–235.

26. *Register of Enlistments in the U.S. Army, 1798–1914* (National Archives [NARA] Microfilm Publication M233, 81 rolls); *Returns from U.S. Military Posts, 1800–1916* (Fort Crawford) (National Archives Microfilm Publication M617, 1,550 rolls), both in Records of the Adjutant General's Office, 1780s–1917, Record Group 94, National Archives, Washington, DC.

27. James L. Hansen, "Crawford County Marriages, 1816–1848," *Minnesota Journal of Genealogy*, no. 1 (May 1984).

28. *Deeds A*, 105–107.

29. Franklin, *American State Papers*, 875.

30. Franklin, *American State Papers*, 875.

31. *Deeds A*, 105–107.

32. *Returns from U.S. Military Posts, 1800–1916* (Fort Crawford); Walt Bachman, *Northern Slave, Black Dakota: The Life and Times of Joseph Godfrey* (Bloomington, MN: Pond Dakota Press, 2013), 25.

33. James L. Hansen, "Prairie du Chien and Galena Church Records, 1827–1829," *Minnesota Journal of Genealogy*, no. 5 (November 1985).

34. Lockwood, "Early Times and Events," 147.

35. Hansen, "Prairie du Chien and Galena Church Records."

36. Hansen, "Prairie du Chien and Galena Church Records"; "Muster Roll of Captain Thomas McNair's Company of Michigan Militia," in *Register of Enlistments in the U.S. Army, 1798–1914* (National Archives Microfilm Publication M233, 81 rolls), Records of the Adjutant General's Office, 1780s–1917, Record Group 94, National Archives, Washington, DC.

37. Hansen, "Prairie du Chien and Galena Church Records."

38. *Ratified Treaty No. 155, Documents Relating to the Negotiation of the Treaty of July 29, 1829, with the Chippewa, Ottawa and Potawatomi Indians* (Washington, DC: National Archives, July 29, 1829), http://digital.library.wisc.edu/1711.dl/History.IT1829no155.

39. *Ratified Treaty No. 155.*

40. *Ratified Treaty No. 156.*

41. *Deeds A*, 130.

42. Bureau of the Census, *Historic Statistics of the United States, Colonial Times to 1970* (Washington, DC: US Department of Commerce, 1975), 163.

43. Tiya Miles, *The Dawn of Detroit: A Chrinicle of Slavery and Freedom in the City of the Straits* (New York: The New Press, 2017), 302n44.

Chapter 3

1. Ronald Rayman, "Frontier Journalism in Kentucky: Joseph Montfort Street and the Western World, 1806–1809," *Register of the Kentucky Historical Society* 76, no. 2 (1978): 98–111.

2. Anthony W. Street to Joseph M. Street, October 4, 1807, in Street Family Papers, MS 946, Yale University Archives, New Haven, Connecticut.

3. *1810 US Federal Census, Kentucky, Henderson County*, Henderson County KyGenWeb Genealogy Site, 334, http://hendersoncountyky.ushalls.com/census/1810/p334.html; Charles Aldrich and George Wilson, "George Wilson: First Territorial Adjutant of the Militia of Iowa," *Annals of Iowa* 4, no. 8 (1901): 563–576.

4. Joseph M. Street to Joseph H. D. Street, October 11, 1836, in Street Family Papers.

5. Rayman, "Frontier Journalism in Kentucky"; E. B. Washburne, ed., *The Edwards Papers: Being a Portion of the Collection of the Letters, Papers and Manuscripts of Ninian Edwards* (Chicago: Fergus Press, 1884), 70, 282.

6. Aldrich and Wilson, "George Wilson."

7. *Laws Passed by the First General Assembly of the State of Illinois, at Their Second Session, Held at Kaskaskia, 1819* (Kaskaskia: Blackwell and Berry, 1819), 354–361.

8. Constitution of 1818, Article VI, Section I, Illinois Digital Archives, www.idaillinois.org/digital/collection/isl2/id/167.

9. Rebecca Schmook, ed., *Gallatin County, Illinois Slave Register 1815–1839* (Harrisburg, IL: Saline County Genealogical Society, 1994), 7–8.

10. Schmook, *Gallatin County*, 7–8.

11. Schmook, *Gallatin County*, 9–10.

12. Schmook, *Gallatin County*, 9–10.

13. Schmook, *Gallatin County*, 2–5, 11, 13, 15, 16–19, 21, 48.

14. Illinois Servitude and Emancipation Records, Illinois State Archives, apps.ilsos.gov.

15. Schmook, *Gallatin County*, 5–6.

16. Estelene Bell to Mary Elise Antoine, February 8, 2019; Street family Bible.

17. Constitution of 1818, Article VI, Section 2.

18. John Musgrave, "Black Kidnappings in the Wabash and Ohio Valleys of Illinois," Hickory Hill Plantation, Old Slave House Preservation Project, 1997, www.illinoishistory.com/blackkidnappings.html.

19. Harris, *The History of Slavery in Illinois*, 28.

20. Washburne and Edwards, *The Edwards Papers*, 283.

21. Washburne and Edwards, *The Edwards Papers*, 282–287.

22. Washburne and Edwards, *The Edwards Papers*, 292.

23. Washburne and Edwards, *The Edwards Papers*, 300, 320–321.

24. Washburne and Edwards, *The Edwards Papers*, 320–321.

25. Washburne and Edwards, *The Edwards Papers*, 317. Joseph M. Street to Ninian Edwards, March 30, 1827, in "Prairie du Chien in 1827," in *Wisconsin Historical Collections*, vol. 9, Collections of the State Historical Society of Wisconsin (1882; repr. Madison: State Historical Society of Wisconsin, 1910), 356.

26. *Deeds A*, 198–199.

27. *Executive Documents Printed at the Order of the House of Representatives at the First Session of the Twenty-third Congress*, vol. 4 (Washington: Duff Green, 1832), 94.

28. Joseph M. Street to Ninian Edwards, November 1827, in "Prairie du Chien in 1827," in *Wisconsin Historical Collections*, vol. 9, 356–362; Judith Gildner and Ronald Rayburn, "Confrontation at the Fever River Lead Mining District: Joseph M. Street vs. Henry Dodge, 1827–1828," *Annals of Iowa* 44, no 4 (1978): 278–295.

29. Letter book of Joseph M Street, June 4, 1834, Joseph Montfort Street papers, 1829–1840, Special Collections, State Historical Society of Iowa, Des Moines, Iowa; Edgar Harlan and Ida M. Street, "Joseph M. Street's Last Fight with the Fur Traders" *Annals of Iowa*, 17, no. 2 (1929): 105–148.

30. Francis Paul Prucha, ed., *Documents of United States Indian Policy* (Lincoln: University of Nebraska Press, 1990), 33.

31. *Executive Documents Printed at the Order of the House of Representatives at the Second Session of the Twenty-first Congress*, vol. 3 (Washington: Duff Green, 1831), 62.

32. Members of the Virginia and North Carolina Triplett families had migrated west and lived in Kentucky and Missouri by the early 1800s. The Triplett

family members living in Kentucky owned enslaved Black men and women. A William Triplett from Missouri established the first smithy in Salem, Jo Daviess County, Illinois. James may have been enslaved by and/or secured his freedom from one of these families living in Kentucky and Illinois. "Virginia Slaves Freed after 1782," Free African Americans, www.freeafrican americans.com/virginiafreeafter1782.htm.

33. *Fourth Census of the United States, 1820* (National Archives [NARA] Microfilm Publication M33, 142 rolls), Records of the Bureau of the Census, Record Group 29, National Archives, Washington, DC.

34. *Executive Documents*, vol. 4 (Washington, DC: Duff Green, 1832), 94; *Executive Documents*, vol. 3 (Washington, DC: Duff Green, 1832), 100.

35. Street family Bible; Estelene Bell to Mary Elise Antoine, February 8, 2019.

36. *1834 US Federal Census, Michigan Territory, Crawford County, Prairie du Chien*, ancestry.com.

37. Bell to Antoine.

38. Prucha, *Documents of United States Indian Policy*, 8–9.

39. *Deeds A*.

40. *Deeds A*.

41. Joseph M. Street to Thomas Street, June 10, 1839, Joseph Montfort Street Papers, 1808–1898, Wisconsin Historical Society.

42. Aldrich and Wilson, "George Wilson"; Harlan and Street, "Joseph M. Street's Last Fight."

43. Harriet Jacobs, *Incidents in the Life of a Slave Girl* (1861; repr. New York: Oxford University Press, 1988), 256.

44. J. N. Davidson, *Negro Slavery in Wisconsin* (Milwaukee: Parkman Club Publications, 1896), 127–128.

45. Aldrich and Wilson, "George Wilson"; Harlan and Street, "Joseph M. Street's Last Fight."

46. Gutman, *The Black Family in Slavery and Freedom*, 211–229.

47. Aldrich and Wilson, "George Wilson."

48. Harlan and Street, "Joseph M. Street's Last Fight."

49. William B. Street, "General Joseph M. Street," *Annals of Iowa* 2, nos. 2–3 (July–October 1895): 81–105.

50. *1870 United States Federal Census, Missouri*, ancestry.com.

51. *Register Officers and Agents, Civil, Military, and Naval in the Service of the*

United States of the Thirtieth September, 1833 (Washington, DC: Francis
Preston Beats, 1833), 92.

52. Harlan and Street, "Joseph M. Street's Last Fight."

53. Charles Kappler, ed., *Indian Treaties, 1778–1883* (New York: Interland Publishing, 1972), 345–348.

54. George W. Cullum, *Biographical Register of the Officers and Graduates of
the U. S. Military Academy at West Point, N.Y.* (Boston: Houghton Mifflin,
1891), 466; Settled Accounts, Army Paymaster, National Archives, NA,
RG 217, E516.

55. Aldrich and Wilson, "George Wilson."

56. Aldrich and Wilson, "George Wilson"; Settled Accounts, Army Paymaster;
Iowa Census Records, *1850 US Federal Census, Iowa*, Random Acts of
Genealogical Kindness, https://raogk.org/census-records/iowa.

57. John B. Cabelle to Joseph H. D. Street, March 10, 1834 in Street Family Papers.

58. *Returns from U.S. Military Posts, 1800–1916* (Fort Crawford) (National Archives Microfilm Publication M617, 1,550 rolls), Records of the Adjutant
General's Office, 1780's–1917, Record Group 94, National Archives, Washington, DC.

59. Harlan and Street, "Joseph M. Street's Last Fight."

60. Walt Bachman, "Bachman Army Slave Database," shared with author October 2021.

61. *Executive Documents, Twenty-fourth Congress, Second Session* (Washington,
DC: Duff Green, 1838), 11.

62. Charles Aldrich and Ida M. Street, "A Second Chapter of Indian History,"
Annals of Iowa 6, no. 5 (1904): 364–375.

63. John Beach, "Indian Agency in Wapello County," *History of Wapello County,
Iowa* 1 (Chicago: J. S. Clarke Publishing Company, 1914), 23.

64. Joseph M. Street to Thomas Street, June 10, 1839, Joseph Montfort Street
Papers.

65. Street to Street, June 10, 1839.

66. Aldrich and Wilson, "George Wilson."

67. Aldrich and Street, "A Second Chapter of Indian History."

68. Aldrich and Wilson, "George Wilson."

69. *Deeds A*, 198–199.

70. *Acts Passed at the First Session of the Legislative Assembly Wisconsin Territory* (Belmont, W.T.: James Clarke, 1836).

71. Aldrich and Wilson, "George Wilson"; Iowa Census Records, *1850 US Federal Census, Iowa, Wapello County, District 13*, Random Acts of Genealogical Kindness, https://raogk.org/census-records/iowa; Henry Triplett to George Wilson, December 15, 1900, Joseph Montfort Street Papers, State Historical Society of Iowa, Cedar Rapids, Iowa.

72. Aldrich and Wilson, "George Wilson."

73. *Constitution of the State of Iowa*, May 18, 1846, Iowa Legislature, www.legis.iowa.gov/docs/publications/ICNST/780453.pdf.

74. Register of Deeds, Wapello County, Ottumwa, Iowa.

75. *The History of Jefferson County, Iowa* (Chicago: Western Historical Company, 1879), 421.

76. *Constitution of the State of Iowa*.

77. Triplett to Wilson, December 15, 1900.

78. Triplett to Wilson, December 15, 1900.

79. Richard Selcer, *A History of Fort Worth in Black & White: 165 Years of African-American Life* (Fort Worth: University of North Texas Press, 2015), 17–18.

80. *1850 US Federal Census, Iowa, Jefferson County, Libertyville; Iowa, State Census Collection, 1836–1925*, ancestry.com.

81. *Iowa, State Census Collection, 1836–1925*, ancestry.com.

82. *1860 US Federal Census, Iowa, Lee County, Keokuk*, ancestry.com.

83. *Roster and Records of Iowa Soldiers, War of the Rebellion, Historical Sketches of Volunteer Organizations*, vol. 5 (Des Moines: E. H. English, 1911), 1585–1590.

84. *US Colored Troops Military Service Records, 1863–1865*, ancestry.com.

85. *1870 US Federal Census, Missouri, Macon County, Macon*, ancestry.com; Alexander W. Wayman, *Cyclopedia of African Methodism* (Baltimore: Methodist Episcopal Book Depository, 1882), 167.

86. *1880 US Federal Census, Missouri, Livingston County, Chillicothe*, ancestry.com.

Chapter 4

1. Settled Accounts, Army Paymaster, National Archives, NA, RG 217, E516.

2. Settled Accounts, Army Paymaster.

3. *U.S. Census Reconstructed Records, 1660–1820* and *1810 United States Federal Census*, ancestry.com.

4. *Returns from U.S. Military Posts, 1800–1916* (Detroit, Fort Howard) (National Archives Microfilm Publication M617, 1,550 rolls), Records of the Adjutant General's Office, 1780's–1917, Record Group 94, National Archives, Washington, DC.

5. Settled Accounts, Army Paymaster.

6. *General Regulations for the Army; or, Military Institutes* (Washington, DC: Davis & Force, 1825), 38, 223, 286–287; Walter Lowrie, *Military Affairs, American State Papers*, vol. 4 (Washington, DC: Gales & Seaton, 1860), 436.

7. Settled Accounts, Army Paymaster.

8. L. D. Ingersoll, *A History of the War Department of the United States* (Washington, DC: Francis B. Mohun, 1880), 205–206.

9. Richard Dalzell Gamble, *Garrison Life at Frontier Military Posts, 1830–1860* (Norman: University of Oklahoma, 1956), 183.

10. Settled Accounts, Army Paymaster; Testimony of Courtney, St. Louis Court Historical Records Project: 1836 Mar Case Number 10—*Courtney, a woman of color v. Rayburn, Samuel*, Washingon University Digital Gateway, repository.wustl.edu/concern/texts/xw42n910s.

11. *Returns from U.S. Military Posts, 1800–1916* (Detroit, Fort Howard); Settled Accounts, Army Paymaster.

12. Harry B. Deas to Spotswood Garland, February 15, 1900, ancestry.com.

13. Francis R. Heitman, *Historical Register and Dictionary of the United States Army, from Its Organization, Sept. 29, 1789 to March 2, 1903*, vol. 1, part 2 (Washington, DC: Government Printing Office, 1903), 299.

14. E. S. Seymour, *Sketches of Minnesota, the New England of the West* (New York: Harper & Brothers, 1850), 103.

15. Marcus L. Hansen, *Old Fort Snelling, 1819–1858* (Cedar Rapids: State Historical Society of Iowa, 1918), 54.

16. Settled Accounts, Army Paymaster.

17. Edward J. Littlejohn, "Slaves, Judge Woodward, and the Supreme Court of the Michigan Territory," *Michigan Bar Journal* (July 2015): 24.

18. Willis Frederick Dunbar, *Michigan: A History of the Wolverine State* (Grand Rapids, MI: Eerdmans Publishing Co., 1965), 200, quoted in Littlejohn, "Slaves, Judge Woodward," 24.

19. Tiya Miles, *The Dawn of Detroit: A Chronicle of Slavery and Freedom in the City of the Straits* (New York: The New Press, 2017), 228–229.

20. Hansen, *Old Fort Snelling*, 74–75.
21. Correspondence with Stephen Osman, retired site director, Fort Snelling, Minnesota Historical Society.
22. Charlotte Ouisconsin Van Cleve, *Three Score Years and Ten: Life-long Memories of Fort Snelling* (Minneapolis: Harrison and Smith, 1888), 61.
23. Edward K. Thomas, *View of Fort Snelling*, circa 1850, oil on canvas, 27" × 34" (68.58 × 86.36 cm), Minneapolis Institute of Art, https://collections.artsmia.org/art/687/view-of-fort-snelling-edward-k-thomas.
24. Van Cleve, *Three Score Years and Ten*, 32–33.
25. Van Cleve, *Three Score Years and Ten*, 32, 40–43.
26. Settled Accounts, Army Paymaster.
27. Livia Appel, "Slavery in Minnesota," *Minnesota History Bulletin* 5, no. 1 (1923): 40–43.
28. "List of Slaves Owned by Lawrence Taliaferro, 1813," Lawrence Taliaferro papers, 1813–1868, Minnesota Historical Society, Minneapolis, Minnesota.
29. List of Slaves, Lawrence Taliaferro Papers.
30. Taliaferro Journal, July 1825–June 1826; Financial Records, 1819–1822, both in Lawrence Taliaferro Papers.
31. James A. Green, *William Henry Harrison: His Life and Times* (Richmond: Garrett and Massie, 1941), 434–435.
32. Helen Dunlap Dick, "A Newly Discovered Diary of Colonel Josiah Snelling," *Minnesota History* 14, no. 4 (1937): 399–406.
33. Miel Wilson and Robert J. Moore, eds., *St. Louis Probate Court Records, Court Ordered Slave Sales* (St. Louis, MO: National Parks Service, 2007), www.nps.gov/jeff/learn/historyculture/upload/Slave%20Sales%20Database.pdf.
34. Response of Defendant, St. Louis Circuit Court Historical Records Project: 1834 Nov Case Number 82—*Rachel, a woman of color v. Walker, William*, Washington University Digital Gateway, repository.wustl.edu/concerns/texts/t722h9873; Joseph Rolette to Major T. F. Smith, May 25, 1839, https://rfrajola.com/binders/Binder37.pdf.
35. Settled Accounts, Army Paymaster.
36. *Returns from U.S. Military Posts, 1800–1916* (Fort Crawford, 1817–1827) (National Archives Microfilm Publication M617, 1,550 rolls), Records of the Adjutant General's Office, 1780s–1917, Record Group 94, National Archives, Washington, DC; Walt Bachman, *Northern Slave, Black Dakota:*

The Life and Times of Joseph Godfrey (Bloomington, Minnesota: Pond Dakota Press, 2013), 7–8.

37. Walt Bachman, *Officer, Gentleman, Slavemaster: Slavery and Racism at West Point and Fort Leavenworth* (self-pub., Walt Bachman, 2020), 41, 174n89.

38. Harriet Jacobs, *Incidents in the Life of a Slave Girl* (1861, repr. New York: Oxford University Press, 1988), 69.

39. Harry B. Deas to Spotswood Garland, February 15, 1900.

40. Settled Accounts, Army Paymaster.

41. Van Cleve, *Three Score Years and Ten*, 28–30, 62; J. Fletcher Williams, "Memoir of Capt. Martin Scott," in *Minnesota Historical Collections*, vol. 3 (St. Paul: Minnesota Historical Society, 1880), 180–187.

42. George W. Cullum, *Biographical Register of the Officers and Graduates of the U. S. Military Academy at West Point, N. Y.*, vol. 1 (Boston: Houghton Mifflin and Company, 1891), 394–395; *Returns from U.S. Military Posts, 1800–1916* (Jefferson Barracks).

43. Charles Aldrich and George Wilson, "George Wilson: First Territorial Adjutant of the Militia of Iowa," *Annals of Iowa* 4, no. 8 (1901): 563–576.

44. Settled Accounts, Army Paymaster.

45. *Records of the Office of the Quartermaster General Consolidated Correspondence, 1794–1915*, National Archives, Record Group 92.

46. Settled Accounts, Army Paymaster.

47. Settled Accounts, Army Paymaster.

48. Settled Accounts, Army Paymaster; *Returns from U.S. Military Posts, 1800–1916* (Fort Snelling); James L. Hansen, "Crawford County Marriages, 1816–1848," *Minnesota Journal of Genealogy*, no. 1 (1984).

49. Settled Accounts, Army Paymaster.

50. *Records of the Office of the Quartermaster General.*

51. Tara Bynum, "Phillis Wheatley on Friendship," *Legacy: A Journal of American Women Writers* 31, no. 1 (2014): 43.

52. *Returns from U.S. Military Posts, 1800–1916* (Fort Crawford).

53. Lawrence Taliaferro, *Auto-biography of Major Lawrence Taliaferro: Written in 1864* (St. Paul: Minnesota Historical Society, 1894), 190–200.

54. Ledger, 1831, Alexis Bailly Papers, Minnesota Historical Society.

55. Wisconsin Census Records, *1850 US Federal Census, Michigan Territory, Crawford County, Prairie du Chien*, Random Acts of Genealogical Kindness, https://raogk.org/census-records/wisconsin.

56. *Wisconsin, US, Compiled Census and Census Substitute, Index, 1820–1890*, ancestry.com; "St. Gabriel's Cemetery Record of Burials," Holy Family Parish, Prairie du Chien, Wisconsin.

57. William H. Bingham and R. I. Holcombe, *Compendium of History and Biography of Minneapolis and Hennepin County, Minnesota* (Chicago: H. Taylor & Company, 1914), 46.

58. Donald Dean Parker, ed., *Recollections of Philander Prescott, Frontiersman of the Old Northwest, 1819–1862* (Lincoln: University of Nebraska Press, 1866), 152.

59. Parker, *Recollections of Philander Prescott*, 152.

60. Bachman, *Northern Slave, Black Dakota*, 42.

61. Henry Hastings Sibley and Theodore Christian Blegen, *The Unfinished Biography of Henry Hastings Sibley* (Minneapolis: The Voyageur Press, 1932), 35.

62. Testimony of Courtney, St. Louis Court Historical Records Project: 1836 Mar Case Number 10—*Courtney, a woman of color v. Rayburn, Samuel*.

63. *Deeds B*, Crawford County Register of Deeds, Prairie du Chien, Wisconsin.

64. *Iowa, State Census Collection, 1836–1925*, ancestry.com.

65. Testimony of Courtney.

66. Jacobs, *Incidents in the Life of a Slave Girl*, 130.

Chapter 5

1. Testimony of Elias T. Langham, St. Louis Circuit Court Historical Records Project: 1834 Nov Case Number 82—*Rachel, a woman of color v. Walker, William*, Washington University Digital Gateway, repository.wustl.edu/concerns/texts/t722h9873.

2. Testimony of Elias T. Langham.

3. *Returns from U.S. Military Posts, 1800–1916* (National Archives Microfilm Publication M617, 1,550 rolls), Records of the Adjutant General's Office, 1780s–1917, Record Group 94, National Archives, Washington, DC.

4. *Returns from U.S. Military Posts*.

5. *Records of the Office of the Quartermaster General, Consolidated Correspondence, 1794–1915*, National Archives, RG 92, Entry 225, NM-81.

6. Zachary Taylor, Last Will and Testament, 1847, in Zachary Taylor Papers: Series 6, Additions, 1820–1863, Library of Congress, www.loc.gov.

7. Charles Fenno Hoffman, *A Winter in the Far West*, vol. 2 (London: R. Bentley, 1835), 1–19.

8. Willoughby Morgan, Probate Estate Files, St. Louis Probate Court, 1833, Missouri Judicial Records, Missouri State Records and Archives, https://s1.sos.mo.gov/records.

9. Hoffman, *A Winter in the Far West*, 1–19.

10. *Records of the Office of the Quartermaster General.*

11. Bachman Army Slave Database, shared with author October 2021.

12. *Returns from U.S. Military Posts, 1800–1916* (Fort Crawford).

13. Settled Accounts, Army Paymaster.

14. Bachman Army Slave Database.

15. *Deeds B*, Crawford County Register of Deeds, Prairie du Chien, Wisconsin.

16. Settled Accounts, Army Paymaster.

17. *Records of the Office of the Quartermaster General.*

18. *Records of the Office of the Quartermaster General.*

19. *Returns from U.S. Military Posts.*

20. Estate of Joseph Klunk, Missouri, Wills and Probate Records, 1766–1988, ancestry.com.

21. *Returns from U.S. Military Posts; Missouri Death Records*; ancestry.com; Testimony of Rachel and Testimony of Thomas B. W. Stockton, St. Louis Circuit Court Historical Records Project: 1834 Nov Case Number 82—*Rachel, a woman of color v. Walker, William.*

22. *Returns from U.S. Military Posts; Records of the Office of the Quartermaster General.*

23. Kelly M. Kennington, *The Shadow of Dred Scott: St. Louis Freedom Suits and the Legal Culture of Slavery in Antebellum America* (Athens: University of Georgia Press, 2017), 17–40.

24. Testimony of Rachel.

25. William Wells Brown, *Narrative of William Wells Brown as Told by Himself* (Boston: The Anti-Slavery Office, 1847), 39–41, 51–52.

26. Brown, *Narrative of William Wells Brown*, 43.

27. Brown, *Narrative of William Wells Brown*, 39–41.

28. Brown, *Narrative of William Wells Brown*, 39–41.

29. Edward E. Baptist, "'Cuffy,' 'Fancy Maids,' and 'One-eyed Men'": Rape, Commodification and the Slave Trade in the United States," *The American Historical Review*, vol. 106, no. 5 (2001), 1619–1650.

30. Brown, *Narrative of William Wells Brown*, 39–41.

31. John Brown, *Slave Life in Georgia: A Narrative of the Life, Sufferings, and*

Escape of John Brown, a Fugitive Slave, Now in England (London: W. M. Watts, 1855), 110–113, https://docsouth.unc.edu/neh/jbrown/menu.html.

32. Petition of Rachel, St. Louis Circuit Court Historical Records Project: 1834 Nov Case Number 82—*Rachel, a woman of color v. Walker, William*.

33. Josiah Henson, *Truth Stranger than Fiction: Father Henson's Story of His Own Life* (Boston: John P. Jewett, 1858), 12.

Chapter 6

1. Kelly Kennington, email to Mary Elise Antoine, September 20, 2020.

2. Lucy Delaney, *From the Darkness Cometh the Light, or, Struggles for Freedom* (St. Louis, MO: J. T. Smith, [189–?]), n.p., Documenting the American South, https://docsouth.unc.edu/neh/delaney/menu.html.

3. *Returns from U.S. Military Posts, 1800–1916* (National Archives Microfilm Publication M617, 1,550 rolls), Records of the Adjutant General's Office, 1780's–1917, Record Group 94, National Archives, Washington, DC.

4. Kelly M. Kennington, *In the Shadow of Dred Scott: St. Louis Freedom Suits and the Legal Culture of Slavery in Antebellum America* (Athens: University of Georgia Press, 2017), 199. In *Redemption Songs: Suing for Freedom before Dred Scott*, Lea VanderVelde provides biographical sketches of some of the men and women who gained their freedom by filing suit in St. Louis Circuit Court.

5. "Before Dred Scott: Freedom Suits in Antebellum Missouri," Missouri Digital Heritage, Missouri State Archives, www.sos.mo.gov/archives/education/aahi/beforedredscott.

6. "Before Dred Scott."

7. Kennington, *In the Shadow of Dred Scott*, 30–32.

8. Kennington, *In the Shadow of Dred Scott*, 42.

9. Petition of Rachel, St. Louis Circuit Court Historical Records Project: 1834 Nov Case Number 82—*Rachel, a woman of color v. Walker, William*, Washington University Digital Gateway, repository.wustl.edu/concerns/texts/t722h9873.

10. Testimony of John, St. Louis Circuit Court Historical Records Project: 1834 Nov Case Number 82—*Rachel, a woman of color v. Walker, William*.

11. Ruling Made in Vacation at Chambers, *Rachel, a woman of color v. Walker, William*.

12. Kennington, *In the Shadow of Dred Scott*, 56.

13. Response to Summons, *Rachel, a woman of color v. Walker, William.*

14. "Before Dred Scott."

15. Complaint of Plaintiff, *Rachel, a woman of color v. Walker, William.*

16. Charge of Trespass, St. Louis Circuit Court Historical Records Project: 1834 Nov Case Number 83—*Henry, James, a boy of color v. Walker, William.*

17. "Before Dred Scott."

18. Kennington, *In the Shadow of Dred Scott,* 58–60.

19. Kennington, *In the Shadow of Dred Scott,* 62–63.

20. Delaney, *From the Darkness Cometh the Light,* n.p.

21. Response of Defendant, *Rachel, a woman of color v. Walker, William.*

22. Summons, *Rachel, a woman of color v. Walker, William.*

23. Summons, *Rachel, a woman of color v. Walker, William.*

24. Attachment, *Rachel, a woman of color v. Walker, William.*

25. Testimony, *Rachel, a woman of color v. Walker, William.*

26. R. Jones, Adjutant General, to Lt. T. B. W. Stockton, November 5, 1835 (National Archives Microfilm Publication M233, 81 rolls), Records Relating to Regular Army Personnel, Record Group 94, Washington, DC.

27. Bill of Exceptions, *Rachel, a woman of color v. Walker, William.*

28. Bill of Exceptions, *Rachel, a woman of color v. Walker, William.*

29. Bill of Exemption, *Henry, James, a boy of color v. Walker, William.*

30. Testimony, *Rachel, a woman of color v. Walker, William.*

31. Delaney, *From the Darkness Cometh the Light,* n.p.

32. Kennington, *In the Shadow of Dred Scott,* 36.

33. David Thomas Konig, "The Long Road to Dred Scott: Personhood and the Rule of Law in the Trial Court Records of St. Louis Slave Freedom Suits," *UMKC Law Review* 75, no. 1 (2006): 53–80.

34. Decision of the Circuit Court, *Rachel, a woman of color v. Walker, William.*

35. Bill of Exemption, *Rachel, a woman of color v. Walker, William.*

36. Testimony of Courtney, St. Louis Court Historical Records Project: 1836 Mar Case Number 10—*Courtney, a woman of color v. Rayburn, Samuel,* Washingon University Digital Gateway, repository.wustl.edu/concern/texts/xw42n910s.

37. Speech of Charles D. Drake delivered in Turner's Hall St. Louis, January 2, 1863, Cornell Digital Collections BookReader, http://reader.library.cornell.edu/docviewer/digital?id=may903604#mode/1up.

38. Testimony of Courtney.

39. Testimony of Courtney.

40. Charges of Courtney, *Courtney, a woman of color v. Rayburn, Samuel.*

41. John Thomas Scharf, *History of St. Louis City and County from the Earliest Period to the Present*, vol. 2 (Philadelphia: Louis H. Everts, 1883), 1260.

42. Wisconsin Census Records, *1840 US Federal Census, Missouri, St. Louis County, St. Louis*, Random Acts of Genealogical Kindness, https://raogk .org/census-records/wisconsin.

43. Testimony of Courtney.

44. Plea of Not Guilty, *Courtney, a woman of color v. Rayburn, Samuel.*

45. Anne Twitty, *Before Dred Scott: Slavery and Legal Culture in the American Confluence, 1787–1857* (New York: Cambridge University Press, 2016), 114–115, 247–273.

46. Plea of Not Guilty, *Courtney, a woman of color v. Rayburn, Samuel.*

47. Brief of Appellant, *Rachel, a woman of color-Appellant, Walker, William-Respondent*, Missouri Supreme Court Historical Database, https://s1 .sos.mo.gov.

48. Adjudgment of Errors, *Rachel, a woman of color-Appellant, Walker, William-Respondent.*

49. Opinion of the Court, *Rachel, a woman of color-Appellant, Walker, William-Respondent.*

50. Defendant's Brief, *Rachel, a woman of color-Appellant, Walker, William-Respondent.*

51. Opinion of the Court, *Rachel, a woman of color-Appellant, Walker, William-Respondent.*

52. Opinion of the Court, *Rachel, a woman of color-Appellant, Walker, William-Respondent.*

53. Of these three cases decided by Missouri courts, *Winny v. Whitesides* was the most important. John and Phebe Whitesides had lived in the Carolinas with an enslaved person named Winny. When the couple relocated north of the Ohio River, they took Winny with them. The Whitesides resided for three or four years in the part of the Northwest Territory that became Illinois, retaining Winny in slavery. The Whitesides then moved to St. Louis in Missouri Territory, once more bringing Winny with them and still holding her in bondage. Winny filed suit to obtain her freedom from Phebe

Whitesides (John Whitesides had died) in the Superior Court of Missouri Territory in 1818. She charged various members of the Whitesides family with trespass, assault and battery, and false imprisonment. Winny argued that because she had lived in Indiana Territory, she and the children who had been born to her while she lived in Indiana Territory should be free.

On February 13, 1822, a jury agreed with the argument that living in any part of the Northwest Territory made a person free and declared Winny and her children free persons. In the opinion of Judge George Tompkins, "The sovereign power of the United States has declared that 'neither slavery nor involuntary servitude shall exist there[']; and this court thinks that the person who takes his slave into said territory, and by the length of his residence there indicates an intention of making that place his residence and that of his slave, and thereby induces a jury to believe that fact, does, by such residence, declared his slave to have become a free man."

The Whitesides appealed the case to the Missouri Supreme Court, which upheld the lower court's verdict. The justices' decision to uphold the lower court verdict was based on the terms of the Northwest Ordinance. In their majority opinion, Justices McGirk and Tompkins stated, "Once free, always free." *Winny v. Whitesides* was the first suit for freedom heard by the Supreme Court of Missouri. The case and the opinion—"once free, always free"—would be used in determining the outcome of future freedom suits filed by enslaved individuals.

54. Timeline of Missouri's African American History, Missouri Digital Heritage, Missouri Office of the Secretary of State, https://sos.mo.gov/mdh/curriculum/africanamerican/timeline/timeline2.

55. "Julia v. McKinney," Elektratig blog, February 6, 2007, elektratig.blogspot.com.

56. Opinion of the Court, *Rachel, a woman of color-Appellant, Walker, William-Respondent.*

57. US Bureau of the Census, *Historical Statistics of the United States, Colonial Times to 1970*, vol. 1 (Washington: US Department of Commerce, 1975), 163.

58. Estate of Joseph Klunk, Missouri, Wills and Probate Records 1766–1988, ancestry.com.

59. General Assembly of the State of Missouri, "Negroes and Mulattoes: An Act Concerning Free Negroes and Mulattoes," Section 8, Approved March 14th, 1835, 414–415, Missouri State Archives, Jefferson City, Missouri.

60. "Freedom Licenses," National Park Service, www.nps.gov/jeff/learn/his toryculture/freedom-licenses.htm.

Chapter 7

1. Bachman Army Slave Database, shared with author October 2021 .

2. *1836 Wisconsin Territorial Census*, *US Federal Census, 1830, Michigan Territory, Crawford County*, ancestry.com.

3. *Returns from U.S. Military Posts, 1800–1916* (Detroit, Fort Howard) (National Archives Microfilm Publication M617, 1,550 rolls), Records of the Adjutant General's Office, 1780's–1917, Record Group 94, National Archives, Washington, DC. *Deeds B*, Crawford County Register of Deeds, Prairie du Chien, Wisconsin.

4. *1836 Wisconsin Territorial Census*; "Richard J. Steimann, "The Wapacootas and the White Man: The Story of the Early Development of Faribault," unpublished manuscript, Oversize Books Collection, St. Olaf Rolvaag Library, Northfield, Minnesota.

5. James L. Hansen, "Crawford County Marriages, 1816–1848," *Minnesota Genealogical Journal* 1 (May 1984); *1850 US Federal Census, Michigan Territory, Crawford County, Prairie du Chien*, Random Acts of Genealogical Kindness, https://raogk.org/census-records/wisconsin.

6. Carl J. Ekberg, "The Flour Trade in French Colonial Louisiana," *Louisiana History* 37 (Summer 1997): 261–282.

7. *Ledger 1837–1841*, Crawford County Clerk of Courts, Prairie du Chien, Wisconsin.

8. James L. Hansen to Mary Elise Antoine, March 18, 2020.

9. *Deeds F*, Crawford County Register of Deeds, Prairie du Chien, Wisconsin.

10. "Schedule of the Census of Crawford County, 1842," Crawford County Register of Deeds, Prairie du Chien, Wisconsin.

11. Fred L. Holmes, ed., *The Wisconsin Blue Book* (Madison: Democrat Printing Company, 1927), 401–403.

12. James L. Hansen, "Soldiers from Wisconsin Territory Who Served in the Mexican War, 1846–1848," part 1, *Wisconsin State Genealogical Society Newsletter*, vol. 60, no. 4 (October 2014): 17–23.

13. Hansen, "Soldiers from Wisconsin Territory."

14. 1850 and 1860 *Federal Census for Michigan Territory, Crawford County, Prairie du Chien*, Random Acts of Genealogical Kindness, https://raogk

.org/census-records/wisconsin; *US Passport Applications, 1795–1925*, ancestry.com.

15. Hansen, "Crawford County Marriages"; *1820 and 1830 US Federal Census, Michigan Territory, Crawford County; 1836 Census Wisconsin Territory, 1850, 1860; and 1870 US Federal Census, Wisconsin, Crawford County*, all on ancestry.com.

16. *1860 US Federal Census, Wisconsin, Crawford County, Town of Prairie du Chien.*

17. Richard H. Zeitlin, *Prairie du Chien: Urban Consolidation and Decline, 1858–1930*, File No. 35 (US Army Corps of Engineers, 1986); *1870 and 1880 US Federal Census, Wisconsin, Crawford County, Prairie du Chien.*

18. *1870 US Federal Census, Wisconsin, Crawford County, Town of Prairie du Chien.*

19. *1880 US Federal Census, Wisconsin, Crawford County, Prairie du Chien; 1880 US Federal Census, Iowa, Plymouth County, Perry Township; and US Federal Mortality Schedules, 1850–1885*, all on ancestry.com

20. *1880 US Federal Census, Iowa, Plymouth County, Perry Township*, Random Acts of Genealogical Kindness, https://raogk.org/census-records/iowa.

Conclusion

1. Walt Bachman, *Northern Slave, Black Dakota: The Life and Times of Joseph Godfrey* (Bloomington, MN: Dakota Pond Press, 2013), 42–43.

2. Kelly M. Kennington, *In the Shadow of Dred Scott: St. Louis Freedom Suits and the Legal Culture of Slavery in Antebellum America* (Athens: University of Georgia Press, 2017), 17–40.

3. *1810 US Federal Census, Southampton, Virginia, 1830 US Federal Census, Missouri, St. Louis County*, ancestry.com.

4. *Returns from U.S. Military Posts, 1800–1916* (Detroit, Fort Howard) (National Archives Microfilm Publication M617, 1,550 rolls), Records of the Adjutant General's Office, 1780's–1917, Record Group 94, National Archives, Washington, DC.

5. "Visit to Dred Scott –His Family—Incidents of His Life—Decision of the Supreme Court," *Frank Leslie's Illustrated Newspaper*, June 27, 1857.

6. Lea VanderVelde, *Mrs. Dred Scott: A Life on Slavery's Frontier* (New York: Oxford University Press, 2009), 76–84.

7. Petition for Leave to Sue for Freedom, Harriet, a woman of color, April 6,

1846, The Revised Dred Scott Case Collection, Washington University Digital Library, http://digital.wustl.edu/d/dre/drexml/dre1846.0002 .002.html.

8. Transcript of *Dred Scott v. Sanford* (1857), National Archives, www.archives .gov/milestone-documents/dred-scott-v-sandford#transcript.

9. "Missouri's Dred Scott Case, 1846–1857," Missouri Digital Heritage, www .sos.mo.gov/archives/resources/africanamerican/scott/scott; Transcript of *Dred Scott v. Sanford*.

10. "Missouri's Dred Scott Case, 1846–1857."

11. Petition for Leave to Sue for Freedom, Dred, a man of color, April 6, 1846, http://digital.wustl.edu/d/dre/drexml/dre1846.0001.001.html; Petition for Leave to Sue for Freedom, Harriet.

12. "Missouri's Dred Scott Case, 1846–1857."

13. "Dred Scott, Plaintiff in Error, v. John F. A. Sandford," Legal Information Institute, Cornell Law School, www.law.cornell.edu/supremecourt/text/ 60/393.

14. *Statutes of the Territory of Wisconsin Passed by the Legislative Assembly 1838–1839* (Albany, NY: Packard, Ven Benthuysen & Company, 1839), 349.

15. *1836 Wisconsin Territorial Census*, *US Federal Census, 1830, Michigan Territory, Crawford County*, ancestry.com.

16. *1836 Wisconsin Territorial Census*; *History of Crawford and Richland Counties, Wisconsin* (Springfield, IL: Union Publishing Company, 1884), 550.

17. Testimony of Elias T. Langham, St. Louis Circuit Court Historical Records Project: 1834 Nov Case Number 82—*Rachel, a woman of color v. Walker, William*, Washington University Digital Gateway, repository.wustl.edu/ concerns/texts/t722h9873.

18. Opinion of the Court, *Rachel, a woman of color-Appellant, Walker, William-Respondent*, Missouri Supreme Court Historical Database, https://s1.sos .mo.gov.

19. George M. Brooke to Major R. Cross, 14 July 1837, National Archives, RG 92, Box 431, Entry 225.

20. Settled Accounts, Army Paymaster, National Archives, NA, RG 217, E516.

21. Joseph Rolette to Major T. F. Smith, 25 May 1839, https://rfrajola.com/ binders/Binder37.pdf.

22. Bachman Army Slave Database, shared with author October 2021.

23. Settled Accounts, Army Paymaster; Bachman Army Slave Database.

24. Settled Accounts, Army Paymaster.

25. John H. Fonda, "Early Reminiscences of Wisconsin," in *Wisconsin Historical Collections*, vol. 5, Collections of the State Historical Society of Wisconsin (Madison: State Historical Society of Wisconsin, 1868), 205–284.

26. Settled Accounts, Army Paymaster; Bachman Army Slave Database.

27. *Pierre, a mulatto v. Chouteau, Gabriel*, 1842, Case Number 125, Washington University Digital Archives, stlouiscourtrecords.wustl.edu.

INDEX

Page numbers in *italics* refer to illustrations.

ABOUT THE AUTHOR

Mary Elise Antoine is president of the Prairie du Chien Historical Society, board member of the Wisconsin Trust for Historic Preservation, and former curator at Villa Louis. She is the author of *The War of 1812 in Wisconsin* and coeditor, with Lucy Eldersveld Murphy, of *Frenchtown Chronicles of Prairie du Chien*.